If You Knew the Gift of God

If You Knew the Gift of God

God

The Classical Church Teaching on Grace

Cliff Ermatinger

Padre Pio Press   Milwaukee

Cover design by Ryan Rogers

Printed in the United States of America

Thanks
To Michele, Dave, Cecile, and Patrick.

A special word of thanks to Fr. Melvin Michalski, the *censor librorum* in my archdiocese. This task was one of the last he carried out in a life of total dedication to the Church in Milwaukee. His insights, suggestions, corrections, and the friendship that developed through our collaboration all meant very much to me. *Requiescat in pace.*

Table of Contents

Introduction...i

Part One: The Theology of Grace............................ 1

- 1- Creation and God's Presence............................ 2

-2- The Supernatural Creation.............................7

-3- What Grace Does... 16

-4- What Sanctifying Grace Produces in Us................. 26

-5- Temples of the Holy Spirit?...........................39

-6- The Gift that Keeps on Giving.........................54

-7- The Birth of the Life of Grace......................... 64

-8- Utter Disaster: The Loss of Grace.......................72

Part Two: Cultivation of Grace............................87

-1- Growth Through the Sacraments........................ 89

-2- Growth Through Virtue.................................102

-3- Growth Through Prayer................................. 110

-4- Fidelity to Grace.. 121

Part Three: Development of Grace 145

-1- The Sinful.. 150

-2- The Purgative Way...................................... 156

-3- The Illuminative Way....................................192

-4- The Unitive Way.. 238

Introduction

Looking at the lives of the saints we see their heroism, extraordinary virtue, profound intimacy with our Lord. They can seem distant, if not in time and place, then certainly in experience and moral stature. A common misunderstanding is to think of them as the fortunate few, almost as if they won the divine lottery. When we read of St. Paul running his race, we, the spiritual *hoi polloi*, run the danger of contenting ourselves with observer status in this most existential and dramatic of all contests.

The problem is that we too often think holiness some arcane subject, when all along, the Church has clearly laid out its itinerary for us through her own spiritual masters and teaching.

Knowledge of the spiritual life requires understanding of the Church's teaching on grace. Spiritual theology deals with understanding the mechanics of this teaching and how to employ it. Lacking this understanding, we are left with the descriptive method that tends to convert the spiritual life into a disjointed collection of experiences. We end up with a more psychological-experiential presentation of the spiritual life than a theological one.

When God created man according to his image and likeness,

he made human nature in a specific way, with a spiritual structure, though natural, capable of receiving the supernatural structure superimposed by grace, of which grace is a part. For example, the intellect, a purely spiritual yet natural faculty within our nature, receives the light of faith through grace and thus assents to truths that can only be known supernaturally. The light of grace affords us the ability to understand things that would otherwise remain hidden to our natural mind. In heaven, in fact, God gives the mind what is called the light of glory, the supernatural grace of being capable of beholding his Face without self-destructing; for *no man can see my Face and live* (Ex 30:20).

A cornerstone of the Classical Tradition teaches us that grace builds on nature. What this means is that God created human nature in such a way that it would be capable of spiritual actions in the natural order – like having a conversation, thinking syllogistically, reading a book, etc. When grace is superimposed on human nature, the spiritual elements of the human nature – namely, the intellect and the will, become capable of realizing supernatural actions, working above and beyond their own nature, while employing it more fully. The theological virtues of faith, hope, and love are examples of this, as are the other infused virtues. All of this is thanks to grace. And grace is the beginning of holiness and indeed, eternal life.

The measure or the perfection of the spiritual life is the degree of participation by the individual Christian in the sanctity and perfection of God. In other words, how holy you are is determined by the degree of sanctifying grace you have. "It is the will of Jesus Christ that the whole body of the Church, no less than the individual members, should resemble Him."[1]

The more you are like God and participate in his nature, the holier you are.

A modern theologian firmly rooted in the Classical Tradition who expressed this teaching with utter clarity was Fr. Royo Marin, OP. Many years ago, I was on my 30-day silent retreat and discovered his diminutive work *Somos Hijos de Dios* ("We are Sons of God")[2]. Its value for my work in the United States was immediately clear. Unfortunately, it was never translated into English and enjoyed a brief life in its original form, only one edition saw the light of day. It seems to be something of a summary of his earlier 1,000 - page work, *The Theology of Christian Perfection*. I considered publishing an English version of it but found that, while his larger book might be too ambitious for some, a direct translation of his opuscule resulted in some phrasing that might prove culturally difficult to understand. Instead of translating the original (which serves as the inspiration and nucleus for this book), I sought to state the argument with the greater reliance on St. Thomas, St. John of the Cross, and St. Teresa of Avila, as well as more recent Papal documents. In addition to this, I added some new sections and excised others that seemed repetitive - but always guided by the sure hand of Fr. Marin. This book is an effort to restate the classical Church teaching on grace: what it is, what it does, and how to grow in it.

15th of August, 2018
The Solemnity of the Assumption of the Blessed Virgin Mary
Milwaukee

---

[1] *Mystici Corporis*, 47. Pius XII.
[2] Biblioteca de Autores Cristianos, Madrid: 1977.

Part One:
The Theology of Grace

- 1 -

Creation and God's Presence

Before speaking about our divine filial adoption, which is brought about by the grace of God in the supernatural order, we have to take a brief glance at man's purely natural condition, which as is stated in the well-known theological aphorism, grace does not come to destroy nature but to perfect it and bring it to its fulfillment.

Man's place in all this

In the purely natural order man is certainly a creature of God since he has received from him his own existence by agency of his biological parents; yet, speaking with theological precision, it cannot be claimed that man is, according to this natural order, a true son of God. As we will discuss further on, true filiation consists in receiving by natural generation, the life and the specific nature of the father. There is no other way to establish the father–son relationship, in its strict sense, except by way of generative causality. If a sculptor faithfully reproduces the image of his son carved in marble, he is certainly the author of that work, but not the father, because he has not transmitted the specific human nature, nor is Geppetto Pinocchio's father for the same reason.

In the purely natural order, God the Creator communicates to us our human nature. Nonetheless, for all that natural man receives from him, man does not receive divine nature. For that to occur grace must intervene.

The Hierarchy of Creation

In the purely natural order we distinguish five grades of perfection.

Minerals: They have received their inert and inanimate nature from the Creator without the least sign of life. Life consists of imminent movement – *vita in motu*. Where there is not one's own movement, actual or potential, there is no life; but not all movement is life (*i.e.*, the moving water over current, the hands of a clock, a locomotive). All inanimate beings receive their possible movements from without, that is, by a cause that is extrinsic to themselves, without which they can bring about no movement at all.

Vegetable life: In plants we discover the first manifestation of life in its most rudimentary form–the so-called vegetative state, which places the lowest weed above the most brilliant diamond.

Animal life: On the scale of creatures, animals are far above the plants. Unlike the plants, animals have five senses, hunt their food, procreate, and follow their instincts to defend themselves.

Human life: Unlike animals, man has a rational soul and is therefore capable of acting beyond his instincts. Man's intellect and free will put him so far above the animals that his actions can be considered virtuous or vicious, heroic or sinful. Unlike vegetables and animals, man is also a spiritual being. He is a union of body and soul. St. Gregory the Great said correctly that man is a sort of microcosm of the universe, a summary, a compendium of all creation: he exists just as the minerals do; he lives as the plants do; he feels and has instincts in a similar way to animals; yet he possesses a soul with understanding and free will, just like the angels.

Angelic life: we know from divine revelation that there exists an angelic world far above our own rational and human existence. There is a vast number of purely spiritual beings without any material admixture. They are gifted with a keen intelligence much more penetrating and sharper than the most brilliant of men.

Infinitely above the highest of angels exists God. *I am who I am* (Ex 3:14) – God's nature is his existence, he is pure act, he is infinite Being. Whatever exists is conserved in existence through God. If God were to suspend his conserving action nothing would exist except God. All that exists is in a state of uninterrupted creation.

God's place in all this

In order that we may understand more clearly God's supernatural presence, let us first consider this natural presence in   things.
God is everywhere – a simple truth too easily forgotten. Yet it is a thought that could change the whole tenor of our lives.

We tire ourselves trying to imagine God as someone far away, and our prayer suffers accordingly. God is spirit, whose presence is not limited to any one place but is to be found in all things. So shall the true adorers of God, we are told, *worship the Father in Spirit and in truth* (Jn 4:23). So, too, the Apostle says, *in him we live and move and have our being* (Acts 17:28). But let's

4

begin at the beginning.

To consider how the least grain of sand on the bottom of the sea or our very own human existence is dependent on its relationship to God is something worth meditating on for our whole life long. And nonetheless, this is only the purely natural order that has nothing to do with sanctifying grace or the supernatural order. Everything that exists, rocks, plants, animals, men, angels– even fallen angels – are linked to God's creating act through his triple presences in the deepest and most hidden part of each creature's being:

Essence: since the creature is receiving its own natural being in every instant (just as a light bulb receives electrical current).

Presence: nothing escapes God's all-seeing eye. Everything is present to him.

Power: our own utter dependence on God's power makes it impossible to escape it. True, we can distance ourselves from God's merciful love and bring upon ourselves his infinite justice, such is the punishment for the unrepentant sinner, thus experiencing God's power in one way; or, on the other hand, the righteous person who experiences the power of his transforming action – such is the work of grace.

Again, *In him we live and move and have our being.* This is the first truth that strikes us at the beginning of our spiritual life, and it would achieve amazing results if only we could make this thought of God's actual presence in all things a reality in our lives.

Even apart from him before all supernatural revelation, reason tells us that God knows and sees us completely and constantly, since he knows and sees all things. *Where can I go from your spirit? From your presence, where can I flee? If I ascend to the heavens, you are there; if I lie down in Sheol, there you are* (Ps

139:7-8). Apart from him we cannot lift a finger. There is nothing, literally nothing, not subject to his governance – not even sin. Even when we sin, God is he who gives us the power to act and sustains us in the act: the only thing that does not come from him is the deprivation of our will. Were we able to do the slightest thing without him, he would not be the first and universal Cause. In other words, he would not be God.

But that is not all. It is not enough that God should watch over us and direct our ways. As the sole and sovereign source of all being he must keep us in existence, giving us in each moment all that we are. Were this divine action to cease for one instant, we, and the universe itself along with us, would vanish like a dream. Once we have understood the necessity for this divine intervention, preserving all that God has created, the tiniest object assumes for us singular greatness, since it is the omnipotent God and he alone who, present in this little creature, saves it from falling into nothingness.

-2-

The Supernatural Creation

Everything discussed in the previous chapter refers to the purely natural human order in which man is a simple creature of God, superior to all of creation, save the angels. In this chapter we will consider what occurs in the soul of man according to the supernatural order.

Original Man

The Church teaches us that man, in his origins, was created in grace and, therefore, raised to the supernatural order. This is called original justice. "From the first moment of his existence, our common father Adam was created in holiness and justice."[3] Just as our first parents were created in friendship with God – in a state of grace – and had intimate knowledge of him, we, for all of our fallenness and consequent intellectual darkness, can know of God through the light of human reason. This is what the First Vatican Council says:

---

[3] *Denzinger*, 1511.

"If anyone shall have said that the one true God, our creator and our Lord, cannot be known with certitude by those things which have been made, by the natural light of human reason, let him be anathema."[4]

An Ugly Reality

Unfortunately, Adam was not faithful to the demands that this supernatural elevation to grace brought with it. Upon transgressing God's commandment through Original Sin, our first parents lost for themselves and their descendants the immense supernatural treasure they had received from God and which all their children would have inherited. The Council of Trent defines this doctrine in the following canons: "If anyone does not confess that the first man Adam, when he transgressed the commandment of God in paradise, and immediately lost his holiness and the justice in which he had been established... Let him be anathema."[5] Further it says,

If anyone asserts that the transgression of Adam has harmed him alone and not his posterity, and that the sanctity and justice he received from God, which he lost, he has lost for himself alone and not for us also; or that he having been defiled by the sin of disobedience has transfused only death and the punishments of the body into the whole human race, but not sin also, which is the death of the soul, let him be anathema, since he contradicts the apostle who says *By one man sin entered into the world, and by sin death, and so does passed upon all men, in whom all have sinned* (Rom 5:12).[6]

---

4 *Ibid.,* 3026.
5 *Ibid.,* 1511.

If anyone asserts that this sin of Adam, which in its origin is one, and by propagation, not by imitation, transfused into all, which is in each one as something that is his own, is taken away either by the forces of human nature or by a remedy other than the merit of the one mediator, our Lord Jesus Christ, who has reconciled us to God in his own blood, made unto us justice, sanctification and redemption; or if he denies that that merit of Jesus Christ is applied both to adults and to infants by the sacrament of baptism rightly administered in the form of the Church, let him be anathema; for there is no other name under heaven given to men, whereby we must be saved.[7]

God's Response to Man's Disaster

The catastrophe brought about by Original Sin makes it, of itself, absolutely irreparable by mere human action. No individual man, nor all men together, can undo the effects of original sin. It is impossible for man to save himself. But God, in his infinite mercy, had compassion on humanity and decreed the incarnation of his own Son, who, *humbled himself, becoming obedient to death, even death on a cross* (Phil 2:8), and through his redemptive death reestablished the possibility of supernatural life for man which was lost through our first parents. St. Paul says the following: *But God, who is rich in mercy, because of the great love he had for us, even when we were dead in our transgressions, brought us to life with Christ (by grace you have been saved), raised us up with him, and seated us with him in the heavens*

---

[6] *Ibid.*, 1512.

[7] Council of Trent, *Decree Concerning Original Sin*, 3.

in Christ Jesus, that in the ages to come he might show the immeasurable riches of his grace in his kindness to us in Christ Jesus. For by grace you have been saved through faith, and this is not from you; it is the gift of God (Eph 2:4-8).

Christ is the only savior and there is no other source of supernatural life. No person has ever received nor can receive a grace outside of Christ, since *from his fullness we have all received, grace in place of grace* (Jn 1:16). With ineffable love and mercy, Christ tells us why he came to this world: *I came so that they might have life and have it more abundantly* (Jn 10:10).

So now we must ask ourselves the question: in what consists this supernatural life that Christ merited through the price of his Precious Blood? Its fundamental root consists of sanctifying grace, that gives us a true and real participation in the life and nature of God himself. And this is the sublime mystery we will now consider.

The Gift of God: Sanctifying Grace

Sanctifying grace is a divine gift, a supernatural quality, infused by God in our soul, which offers us a true and formal participation in God's nature, making us similar to him. We shall now consider this statement word for word.

Sanctifying grace: it is called thus because it truly does sanctify the person fortunate enough to possess it. Within the order of sanctification there are many degrees, as we shall see; by its mere possession in a minimal degree – as in the case of a recently baptized baby – it essentially sanctifies the one who receives it. Between the baby recently justified through the possession of sanctifying grace and the greatest saints in heaven is a difference of degree. This is an accidental, not an essential, difference.

Divine gift: one of the most noteworthy characteristics of sanctifying grace is that it is a gift, that is, something God gives gratuitously to the soul. No created or creatable nature, human or angelic, has a right to such a gift. No heroic action can merit it. No amount of goodwill can earn it. Grace resides beyond all human capability. It is therefore, supernatural, exceeding infinitely every human or angelic possibility. No matter how perfect a man or an angel may be according to nature they can do nothing to save themselves. St. Augustine often repeated that human or angelic natures are related to grace as inanimate matter is related to the life principle. Matter, in and of itself, is dead. It cannot give itself life, because it exists in another order. The Angelic Doctor, Thomas Aquinas, says the following: "The gift of grace surpasses every capability of created nature, since it is nothing short of a partaking of the divine nature, which exceeds every other nature. And thus, it is impossible that any creature should cause grace. For it is as necessary that God alone should deify, bestowing a partaking of the divine nature by a participated likeness, as it is impossible to anything save a fire should enkindle."[8]

Sanctifying grace is therefore divine in the fullest extension of the word. Everything in the natural order is a gift of God, but not necessarily a divine gift. Divine gifts belong to the order of sanctifying grace, because only this order offers us a real and true participation in the very nature and life of God. The sun that warms us, the water we drink, the air we breathe, the foods we eat, are all gifts of God; but none of them are divine as is sanctifying grace.

Supernatural quality: the nature of sanctifying grace bears

---

[8] Summa Theologica, I-II, 112, 1.

within it a habitual quality in this supernatural order; that is, something accidental received in the essence of the soul that divinizes it.

Just as something good has the quality of goodness, in other words, it participates in goodness in an accidental way; so too, grace is a quality that makes man pleasing in God's eyes: he becomes justified, a friend, a son, and an inheritor of God. By sanctifying grace, this supernatural quality makes man similar to God in his very divine nature.

Infused by God into our soul: this is something that Protestant theology denies with its extrinsic imputation of the merits of Christ, but this is a truth of the Faith expressly defined by the Council of Trent with the following words: "If anyone shall say that men are justified either by the sole imputation of the justice of Christ, or the sole remission of sins, to the exclusion of grace and charity, which is poured forth in their hearts by the Holy Spirit and remains in them, or even that the grace by which we are justified is only the favor of God: let him be anathema."[9]

Aquinas says, "The love of God infuses and creates goodness."[10] This is the principal difference between human and divine love. Our own experience is that we find (or imagine) something good in the object or person loved. God on the other hand, makes the creature good by loving it. Once he has given his love, he can never retract it. A lover delights in that which is similar to him in the beloved, sanctifying grace elevates us to the level of "friends" of God, deifying us through a formal participation in his own divine nature. In a word, God loves men with supernatural love that makes the man pleasing

---

[9] Denzinger, 1561.
[10] *S. Th.* I, 20,2.

in God's sight. Just as the supernatural love of God is the cause of that which he loves, it follows that it also must produce in man that which makes man pleasing to God, the reason of his supernatural goodness that is, sanctifying grace.

Which offers us a true and formal participation in God's nature: we have already mentioned that sanctifying grace constitutes a true participation in divine nature. Nonetheless, we must be more precise in saying that this true and authentic participation is quasi physical, as St. John of the Cross puts it: like wood put in a fire which takes upon itself the very attributes of fire without losing its own nature as wood. By formal participation, we mean that grace penetrates the soul and transforms the soul to such an extent that it becomes deiform. In other words, it is not simply a coating on the soul, or something merely extrinsic to it.

That grace truly makes us participants in divine nature is a truth of the Faith revealed in Sacred Scripture. The Apostle St. Peter says, *"through these, he has bestowed on us the precious and very great promises, so that through them you may come to share in the divine nature, after escaping from the corruption that is in the world because of evil desire"* (2 Pet 1:4).

Following the principle of *lex orandi,* the Church teaches us in the *Preface for the Solemnity of the Ascension of the Lord* that, "He ascended into heaven in order to make us participants in his divinity."

St. Leo the Great enjoins his hearers to "recognize your dignity, O Christian, made participant in the divine nature, that you not return to your vile, previous condition."[11]

The sublime divine nature now, by the infinite power of its equally infinite love, draws our nature unto itself, receives it

---

[11] Sermo 22 in nat. Dom., 3: PL 54, 192c.

into its divine bosom, immerses it into itself as iron is dipped into the furnace, and thus we belong to God's kind in the same manner as the palm tree belongs to the class of plants, and the lion to that of animals. As Scheeben explains:

> If out of so many millions of men and angels, God selected a single soul, and bestowed upon it this unheard of dignity, the soul, if it were visible, would darken the beauty of the sun, of all nature, and of all heavenly spirits, and would so amaze not only mortal men, but also the angels, that they would be inclined to adore it as they adore God himself. How is it possible that we despise the same gift when it is so profusely, we might say, extravagantly lavished upon all, and that our ingratitude increases in the proportion in which God will be more liberal towards us?[12]

Making us similar to him: This is the logical and natural consequence of everything we have said thus far. Making us participants of his own divine nature, God elevates us to his own level, making us similar to him. Nonetheless, we must explain in what consists this sublime similarity.

Certainly, all creatures are similar to God in their own respective way. Minerals are similar to God in that they exist. Plants are similar to God in that they live. Men and angels are similar to God in that they are spiritual beings with an intellect and a free will. But it is precisely grace which makes men similar to God as God is God – and not in any other way. The soul in a state of sanctifying grace is placed on a level with God,

---

[12] M. Joseph Scheeben, The Glories of Divine Grace, New York: Benzinger Brothers, 1886, 42-43.

a level to which it is impossible for him to rise by his own power. St. Thomas tells us: "The good of the universe is greater than the particular good of one, if we consider both in the same genus. But the good of grace in one is greater than the good of nature in the whole universe."[13]

---

[13] *S Th* I-II, 113, 9 ad 2.

-3-

What Grace Does

Having glanced at the nature of sanctifying grace, albeit with broad brush strokes, let us now consider the effects it produces in the soul justified by grace.

All the effects of sanctifying grace are contingent on this unique participation in the divine nature. St. Paul indicates three effects in the following sacred text:

For you did not receive a spirit of slavery to fall back into fear, but you received a spirit of adoption, through which we cry, "Abba, Father!" The Spirit itself bears witness with our spirit that we are children of God, and if children, then heirs, heirs of God and joint heirs with Christ, if only we suffer with him so that we may also be glorified with him (Rom 8: 15-17).

Building on this text we will indicate, in the first place, the three principal effects produced in our souls by sanctifying grace.

Grace makes us truly adoptive sons of God

To be a father – as we have seen– it is absolutely necessary to transmit to another being one's own specific nature. A painter is not the father of this painting, and the author is not the father of his book. The product of one's work does not possess one's nature. On the other hand, our own biological parents have transmitted to us their own proper human nature.

Is this divine filiation that God transmits to us by way of sanctifying grace natural in any way? By no means. God the Father has only one Son according to his own nature: the Eternal Logos. God the Father is eternally transmitting his nature to him who alone has been generated according to the divine nature. In virtue of this natural generation, the second Person of the Blessed Trinity possesses the same divine essence as the Father; he is God as much as the Father is God. As a result, Jesus Christ, whose human nature is hypostatically united to the Person of the eternal Logos is not an adoptive son of God, but naturally his Son with all the rigor of the term. St. Thomas says,

> Sonship belongs properly to the hypostasis or person, not to the nature; wherefore we have stated that filiation is a personal property. Now in Christ there is no other than the uncreated Person or Hypostasis, to whom it belongs by nature to be the Son. But it has been said above that the sonship of adoption is a participated likeness of natural sonship: nor can a thing be said to participate in what it has essentially. Therefore Christ, who is the natural Son of God, can nowise be called an adoptive son.[14]

---

[14] *S Th* III, 23,4.

Our own divine affiliation by way of grace is quite distinct. It is in no way a natural filiation, but rather an adopted filiation. Nonetheless, we should avoid diminishing the grandeur of this adoptive state. This merits some explanation.

Adoption implies the gratuitous admission of a stranger into a family, who is from that moment onward considered a son, enjoying the rights of inheritance and all the goods that come with it. Human adoption demands three conditions: first, the one adopted must be a human person. Adoption requires a similarity of nature with the adoptive parent. No one can adopt a statue or a book or an animal. Second, the one adopting exercises gratuitous love and free choice. No one has a right to be adopted and, as a result, no one has a duty to adopt. It is a gift. And third, regarding inheritance and the goods accompanying the adoption, these must be real, or the adoption is an illusion, fictitious.

Thus, sanctifying grace grants us a divine adoption which perfectly fulfills all these conditions - and goes far beyond them. In fact, divine filiation is truer than the legal process of human adoption. What occurs in the legal process of adoption is a legal fiction. The court declares that the child belongs to the parents, all the while knowing that it is not, strictly speaking, true. "Son," In this case, is still an extrinsic reality. The son does not have the blood of his adoptive parents.

On the other hand, when God adopts us, he infuses sanctifying grace that gives us, as we have seen, a true, formal participation in his own divine nature. This is a case of intrinsic adoption that inserts the divine reality into our soul. Metaphorically, we can say that the soul in a state of grace has God's very blood running through his veins.

Through sanctifying grace, a true spiritual generation occurs, a super natural generation and, analogically, reminds us of the generation of the eternal Logos of God. Echoing St. John the Evangelist, sanctifying grace does not only make us merely children by adoption, but rather makes us children indeed: *See what love the Father has bestowed on us that we may be called the children of God. Yet so we are* (I Jn 3:1). If this truth of the faith were not divinely revealed, we would consider it too fantastic to believe.

Grace makes us inheritors of God's Kingdom

As a consequence of our divine filiation we also become true inheritors of God's kingdom. St. Paul says *If [we are] children, then [we are] heirs* (Rom 8:17). Here too, we find prominent distinctions between human inheritance and divine inheritance: A legal inheritance is received upon the death of one's father and the more inheritors, the less the inheritance. But our Father in heaven will live eternally and with him we possess the inheritance that, in spite of the immense number of participants, is not diminished in any way.

Our inheritance is more than God's possessions, it is God himself and his infinite majesty. As the father said to the older of the two sons in the parable of the prodigal son, *everything I have is yours* (Lk 15:31). The Blessed Trinity, three Persons in one God, infinite Divinity, adds to that: "and I Am is yours, as well."

The principal part of the inheritance is the beatific vision. Our simple human nature is unequipped to see God. In fact, in the Book of Exodus it says that no man can see God and live (Ex 33:20). Just as our human nature is not equipped to live underwater without oxygen tanks, so too, our human nature is not equipped to live in heaven. Sanctifying grace makes adequate our naturally inadequate nature for it to survive heaven.

Grace confers upon the soul the riches of divinity and everything that constitutes the happiness of God. This is an indescribable joy. After communicating to us his divine nature and his own happiness, God will share with us his exterior goods such as his honor, his glory, his dominion, his royalty. The soul in sanctifying grace receives all these joys without the possibility of losing them. Our every joy and desire will be fulfilled.

Although sanctifying grace is an unmerited gift, once it is possessed, the soul in grace can merit heaven as a title of justice. Aristotle says that acts follow the nature of a being, as a result the value of all work proceeds from the dignity of the one who carries it out; and since grace is a divine form inherent in the justified soul, whatever supernatural action is carried out - having grace as its foundation and root – speaks of an intrinsic relationship to glory and bears within it all the demands and consequences.

Therefore, grace and glory are situated on the same plane, they are substantially the same life. There is only a difference of degree: it is the same life either in its initial stage or its perfected stage. A young child and a mature adult have the same life; the only difference is that of degree. This also occurs in the life of grace and glory. St. Thomas says: "For grace is nothing else than a beginning of glory in us."[15]

Grace makes us brothers of Christ and co-heirs with Him

This is the third affirmation St. Paul makes in his *Letter to the*

---

[15] *S Th* II-II, 24, 3, ad 2.

Romans already cited. As such, this relationship derives immediately from the previous two affirmations. St. Augustine says: "To whom do we say, 'Our Father?' to the Father of Christ. He then, who says 'Our Father' to the Father of Christ, says to Christ, what else but 'our Brother'?"[16]

As grace communicates to us a full participation in the divine life of Christ it therefore makes us his brothers. The Church teaches us in the *Preface for the Ascension*: "For after his resurrection he plainly appeared to all his disciples and was taken up to heaven in their sight, that he might make us sharers in his divinity." *For those he foreknew he also predestined to be conformed to the image of his Son, so that he might be the firstborn among many brothers* (Rom 8:29). Of course, we are not brothers of Christ according to nature, nor are we sons of God in the same form as he is. Christ is the only Begotten Son in the order of nature, but through grace we are conjoined to Christ, we become children in the Son of God.

For this reason, the Father deigns to look upon us as if we were one with the Son. He loves us as he loves his Son; he looks on Christ as our Brother in virtue of the title granting the same heritage. We are co-heirs with Christ. He has the natural right to the divine heritage, since he is the Son who was constituted inheritor of all, for which reason he made the world.

Consequently, *"it was fitting that he, for whom and through whom all things exist, in bringing many children to glory, should make the leader to their salvation perfect through suffering. He who consecrates and those who are being consecrated all have one origin. Therefore, he is not ashamed to call them "brothers," saying: "I will proclaim your name to my brothers, in the midst of the assembly I will*

---

[16] *In Joh* 21, 3.

praise you" (Heb 2:10-13).

Therefore, the brothers of Christ must share with him the love and heritage of the heavenly Father. God has modeled us on Christ; with Christ, we are sons of the same Father who is in heaven. All this will be affected by realizing the supreme desire of Christ: that we be one with him as he himself is one with the Father.

Grace bestows upon us supernatural life

This formal participation in the nature of God – which constitutes the very essence of grace – far supersedes, in fact, infinitely supersedes, all of the demands and possibilities of any created nature, whether human or angelic.

Through grace man is elevated above human nature and angelic nature. He enters the level of the divine and is made a part of the family of God, he begins to live in a divine way. Grace confers a super-imposed, infinitely superior life to that which corresponds to man by nature: this is supernatural life.

Grace makes man just and pleasing in God's sight

Regarding the justification of the sinner through sanctifying grace, the Council of Trent teaches us with these beautiful words:

Justification itself follows this disposition or preparation, which is not merely remission of sins, but also the sanctification and renewal of the interior man through the voluntary reception of grace and gifts, whereby an unjust man becomes a just man, from the state of enemy he becomes a friend, that he may be *an heir according to hope of life everlasting* (Titus 3:7)....

Finally the unique formal cause is the justice of God, not that by which he himself is just, but by which he makes us just, that, namely, by which, when we are endowed with it by him, we are renewed in the spirit of our mind, and not only are we reputed, but we are truly called and are just, receiving justice within us, each one according to his own measure, which the *Holy Spirit distributes to everyone as he wills* (1 Cor 12:11), And according to each one's own disposition and cooperation.[17]

Adorned by sanctifying grace, the soul becomes beautiful and resplendent before the eyes of God. God looks with love and joy at the soul in grace in which he finds his very own reflection, his own beauty, his own infinite goodness.

The beauty of a soul in the state of grace is so sublime, that the heavenly Father told St. Catherine of Siena of the following: "My daughter, if I were to show you the beauty of the soul in grace it would be the last thing you see in this world, because its splendor and beauty would be too much for you and you would perish."[18]

Grace makes it possible for man to supernaturally merit

Outside of the state of grace, natural works of man, even the most heroic, would have absolutely no value in the order of eternal life.

St. Thomas says, "Man without grace may be looked at in two states: The first, a state of perfect nature, in which Adam was before his sin; the second, a state of corrupt nature, in which we are before being restored by grace. Therefore, if we speak of man in the first state, there is only one reason why man cannot merit eternal life without grace, by his purely natural endowments, viz. because man's merit depends on the divine

---

[17] Denzinger, 1528-29.
[18] Dialog, 14.

pre-ordination.

Now no act of anything whatsoever is divinely ordained to anything exceeding the proportion of the powers which are the principles of its act; for it is a law of divine providence that nothing shall act beyond its powers. Now everlasting life is a good exceeding the proportion of created nature; since it exceeds its knowledge and desire, according to 1 Cor 2:9 *eye has not seen, nor ear heard, neither has it entered into the heart of man.*

Consequently, no created nature is a sufficient principle of an act meritorious of eternal life, unless there is added a supernatural gift, which we call grace. But if we speak of man as existing in sin, a second reason is added to this, viz. the impediment of sin. For since sin is an offense against God, excluding us from eternal life, no one existing in a state of mortal sin can merit eternal life unless first he be reconciled to God, through his sin being forgiven, which is brought about by grace. For the sinner deserves not life, but death, according to Romans 6:23, *The wages of sin is death.*[19]

As a result, in the supernatural order, a man outside of grace is a walking cadaver, and a spiritually dead soul cannot merit anything. Supernatural merit supposes a radical possession of the supernatural life that can only come through the possession of sanctifying grace. St. Paul alludes to the requirement of sanctifying grace for our works to have supernatural merit with the following words: *If I speak in human and angelic tongues but do not have charity, I am a resounding gong or a clashing symbol. And if I have the gift of prophecy and comprehend all mysteries and all knowledge; if I have all faith so as to move mountains but do not have love, I am nothing. If I give away everything I own, and if I hand my*

---

[19] *S Th* I-II, 114, 2.

body over so that I may boast but do not have charity, I gain nothing (1 Cor 13:1-3).

Grace unites us intimately to God

We have seen that in this simple order of nature God's conserving action makes him present to everything he has created by essence, presence, and power.

Sanctifying grace increases his presence in an indescribable way through union, thus transforming it and elevating it to an infinitely superior plane. In virtue of this new union, God is truly present in the justified soul in the quality of friend – not merely as Creator or Conserver – establishing a mutual current of love and friendship between the soul and God in a sort of transfusion of lives: *God is love, and whoever remains in love remains in God and God in him* (1 Jn 4:16).

-4-

What Sanctifying Grace Produces in Us

Sanctifying grace, as we have seen in the preceding pages, elevates us to a divine plane giving us our participation in the very nature of God. Grace is the principle and foundation of our supernatural life and that which makes us truly children of God.

Nonetheless, we must make mention that sanctifying grace is not immediately operative. It is given to us in the order of being, and not in the order of operation. It divinizes the very essence of our soul, just as fire transforms iron into its own incandescent being; but it is limited to that alone. Grace does not work of its own accord and does nothing of itself. In theological language, we speak of an entitative - and not operative - habit. It gives us a supernatural life but not supernatural operation.

Christian life must grow and develop in us based on supernatural actions, without which we would remain static and immobile – which is a precarious existence for the spiritual life and ultimately leads to sloth and spiritual death. Life is manifested by movement and action.

God has foreseen this and, as a result, conferred upon the soul in grace all the necessary elements for it to realize and carry out supernatural acts corresponding to the supernatural life whose basic and stable principle is sanctifying grace. Joined to this, he infuses in the soul a series of supernatural energies – operative habits – capable of producing supernatural acts corresponding to divine life. Such are the infused virtues and the gifts of the Holy Spirit to which we also must add the influence of what is called actual grace, which puts these things supernaturally in movement. These are the new divine realities that we will study in the following two chapters.

Infused, supernatural virtues

To have a clearer understanding of the meaning of these supernatural or infused virtues, which come about because of the presence of sanctifying grace in the soul at the moment of justification through baptism or penance, it might help to compare to and distinguish them from natural or acquired virtues.

Natural or acquired virtues

We know from experience that a series of repeated acts corresponding to a determined activity bring about a habit. If the repeated actions are bad, theology calls the subsequent habit a vice. On the other hand, if the actions that are repeated are good, theology then calls this habit a virtue. These virtues are acquired naturally: for example, prudence, justice, loyalty, sincerity, honor, etc. these are all acquired by repeated actions.

These natural or acquired virtues beautify human life in the intellectual and moral order and they can even be exercised to a heroic degree as we have seen throughout human history. But this heroism of acquired virtues will always remain on the purely natural plane and they can never bridge the gap between the natural and supernatural regardless of how intense or extreme they may be. The supernatural order is infinitely above the most heroic in the natural order. These are two different universes on two totally different planes. This is the doctrine of the Church as defined against the Pelagians and the Semi-Pelagians. Virtue is not a grace. As St. Thomas Aquinas says:

in the sense that we speak of grace as much as it makes man pleasing to God, or is given gratuitously – and of virtue in as much as it empowers us to act rightly…. Virtue is a disposition of what is perfect – and I call perfect what is disposed according to its nature. Now from this the virtue of a thing has reference to some pre-existing nature, from the fact that everything is disposed with reference to what befits its nature. But it is manifest that virtues acquired by human acts are dispositions, whereby a man is fittingly disposed with reference to the nature whereby he is a man; whereas infused virtues dispose man in a higher manner and toward a higher end, and consequently in relation to some higher nature, i.e., in relation to a Divine Nature, according to 2 Peter 1:4, *He has given us the greatest and most precious promises; that by these you may be made partakers of the Divine Nature.* And it is in respect of receiving this nature that we are said to be born again sons of God.

And thus, even as the natural light of reason is something besides the acquired virtues, which are ordained to this natural light, so also the light of grace which is a participation of the divine nature is something besides the infused virtues which are derived from and ordained to this light... For as the acquired virtues enable a man to walk, in accordance with the natural light of reason, so too the infused virtues enable a man to walk as befits the light of grace.[20]

Further, natural or acquired virtues, even the most beautiful and dignified, are inept and disproportionate to the supernatural life expected of the Christian elevated by grace that is immensely superior to the natural plane. Since sanctifying grace is a purely static, that is not an operative reality, it has as its object to grant us supernatural life, but not its corresponding operations. Therefore, the soul needs some supernaturally principled operative energies to realize the corresponding actions of supernatural life in the order of grace. It is evident that these operative supernatural principles cannot be acquired by man through repetition of natural actions – this is absurd and contradictory; rather, man must receive them by divine infusion joined to sanctifying grace. Such are the infused virtues and the gifts of the Holy Spirit that we will study now.

Supernatural and infused virtues

As we indicated above, supernatural or infused virtues are operative habits infused by God in the powers of the soul to dispose it to work supernaturally according to the dictates of reason illumined by faith. Let's look at each word of this definition.

Operative habits: This is the generic element of the definition common to all virtues both natural and supernatural.

Infused by God: Here we have one of the most radical differences

---

[20] *S Th* I-II, 110, 3.

between natural or acquired virtues and those given by God. Supernatural virtues can only be acquired through divine intervention per infusion, hence the name "infused virtue".

In the powers of the soul: Supernatural virtues are infused by God in the powers of the soul (the understanding and the will, principally), unlike sanctifying grace that is infused and resides in the essence of the soul it transforms and divinizes. The infused virtues have as their mission the perfecting of the powers of the soul, elevating them to a supernatural level and capacitating them for its work in order to produce supernatural acts. The supernaturally virtuous act springs from the union of the natural power and of the virtue infused that perfects it. For example, the supernatural act of charity springs from the natural will and from the infused virtue of charity, which elevates the will to a supernatural order.

To dispose it to work supernaturally: This is the principal and specific difference between natural and infused virtues. Naturally acquired virtues operate naturally always; infused virtues operate supernaturally. The first follow the dictates of simple natural reason; the infused virtues follow the dictates of reason in bloom and by faith. There is an abyss between these two.

As a result, infused virtues can be possessed – at least in germ form – without having the corresponding acquired virtues (for example, a recently baptized child or a hardened sinner who has just repented). Conversely, one can have some natural virtues (such as honor, justice, etc.) without having any of the infused virtues because the soul finds itself in the state of sin.

According to the dictates of reason illumined by faith: The illumination of faith is the distinguishing mark here. Further, the gifts of the Holy Spirit are not directed by reason illumined by faith but rather, by the Holy Spirit - directly and immediately - as we shall see in a moment.

The number of the infused virtues

St. Thomas Aquinas, in his *Summa Theologica,* identifies more than 50 infused virtues. We can catalog them in two fundamental groups: theological and moral virtues. There are three theological virtues and they are by far much more perfect than the moral virtues.

The infused moral virtues can be subdivided into cardinal virtues – that is, prudence, justice, fortitude, and temperance – and those derived from the cardinal virtues (for example, humility, obedience, patience, perseverance, chastity, etc.) in a perfect analogy and parallelism with their corresponding acquired virtues. The theological virtues are strictly divine – because they have as their direct and immediate object God himself. They have no corresponding virtues in the natural order.

Later in this text we will study the way of growth and correspondence with sanctifying grace to the practice of supernatural virtues under the influence of actual grace that puts them in movement. For the moment we will content ourselves with these broad brush-strokes.

The Gifts of the Holy Spirit

The infused virtues, although strictly supernatural, are not enough to make us live the divine life in all its grandeur and perfection, proper to the Christian in grace. Precisely because it has to do with a truly divine life – something infinitely superior to purely natural or human life, any human element that is mixed in with it tarnishes its brilliance and splendor. Without a doubt, they can act and in fact, do act, making us live the divine life proper to grace, but not in all their strength and perfection. For that, we require the gifts of the Holy Spirit.

The infused virtues are moved and governed by the dictates of reason illumined by faith. Since the natural reason is illumined by faith it is a thousand times above itself according to the natural order, leaving far behind it the natural light proper to it. In this sense, the infused virtues are far above the natural or acquired ones which are governed by the lights of human reason abandoned to its own efforts without the supernatural light of faith. For example, the natural virtue of temperance avoids those things that can endanger one's health through excess or endanger one's reputation before the eyes of the world, yet it has nothing to do with mortification made in the will, moved by charity for one's own spiritual gain and is distant from the imitation of Christ. Infused virtues are, evidently, much more refined and perfected than their corresponding natural or acquired counterparts.

Within the workings and the mechanism of infused virtues, inevitably human involvement is present and, when active, natural reason illumined by faith is still natural. It is, indeed, natural reason that directs and governs the infused virtues, and as a result, it inevitably leaves a human imprint in virtue of its human modality, since this modality is the proper characteristic of natural reason even under the illumination of supernatural faith.

As has already been noted, the human modality proceeding from natural reason is a foreign and profoundly disproportionate element to that of the divine and supernatural nature of the infused virtues. By their very nature, these require the aid of divine modality to reveal themselves in all their marvelous splendor. Therefore, even though they may be submitted to the dictates of natural reason that allows them to work within the human context – infused virtues still cannot move and act with full freedom yet. They can only grow and develop to a certain extent and, as a result, will always remain in a precarious position: incomplete and imperfect, incapable of reaching the heights of divine perfection since they are deprived of the divine oxygen that they require proper to their own nature as divine realities.

Such is the role and *raison d'etre* of the gifts of the Holy Spirit. These too are supernatural and infused habits – and in the sense of genus coincide with infused virtues that accompany them – but their mechanism and working is completely distinct. This is not a case of human reason illumined by faith as governor and regulator, but rather something that is proper to the Holy Spirit himself, using them as his own direct and immediate instruments. He is the one who directly moves and acts through them.

As such, since human reason does not intervene in any way, rather, all of the motion regulation proceeds directly in the meetings immediately from the Holy Spirit it is precisely the Holy Spirit who imprints upon the act his own gifts with his own modality which is absolutely divine, and not human, because the proper modality which is specific to the Holy Spirit who acts directly on it is divine and has nothing human about it, which should be clear and evident. Thus, supernatural acts proceeding from the gifts of the Holy Spirit are not only supernatural since their substance – but too, they are supernatural in their mode, and in this sense are far above the quality and perfection of those infused virtues which are governed by the simple human reason illumined by faith.

The gifts of the Holy Spirit are supernatural operative habits infused by God in the powers of the soul in order to receive and facilitate the motions proper to the Holy Spirit in its own divine and superhuman mode.

We will now briefly consider the specific functions of each one of the seven gifts of the Holy Spirit. St. Thomas Aquinas has laid this out for us with great precision. Each one of them has its own specific and direct mission in the order of perfecting some of the fundamental virtues: the three theological virtues and the four cardinal virtues, having repercussions on all the other infused virtues derived from them as well as influencing the sum of the Christian life.

The gift of wisdom

This gift perfects the virtue of charity, allowing it to breathe the air of the divine and fulfill all that is demanded by its exalted condition as the most perfect of the theological virtues. Under this divine influence a person in grace can love God with an extremely intense love.

Under inspiration of this gift one begins to see things through the prism of God and to judge things by divine reason with the sense of eternity, almost as if he had penetrated the frontiers of the beyond. When this gift is active normal human instinct remains dormant and the action proceeds according to divine and supernatural instinct. For the person under the sway of the gift of wisdom eternity has already begun. Paul refers to the action of this gift when he writes, *our citizenship is in heaven* (Phil 3:20).

The gift of understanding

The gift of understanding perfects the virtue of faith,

conferring upon it a profound penetration of the great supernatural mysteries, the Trinitarian indwelling, the mystery of redemption, or incorporation into Christ, the holiness of the Blessed Virgin Mary, the infinite value of the Holy Sacrifice of the Mass, and other similar mysteries acquired, under the influence of the gift of understanding; these are truly extraordinary.

Obsessed for the things of God, these people experience a profound intensity that only one who understands himself to be a pilgrim in this world could experience.

The gift of knowledge

In a certain sense this gift perfects another aspect of the virtue of faith as well as the virtue of hope, teaching us to judge correctly the value of created things, seeing in all of them a vestige of the divine which grants upon them their own value and beauty. St. Francis of Assisi is an example of a saint infused with this gift, illumined to such an extent that he could recognize his own relationship with all created reality in relationship to Christ. This is the intuition of the saints who know how to see with the eyes of God what is deemed foolishness in the eyes of the world (*cf.* 1 Cor 3:19).

The gift of counsel

This gift provides services to the virtue of prudence, not only in those great determinations which orient the direction of one's life (such as vocation, election of state of life, etc.) but even in the small details of the apparently monotonous and banal realities that make up our daily life. These are lights of the Holy Spirit, intuitions providing us with opportunities to discover within the events, not only their value but what we are to do during them.

The gift of piety

This gift serves to perfect the virtue of justice. Its mission is to awaken the will by the prompting of the Holy Spirit to a filial affection for God, considering him as a most loving Father, and bestows upon the soul in grace a sense of universal fraternity towards other men and women – seeing them as children of the same Father and experiencing in a supernatural way a divine affection for them.

Under the influence of the gift of piety the words *Our Father* have a new meaning. Under its influence, such people live abandoned to divine love and experience a profound tenderness of the Blessed Virgin Mary, their most holy Mother, and a sweet filial affection for the Vicar of Christ ("the sweet Christ on earth", as St. Catherine of Siena called him).

The gift of fortitude

This gift strengthens its namesake virtue, bringing it to a heroic degree - even perfection - in two fundamental aspects: resistance and perseverance amid every sort of attack and danger, as well as promptness in carrying out its tasks even amidst the greatest of difficulties.

The gift of fortitude shines in the martyrs, in those great Christian heroes and the silent virtue of those Christians who understand their own dignity, carrying out their duties day to day, whether in the silence of a cloister, in one's home, or in the workplace. This is the gift of heroism in the little things, a sort of silent martyrdom available to all in the state of grace.

The gift of fear the Lord

This gift perfects two virtues: firstly, the theological virtue of hope, because it roots out presumption, which is opposed to it by excess; and offers us unique support with the aid of God who is the formal end of hope.

Secondly, it perfects the cardinal virtue of temperance, since the remembrance of divine punishment puts an immediate break on disordered appetites. Considering the possibility of the most minute of sins, the saints trembled. They understood well the greatness and majesty of God on the one hand and the vile degradation of sin on the other.

Fruits of the Holy Spirit and his blessings

When a person in grace faithfully corresponds to the divine motion of the gifts of the Holy Spirit, what result are acts of supernatural virtue that are so perfect that they are called the fruits of the Holy Spirit. The most sublime fruits of the Holy Spirit correspond to the evangelical beatitudes that signal a crowning moment in the life of the pilgrim here on this earth, becoming something to a prelude to the eternal beatitude.

St. Paul enumerates some of the principal fruits of the Holy Spirit when he writes to the Galatians, *In contrast, the fruit of the Spirit is love, joy, peace, patience, kindness, generosity, faithfulness, gentleness, self-control. Against such there is no law* (Gal 5:22-23).

Certainly, he did not intend to enumerate them all. They are, as has been mentioned, the acts proceeding from the gifts of the Holy Spirit that have a special and perfecting character.

The same can be said about the Beatitudes. In the Sermon on the Mount, Christ mentions eight: poverty of spirit, meekness, mourning, hunger and thirst for justice, mercy, purity of heart, peace, and persecution for the cause of justice. We can add that this is a symbolic number and the beatitudes are not limited to eight. They are the heroic works of the saints that give them a foretaste of the eternal beatitude of heaven.

-5-

Do You Not Know that You are Temples of the Holy Spirit?

Among the sublime effects produced in us by sanctifying grace there is one which infinitely exceeds grace itself: the divine indwelling of the Blessed Trinity in the soul of the just, which constitutes the so-called uncreated grace. This is distinguished from actual grace, which is a created reality. Grace, in effect, gives us a created participation in the uncreated nature of God. But the divine indwelling – absolutely inseparable from sanctifying grace – confers God himself to the soul; that is the very uncreated reality that constitutes the essence of God himself.

The foundation of this teaching

The indwelling of the Blessed Trinity in the just is one of the most explicitly taught truths manifested in the New Testament. This doctrine has been reiterated in the New Testament to underscore the sovereign importance of this mystery:

Whoever loves me will keep my word, and my Father will love him, and we will come to him and make our dwelling with him (Jn 14:23).

We have come to know and to believe in the love God has for us. God is love, and whoever remains in love remains in God and God in him (1 Jn 4:16).

Do you not know that you are the temple of God, and that the Spirit of God dwells in you? If anyone destroys God's temple, God will destroy that person; for the temple of God, which you are, is holy (1 Cor 3:16-17).

Do you not know that your body is a temple of the holy Spirit within you, whom you have from God, and that you are not your own? (1 Cor 6:19).

What agreement has the temple of God with idols? For we are the temple of the living God; as God said: "I will live with them and move among them, and I will be their God and they shall be my people (2 Cor 6:16).

Guard this rich trust with the help of the holy Spirit that dwells within us (2 Tim 1:14).

Clearly, Sacred Scripture employs different formulas to express this singular truth: God dwells in the depths of the soul in the state of grace. Regarding this mystery, the Holy Spirit has a primordial role; not because he is not equal to the Father or the Son, rather for the sake of appropriation; that is that the divine indwelling is principally a work of God's love and the Holy Spirit is essentially the love of God within the Blessed Trinity.

The Church Fathers, especially St. Augustine, have dedicated many beautiful pages to this ineffable mystery of the divine indwelling of the Blessed Trinity in the just.

Modes of Divine Presence

To better understand the nature of the divine indwelling of the Blessed Trinity in the human person, it will be helpful to distinguish it from other forms of divine presence according to Catholic theology.

The personal or hypostatic presence: This is proper and exclusive to Jesus Christ, God made man. In him the Divine Person of the eternal Logos does not reside as in a temple, but rather assumes a human nature to Himself, uniting it to His person so that without any change to the Divine Substance, it is true that the Person of the Son is both true God and true man, one Person having two natures.

The Eucharistic presence: God is present in the Eucharist in the special way that is proper to it. He is the Eucharistic Presence, which in a certain sense affects the Body of Christ in a unique and direct way, and indeed all three persons of the Blessed Trinity: the Logos in virtue of its personal union with humanity of Christ, and the Father and the Holy Spirit, in virtue of the divine "circumincession" – that is, the mutual presence of the three Divine Persons in themselves which makes them absolutely inseparable. Where One of Them is, necessarily the Other Two are.

The presence of vision: God is present in all places by essence, presence, and power, as we have seen already. Nonetheless, he is not visible everywhere. The beatific vision in heaven can be considered as a special presence of God distinct from the other types of presences. In heaven God allows himself to be seen.

The presence of immensity: One of the essential divine attributes is immensity. God is truly present everywhere and, in all things, without whom nothing and no place can exist. It is precisely God's immensity which gives everything its continued existence: by his essence - that is, giving each thing its being; by his presence - that is remaining always before his divine gaze; by his power - that is, submitted totally to his divine power.

The indwelling presence: This is the special presence established by God through grace. Yet, how would we distinguish between the presence of the indwelling from the presence of immensity?

They say that God is present and exists in all things, "by His power, in so far as all things are subject to His power; by His presence, inasmuch as all things are naked and open to His eyes; by His essence, inasmuch as he is present to all as the cause of their being." (St. Th. Ia, q. viii., a. 3). But God is in man, not only as in inanimate things, but because he is more fully known and loved by him, since even by nature we spontaneously love, desire, and seek after the good.

Moreover, God by grace resides in the just soul as in a temple, in a most intimate and peculiar manner. From this proceeds that union of affection by which the soul adheres most closely to God, more so than the friend is united to his most loving and beloved friend and enjoys God in all fullness and sweetness.

Now this wonderful union, which is properly called "indwelling," differing only in degree or state from that with which God beatifies the saints in heaven, although it is most certainly produced by the presence of the whole Blessed Trinity- "We will come to Him and make our abode with Him," (John xiv. 23.) -nevertheless is attributed in a peculiar manner to the Holy Ghost.

While traces of divine power and wisdom appear even in the wicked man, charity, which, as it were, is the special mark of the

Holy Ghost, is shared in only by the just. In harmony with this, the same Spirit is called Holy, for He, the first and supreme Love, moves souls and leads them to sanctity, which ultimately consists in the love of God. Wherefore the apostle when calling us to the temple of God, does not expressly mention the Father or the Son, or the Holy Ghost: "Know ye not that your members are the temple of the Holy Ghost, who is in you, whom you have from God?" (1 Cor. vi. 19).[21]

Certainly, this special presence of the divine indwelling presupposes the preexistence of the general presence by immensity without which nothing would be possible. But we add to this general presence two fundamental things: divine paternity and divine friendship. The former has a foundation in sanctifying grace; the latter has its foundation in supernatural charity. What does this mean?

Divine paternity: As we have already said, properly speaking, it cannot be maintained that God is Father of creatures in the natural order. True, everything is a product of his making – and he continues to create by means of creating agencies – but this fact constitutes God as Author and Creator of everything, but in no way as Father of everything.

To be precise, fatherhood requires the transmission of one's own life to another, according to one's proper and specific nature to another being of the same species.

Therefore, if God wanted to be our Father as well as our Creator it would be necessary for him to transmit his own divine nature in all of its fullness – and this is the case with Jesus Christ, the Son of God by nature. The other possibility is a real and true participation of the same nature; and this is the

---

[21] Divinum Illud Munus, 9. Leo XIII.

case of the person justified by grace.

In virtue of sanctifying grace which grants the justified person a mysterious participation, and nonetheless true and authentic, in the divine nature (*cf.* 2 Pet 1:4), thus justified, one is made truly a child of God by an intrinsic adoption far above every sort of human adoption, which will always remain on a juridical and extrinsic level – regardless of the degree of human affection involved.

From this moment onwards, God, who already resided in the soul through the general presence of immensity, begins to be present in the soul as Father and to see the soul as his true child. This is the first aspect of the presence of divine indwelling, incomparably superior, as can be seen, to the simple presence of immensity.

The presence of immensity is common to everything that exists; even, as we have said, in grains of sand, demons, and condemned souls. The divine indwelling, on the other hand, is proper and exclusive to the adopted children of God. This status presupposes sanctifying grace and cannot be granted without it.

Divine Friendship: Divine adoption is a feast for the soul. When sanctifying grace arrives to the soul it never comes to the festival alone. Among the courtiers to accompany sanctifying grace are the infused virtues; and among them the principle virtue is supernatural charity. Supernatural charity establishes a true and mutual friendship between God and man: it is his very essence.

Therefore, infusing himself in the soul by way of sanctifying grace and through the presence of supernatural charity, God begins to be in the soul in a new way: not simply as Author, but as well as true Friend. This is the second aspect of the divine indwelling.

Not every love has the character of friendship, but that love which is together with benevolence, when we love someone we wish only good for him. If, however, we do not wish good to what we love, but wish good for ourselves (such as one who is said to love wine, or a horse, etc.), it is not a love of friendship, but a kind of concupiscence.

Yet neither does well-wishing suffice for friendship, for a certain mutual love is requisite, since friendship is between friend and friend: and this well-wishing is founded on some kind of communication.

Thus, there is a communication between man and God, in as much as he communicates his happiness to us. *God is faithful: by whom you are called on to the fellowship of his son* (1 Cor 1:9). The love, which is based on this communication, is charity: wherefore it is evident that charity is the friendship of man for God.[22]

The goal of the divine indwelling: It should not surprise us that the Trinitarian indwelling in our souls has a most exalted goal. This is the greatest gift of God, the foremost and greatest of all possible gifts, since it gives us a true and authentic possession of the very being of the infinite God. Sanctifying grace itself, an invaluable gift of unimaginable value, is of infinitely less value than the divine indwelling. Theology gives the name "uncreated grace" to the divine indwelling, as distinguished from habitual or sanctifying grace, which is so designated as created grace. There is an abyss between a creature– no matter how perfect it may be – and its Creator.

The divine indwelling is something akin to the hypostatic union in the person of Jesus Christ, although not quite the same.

---

[22] *S Th* II-II, 23,1.

Rather, it is sanctifying grace that constitutes us formally as adoptive children of God. Sanctifying grace, as we have seen, penetrates and formally imbues the divine presence in the soul, thus divinizing it. Nonetheless, the divine indwelling is something like the incarnation in our souls in that the absolutely divine comes into the human: the very being of God such as he is - One in essence and Three Persons - takes up his residence in the human soul.

The Blessed Trinity has three goals in mind in bringing this about: to make us intimate participants in the life of God; to constitute God as the mover and standard for our actions; and to share with us the joy of the Divine Persons.

To make us intimate participants in the life of God

To say that God dwells in our souls or inhabits us as in a temple, we are expressing a truth that is immediately supported by the famous texts of St. Paul already cited.

To better understand this ineffable mystery it is helpful to remember that grace comes to us as a sort of *seed of God* (*cf.* 1 Jn 3:9), which engenders new life within us: a true participation in divine life by which we not only call ourselves children of God, but are, in fact precisely that: *Yet so we are* (1 Jn 3:1).

This true participation in the divine life is not communicated to us by a passing act, as is the case in human generation, in which the child begins to be and to live independently of the existence of his biological father, from whom he has his origin. As long as the soul remains in a state of sanctifying grace God is continually and in an uninterrupted way communicating his grace and friendship. Just as if God the Creator were to retire his conserving action just for a moment from all created beings they would, therefore *ipso facto* fall into nothingness – just as a light bulb has the current of electricity cut from it; so too, if God were to take back just for a moment the conserving action of grace in the soul of the just, that grace would be instantaneously extinguished and the soul would cease to be a child of God.

Much like an embryo is continually receiving nutrition and health from its mother in a direct way, so too, the soul in grace is continually receiving supernatural, divine life from God in a direct way. Our entire spiritual life depends upon it. For this Christ came to the world, *that they might have life and have it more abundantly* (Jn 10:10). With these words we understand Paul's mysterious expression somewhat better: *Yet I live, no longer I, but Christ lives in me* (Gal 2:20).

This divine adoptive generation has a certain similarity to the generation of the eternal Logos in the interior life of the Father; and our union with God by grace is similar, in a certain way, to the union which exists between him and the Father and the Holy Spirit. No theologian would have dared to state such a thing had it not been revealed by Christ himself in Sacred Scripture in his sublime priestly prayer on the night of the Last Supper:

> *I pray not only for them, but also for those who will believe in me through their word, so that they may all be one, as you, Father, are in me and I in you, that they also may be in us, that the world may believe that you sent me. And I have given them the glory you gave me, so that they may be one, as we are one, I in them and you in me, that they may be brought to perfection as one, that the world may know that you sent me, and that you loved them even as you loved me* (Jn 17:20-23).

The Son of God is one with the Father by his unity of nature and we are one with God by a formal participation in that same divine nature, and this is sanctifying grace. The Son lives of the Father and we live, in a participating way, of God. He is in the Father and the Father is in him; and we as well are in God and God in us.

As a result, by way of grace, we are introduced into the Trinitarian life which is the very life of God who lives within us communicating his life to us. This is a work of the entire Blessed Trinity, not of one Person of the Trinity or another but of all Three in one common work.

Within the soul justified by grace, the three Persons live in their internal relations, introducing themselves to the soul, vivifying the soul by love and knowledge in the most intimate relations. There the Father engenders the Son truly. So too, from the Son and the Father proceeds the Holy Spirit truly, bringing about within the soul the sublime mystery of the unity of the Trinity which is the very life of God, without beginning or end.

To constitute God as the mover and standard for our actions

Life is essentially movement, dynamism, activity. In fact, we know of the existence of a vital form by the nature of its activity and its development. Since grace is a divine form, it too must have divine activity. This is an intrinsic exigency of grace itself in as much as it is a formal participation in the very nature of God. To live supernaturally is to act supernaturally.

As we have seen, this is precisely the function and the finality of the gifts of the Holy Spirit. Human reason, even when illumined by faith, which is the recipient of the infused virtues, is too poor a motor for such activity. Human activity, even when supported from on high, is incapable of reaching God.

It is true that the theological virtues have as their immediate object God himself, yet, as long as they are submitted to the regulation of human reason – even a reason illumined by supernatural faith – they therefore have to accommodate themselves to the human mode which is the created reason, and as such remain hemmed in by this all too human atmosphere, with its limited context. This is the reason that the Angelic Doctor uses to prove the existence of the gifts of the Holy Spirit which, perfecting the infused virtues, also as he communicates to them his divine mode of operation and puts them on a different level – a strictly supernatural one - demanded by the nature of grace and the infused virtues themselves. Human reason under the influence and motion of the gifts is prompted to operate and the acts are materially human but formally divine. Only in this way do we manage to live in the fullness of the divine life received by sanctifying grace.

Thus, the divine action of the gifts of the Holy Spirit is quite distinct from the divine action that is set in motion by the infused virtues. In the case of the divine activity in the infused virtues it corresponds to man to responsibly cooperate with the action as a motor and immediate cause of the same.

Therefore, the acts of the virtues are completely ours, since they are born of us, of our reason and our own free will, even though they are under the influence of God as the first cause, without whom their potency would never move to act - neither in the natural order nor in the supernatural order. But in the case of the gifts, the divine motion is completely distinct: the singular mover is God himself who puts the habit of the gifts in act limiting man to mere recipient of divine motion and seconding it by simply offering no resistance or any sort of modification to change its direction.

Thus, the acts resulting from the gifts are, in a certain way, divine, just as the melody an artist produces on his instrument is materially from the instrument but formally from the musician who plays it. The fact that God is the prime mover in all of this does not diminish in any way the merit of the person who docilely seconds the divine motion. Although God is the principle mover, that person must adhere with all his strength to the divine motion allowing himself to be used, as a channel, offering no resistance. The passivity required under the influence of the gift is relative, that is, only with respect to the initiative of the act which corresponds entirely and exclusively to God. Yet once this motion has been produced, one must freely react in associating oneself intimately with this divine action with all the vital strength and with the fullness of its free will one can muster. As a result, there is a confluence and cooperation of the divine initiative and the human response. The fruit of this free correspondence is supernatural merit.

By the action of the gifts of the Holy Spirit, God dwells in the depths of the just and takes the reins of one's spiritual life. This is no longer a case of human reason illuminated by faith with the human aspect dominating and governing; rather, God himself acts as the motor and the standard of our supernatural actions, putting in movement the entire spiritual organism and bringing it to its full development.

To share with us the joy of the Divine Persons

This is a phenomenon experienced and testified to by mystics throughout the history of the Church.

They experience the intense action of the Blessed Trinity at work within. St. Teresa of Avila says the following: "I have been visited by such a sense of the presence of God that in no way could I doubt that he was within me and I was engulfed by him."[23]

Each day the soul wonders more, for she feels that they (the Three divine Persons) have never left her, and perceives quite clearly, in the way I described, that They are in the interior of her heart – in the most interior place of all and in its greatest depths. She feels within herself this divine companionship.[24]

Volumes of other similar citations could be published. This experience is so clear and unequivocal in the experience of many mystics who came to the knowledge of the mystery of the divine indwelling without having been taught its doctrine, as is the case of St. Elizabeth of the Holy Trinity, recently canonized Carmelite.

The experience of the mystics does nothing but confirm the sublime teaching of the Church on the subject. St. Thomas Aquinas, the prince among theologians, writes the following:

By the gift of sanctifying grace, the rational creature is perfected so that it can freely use not only the created gift itself but *enjoy also the divine Person Himself.* The rational creature does sometimes attain thereto, as when it is made partaker of the divine Word and of the Love proceeding so as freely to know God truly and to love God rightly.[25]

This is the sublime greatness of the finality of the divine indwelling. God Himself, One in essence and Triune in Persons, constitutes the objective of this indescribable experience. The divine Persons surrender themselves to us so that we may enjoy them, according to Thomas' description. When this experiential joy reaches its heights, it is called transforming union. St. Teresa

---

[23] *Life,* 10, 1.
[24] *First Mansions,* 7.
[25] *S Th* I, 43,1.

of Avila speaks of this in her book on the seven mansions of the interior life, *Interior Castles*, which we will consider later in this book. Those who have reached these heights lose all ability to express with human language what they experience; rather, they prefer to be silent and alone in the intimate union with the Blessed Trinity to savor the experience rather than air it publicly. Some of those who have achieved the heights of mysticism also have a certain mystical charism, the ability to express this experience. We see the foundation for this charism in the *First Letter of St. John*:

What was from the beginning, what we have heard, what we have seen with our eyes, what we looked upon and touched with our hands concerns the Word of life—for the life was made visible; we have seen it and testify to it and proclaim to you the eternal life that was with the Father and was made visible to us—what we have seen and heard we proclaim now to you, so that you too may have fellowship with us; for our fellowship is with the Father and with his Son, Jesus Christ (Jn 1:1-3).

St. John of the Cross, who definitely had the charism, said he preferred not to speak about his experience: "The delicateness of delight felt in this contact is inexpressible. I would desire not to speak of it to avoid giving the impression that it is no more than what I describe. There is no way to adequately express the sublime things of God that occur in the spiritual life of these favored ones. The appropriate language for the persons receiving these favors is that they understand them, experience them within themselves, enjoy them, and remain silent.... Thus, one can only say, and truthfully, 'That tastes of eternal life.' Although one does not have perfect fruition in this life as in glory, this touch, nevertheless, since it is a touch, taste of eternal life."[26] Consequently, St. John is never autobiographical, rather he approaches the mystical experience through the rigors of Scholastic theology, mapping out the itinerary of our cooperation with grace with lucidity and theological precision.

What the intellect knew by faith is now experienced in the depths of the soul in an almost tangible, visible way. St. Teresa of Avila says about this: "What we hold by faith the soul may be said here to grasp by sight, although nothing is seen by the eyes, neither of the body or of the soul, for it is no imaginary vision.

Here all three Persons communicate themselves to the soul and speak to the soul and explain to it those words which the Gospel attributes to the Lord – namely, that he and the Father and the Holy Spirit will come to dwell with the soul which loves him and keeps his commandments (cf. Jn 14:23).[27]

This experiential knowledge of God, although substantially the same, is infinitely superior because the mode of knowing him by means of the reason is illumined by faith. From the pen of St. Teresa: "Oh, God help me! What a difference there is between hearing and believing these words and being led in this way to realize how true they are!"[28] The reason for this inequality and difference between the knowledge by faith and knowledge by experience is quite clear – but only fully understood by those who have the mystical experience.

---

[26] Living Flame of Love, 2, n. 21.
[27] Seventh Mansion, 1, n.6.
[28] Ibid., 1, n. 7.

-6-
The Gift that Keeps on Giving

The divine indwelling, sanctifying grace, infused virtues, and the gifts of the Holy Spirit: such is the immense treasure granted to the just – all of this equips us with a supernatural organism and mechanism. And nonetheless something is still lacking to enable us to carry out the most minute of supernatural actions. To have the most advanced technology, and in fact, an entire factory filled with them, would serve no purpose if there were no electricity to power them. The supernatural electrical current that puts the spiritual organism in movement is called actual grace; without which one would be totally incapable of carrying out the smallest of supernatural actions.

The divine indwelling and sanctifying grace are static elements, not dynamic: they are ordered towards being and not operation. Regarding infused virtues and the gifts of the Holy Spirit, they are certainly dynamic elements, but they cannot be moved without a previous push by actual grace which is, once again, the electrical current which puts the technological apparatus to work. This is the supernatural element we will examine now.

The nature of actual grace

As its name indicates, actual grace is transitory, ethereal, and not permanent as is the case with sanctifying grace, the virtues, or the gifts of the Holy Spirit. Ordered towards the habitual and infused habits by their nature, the role of actual graces is to dispose us to receive them when they are lacking.

In other words, the actual grace of repentance in the case of one in the state of sin or, in the case of another in grace, is to dispose that person to better cooperate with grace. As might be imagined, it is impossible to enumerate actual graces.

Actual grace can be defined in this way: It is an interior and transitory supernatural help with which God illumines our understanding and fortifies our will to carry out supernatural actions proceeding from the infused virtues or the gifts of the Holy Spirit.

Interior: Actual grace has as its object to illuminate the intellect and move the will to carry out supernatural actions, and in this sense is called interior. But sometimes God disposes of something external to us to send us an actual grace i.e., a sermon, a book, good spiritual counsel, the death of a loved one that leaves a supernatural impression, etc. Other times it is God himself who moves our understanding with a good inspiration or moves our will, gently inducing us to carry out the good.

Transitory: Unlike sanctifying grace or habitual grace as it is called, which resides permanently within us if it is not expelled by grave sin, actual grace is a transitory aid which disappears in the very moment in which God ceases to communicate it. It is not a habit but rather an act; hence the name actual.

Supernatural help: This is well above our simple nature. It does not find its roots in us nor can we demand it or exercise it naturally. It is a great gift of God, completely gratuitous. God will not deny it to anyone who asks for it humbly and many times he sends us these aids without our asking for them simply because he is good and merciful.

Which illumines our understanding: It grants us insights into what we must do to be saved and be sanctified.

Fortifies our will: Actual grace helps the will by moving it to desire and carry out what it has understood under the light of grace that which is necessary or useful for our salvation and sanctification. It is not enough to understand what we ought to do; we must carry it out.

To carry out supernatural actions: This is the reason God communicates such graces to us. The supernatural actions to which these graces are ordered are three different types: the sinner who does not possess sanctifying grace is moved to repentance; the imperfect Christian who is called to a greater surrender to God's will; the saint is called to greater abnegation of himself and to absolute surrender to God.

Proceeding from the infused virtues are the gifts of the Holy Spirit: without actual grace, the virtues and the gifts would remain completely paralyzed and inactive. Even in the state of grace one would find it impossible to carry out any sort of supernatural act. If one in a state of grace is not capable of this, how much more the person in the state of mortal sin? The sinner could never repent enough to recover the grace of God if God had not previously granted him the actual grace of repentance. No one can utter in a meritorious way the Holy Name of Jesus unless previously moved by the help of actual grace (*Cf.* 1 Cor 12:3). Christ himself tells us: *No one can come to me unless the Father who sent me draw him* (Jn 6:44). And another place he says: *I am the vine, you are the branches. Whoever remains in me and I in him will bear much fruit, because without me you can do nothing* (Jn 15:5).

Every action of infused virtue or a gift of the Holy Spirit in action presupposes a previous actual grace which has put it in movement. This is what St. Paul means when he says: *Not that of ourselves we are qualified to take credit for anything as coming from us; rather, our qualification comes from God* (2 Cor 3:5). And further he says, *For God is the one who, for his good purpose, works in you both to desire and to work* (Phil 2:13).

The division of actual graces

Although actual graces are innumerable we can categorize them into certain fundamental groups according to their specific function.

Operating and cooperating grace: Operating grace is that grace which proceeds exclusively from God and is attributed to him alone: we are moved rather than move of our own accord. Cooperating grace is that grace in which the person is impelled by God and at the same time moves itself, cooperating with divine action. About this, Thomas says the following:

> For the operational effect is not attributed to the thing moved but to the mover. Hence in that effect in which your mind is moved it does not move of itself, but rather God is the sole mover, the operation is attributed to God, and it is with reference to this that we speak of operating grace. But there is another, exterior; and since it is commanded by the will, the operation of this is attributed to the will. And because God assists us in this, both by strengthening our will interiorly so as to attain to the act, and by granting outwardly the capability of operating, it is with respect to this that we speak

of cooperating grace.[29]

Awakening grace and helping grace: The first works as an impulse to the person who is either distracted or inactive; the second works as a help to the one who has already decided to act supernaturally.

Prevenient grace, concomitant grace, fulfilling grace: The first precedes the act, moving, disposing the will to desire it. The second accompanies the act of man during the carrying out of it. And finally, the third is related to the other two that have preceded it, helping the person to carry out an act that God has already initiated. Another name for these last two is "subsequent grace," following on the heels of fruitful and realized prevenient grace.

Internal and external grace: The first effects directly and intrinsically the powers of the soul, the intellect and the will *i.e.,* an inspiration of God that enlightens the intellect is more properly called "illuminating grace"; while God's work directly on the human will is called "inspiring grace." External grace that influences the person from without, i.e., externally, such as a good example, hearing a powerful sermon, Sacred Liturgy, etc. These external graces dispose us to receive further internal graces.

Gratia gratis data: Although every grace is *gratis data*, i.e. a free gift of the Divine Goodness - the term *Gratia gratis data* means those graces granted to particular persons for the salvation of others. To this class belong such extraordinary gifts of grace as charismatic graces (prophecy, gift of miracles, gift of tongues, the priestly power of consecration, the hierarchical power of

---

[29] *S Th* I-II, 111, 2.

jurisdiction).

The possession of these gifts is independent of the personal moral composition of their recipient. However,

> Extraordinary gifts are not to be sought after, nor are the fruits of apostolic labor to be presumptuously expected from their use; but judgment as to their authenticity and proper use belongs to those who are appointed leaders in the Church, to whose special competence it belongs, not indeed to extinguish the Spirit, but to test all things and hold fast to that which is good.[30]

Sanating grace: Divine grace in its function of healing (*sanare*, to heal) the wounds of sin, original and personal, in human nature. This healing process addresses both the mind and the will. Grace heals the will by giving strength to desire and accept the known will of God, and joy in its performance. This grace is also necessary to heal the memory of past wounds, so they do not fester and turn the person to rancor and bitterness.

Sufficient and efficient grace: In the case of the first, it is enough for the person to not resist it for it to set in motion divine action (such as all of the external graces and many of the internal inspirations). This grace gives the recipient the power to accomplish the salutary act. The second is of the sort that moves us internally in such an efficacious way that it infallibly carries out that which God intended without compromising human freedom. It accomplishes the act.

Regarding this, St. Bernard of Clairvaux asked if this was a question of 50% human freedom and 50% God's grace at work;

---

[30] Lumen Gentium, 12.

he solved the issue by determining that it was a question of cooperation of 100% on both sides, for at this point the person is so well disposed to do the will of God that the cooperation is connatural. Without the first sort of grace we cannot work; with the second we work infallibly. The first leaves us with no excuse before God for not desiring to carry it out – such as not following a good counsel or a good inspiration. The second is a gratuitous effect resulting from the infinite mercy of God, helping us to want exactly what God wants.

This last division of grace is of great service to us to understand God's mercy. St. Paul tells us that God wants that all men be saved (1 Tim 2:4); and as a result, he gives everyone, without exception, Christians and pagans, the actual graces that they need – sufficient for them to be saved if they want to take advantage of those graces. If one does not resist those graces and, under their influence, does what he must to correspond perfectly with them, God will, as a result, grant him efficient graces with which to achieve eternal salvation. Condemnation does not come without personal responsibility. God does not condemn anybody without first having given the person sufficient means with which to cooperate with his will in order to be saved. But the person must cooperate with his will and desire to cooperate with his will; or else he will assume responsibility for his own perdition.

Actual grace and our responsibility

God grants all men sufficient graces to carry out his will to overcome temptation. Precisely because these actual graces that God showers us with are so many, so great, and so continuous, our responsibility only increases. St. Paul says, *work out your salvation with fear and trembling* (Phil 2:12). And in another place:

we appeal to you not to receive the grace of God in vain (2 Cor 6:1).

It is theologically sound to maintain that of all the graces our Lord has planned to shower us with throughout our entire life, posterior graces are dependent upon anterior graces and our cooperation with them. Willful infidelity to one grace can cut the entire chain of subsequent graces of linked graces God had planned for us – graces irretrievably lost.

Our Lord refers to this with the following parable:

There was once a person who had a fig tree planted in his orchard, and when he came in search of fruit on it but found none, he said to the gardener, 'For three years now I have come in search of fruit on this fig tree but have found none. [So] cut it down. Why should it exhaust the soil?' He said to him in reply, 'Sir, leave it for this year also, and I shall cultivate the ground around it and fertilize it; it may bear fruit in the future. If not you can cut it down' (Lk 13:6-9).

It is a frightful thing to consider that God might tire of giving us grace upon grace when we are indolent and sterile, as in the case of the sterile fig tree (*cf.* Mt 21:19).

If Divine Mercy is infinite, and we know that it is, God's respect for human freedom is also remarkable, especially when we abuse it:

Then he began to reproach the towns where most of his mighty deeds had been done, since they had not repented. "Woe to you, Chorazin! Woe to you, Bethsaida! For if the mighty deeds done in your midst had been done in Tyre and Sidon, they would long ago have repented in sackcloth and ashes. But I tell you, it will be more tolerable for Tyre and Sidon on the day of judgment than for you

(Mt 11:20-22).

Above all we should not forget that the one who is to judge us is the crucified God. Crucified for our sins. And nonetheless he is the one who has showered us with grace upon grace, many of which have not reached their end or worse, we have spurned by our selfishness. They literally cost him his Blood. With reason St. Paul alludes to this Precious Blood saying: *For you have been purchased at a price. Therefore, glorify God in your body* (1 Cor 6:20). St. Peter insists on the same: *realizing that you were ransomed from your futile conduct, handed on by your ancestors, not with perishable things like silver or gold but with the precious blood of Christ as of a spotless unblemished lamb* (1 Pet 1:18-19).

Grace and efficient actual graces

Catholic theology teaches that efficient actual graces – that is, those that always and infallibly produced their effect – cannot be merited in the strict sense, not even by those who already possess habitual or sanctifying grace. Nonetheless, even though we cannot merit them we can attain them infallibly through prayer under certain circumstances.

It is not the same thing to merit something by means of justice as to attain it infallibly by means of impetration; that is, to beg for it. The worker has merited his pay at the end of the day and therefore this is a thing of justice. The beggar, on the other hand, receives his unmerited alms, in consequence of the generosity of the benefactor hearing his petition. The important thing here is not whether we merit it or achieve it through asking for it; the most important thing is that we receive it and know how to attain it.

For sure, this Catholic doctrine is firm and certain, founded on the promise of Christ. This begging prayer has certain conditions: humility, trust, perseverance without tiring – all of this by the merits of Christ. These are the necessary conditions to attain actual graces. In doing so and by living in a Christian way we will most definitely finally reach our destiny, eternal salvation. Christ expressly promised this with the following words: *Ask and it will be given to you; seek and you will find; knock and the door will be opened to you. For everyone who asks, receives; and the one who seeks, finds; and to the one who knocks, the door will be opened* (Mt 7:7-8).

These are the words of Christ, the eternal Logos. We know that the heavens and the earth will pass but the words of Christ will be fulfilled perfectly. If we do not grow weary in prayer, if we do not tire of incessantly asking for our own salvation we can have the absolute security that we will attain the infinite mercy of God by the merits of Christ the Redeemer.

-7-

The Birth of the Life of Grace

Before considering the sacraments and the grace they impart, we ought to understand that they have been entrusted to the Catholic Church for their administration.

It was possible for [Christ] to impart these graces to mankind directly; but He willed to do so only through a visible Church made up of men, so that through her all might cooperate with Him in dispensing the graces of Redemption.

As the Word of God willed to make use of our nature, when in excruciating agony He would redeem mankind, so in the same way throughout the centuries He makes use of the Church that the work begun might endure.

The spiritual birth of the Christian to the life of grace begins with the sacrament of baptism, which, as a result, has received the name of the sacrament of regeneration. It is also called correctly the sacrament of adoption, because it infuses within us sanctifying grace, thus we become adoptive children of God, as we have seen. Further, it is called the sacrament of Christian initiation because in it the process of our Christian life begins – something that must be developed progressively until we reach the age of perfection according to the measure of Christ's plan.[31]

In this chapter we will consider the nature of baptism, the effects it produces, and the principal exigencies it brings with it.

The nature of baptism

We know by faith that Christ instituted the sacrament of baptism as well as the other six sacraments.

Baptism comes from the Greek word *baptismos*, derived from the verb *baptizein*, which means "to submerge." The external symbol of baptism – ablutions with water – exteriorizes what is happening within the soul: a purification of sin and the infusion of sanctifying grace.

Baptism is a sacrament of spiritual regeneration by way of ablution with water and the express invocation of the three Persons of the Blessed Trinity.

Sacrament: This is the approximate genus common to all of the sacraments. Proper to them is to be outward signs of inward grace that they confer.

Spiritual regeneration: This is the specific difference that distinguishes baptism from the other sacraments. Through this spiritual generation the soul bears within itself many gifts - as we will see when discussing the effects of baptism.

By way of ablution with water: This is the matter proper to baptism since it is a sacrament. In other cases, there is the possibility of a baptism of blood – martyrdom suffered for Christ; and the baptism of desire – the charity or perfect contrition of a sinner not baptized, under the impulse of an prevenient grace.

---

[31] Mystici Corporis, 12.

The express invocation of the three divine Persons of the Blessed Trinity: This is the proper form of the sacrament of baptism, indispensable for its validity. The invocation of the divine persons must be explicit: "I baptize you in the name of the Father, and of the Son, and of the Holy Spirit". Any other utterance such as "I baptize you in the name of the Blessed Trinity", or "In the name of Creator, the Redeemer, and the Sanctifier" or in the "Name of Jesus Christ" does not affect a valid baptism.

Not having received baptism one may not receive validly any other sacrament. If, for example, an unbaptized person receives the Eucharist he will not receive the grace proper to the Eucharist – even if that person were in a state of grace thanks to perfect contrition or perfect charity. That is why baptism is called the gateway to all the other sacraments because without having received it one may not receive any other sacrament validly.

The effects produced by baptism

The sacrament of baptism produces a series of divine wonders in the soul. First, it infuses sanctifying grace under the auspices of regeneration that is proper to baptism thereby capacitating the soul to receive the subsequent sacraments.

Second, it transforms the baptized person into a living temple of the Blessed Trinity prepared for the divine indwelling through race.

Third, it plants the seeds of all the infused virtues and the gifts of the Holy Spirit.

Fourth, it makes the baptized into a living member of Jesus Christ as a branch on the vine (*cf.* Jn 15: 1-5). If that vital principle, by which the whole community of Christians is sustained by its Founder, be considered not now in itself, but in the created effects which proceed from it, it consists in those heavenly gifts which our Redeemer, together with His Spirit, bestows on the Church, and which He and His Spirit, from whom come supernatural light and holiness, make operative in the Church. The Church, then, no less than each of her holy members can make this great saying of the Apostle her own: *And I live, now not I; but Christ lives in me.*[32]

Fifth, it imprints a baptismal character that incorporates us as living members of the Mystical Body of Christ - that is, the Church, and thereby gives us a real and true participation, albeit incomplete, in the priesthood of Christ. This priestly participation is perfected with the character of confirmation and requires its fullness in the character of priestly ordination.

Sixth, it totally erases original sin from the soul and all actual sins anyone may have committed before baptism. Grace does not simply cover our sins, as some Protestants maintain, but rather erases them, making them disappear totally. This has been expressly defined by the Council of Trent:

> If anyone denies that by the grace of our Lord Jesus Christ which is conferred in baptism, the guilt of original sin is remitted, or says that the whole of that which belongs to the essence of sin is not taken away but says that it is only canceled or not imputed, let him be anathema."[33]

Seventh, it remits all punishment due to sin whether temporal or eternal. For example, if a hardened sinner receives

---

[32] Mystici Corporis, 58.
[33] Denzinger, 1515.

baptism shortly before his death he enters immediately into heaven without passing through purgatory. The Council of Florence teaches this explicitly: "The sacrament is the remission of every sin, original and actual, also of every punishment which is due to the sin itself. Therefore, no satisfaction must be enjoined for past sins and if they die before committing any fault they immediately attain the kingdom of heaven and the vision of God."[34] The Council of Trent reiterates this.[35]

Baptism and its demands

It is understandable that a reality such as the one we are considering should bring with it immense demands upon the recipient to correspond with the grace received. Of the two principal commands the first is negative and the second positive: to die definitively to sin and to begin a new life for God in Christ Jesus.

St. Paul elaborates on these responsibilities:

How can we who died to sin yet live in it? Or are you unaware that we who were baptized into Christ Jesus were baptized into his death? We were indeed buried with him through baptism into death, so that, just as Christ was raised from the dead by the glory of the Father, we too might live in newness of life.

For if we have grown into union with him through a death like his, we shall also be united with him in the resurrection. We know that our old self was crucified with him, so that our sinful body might be done away with, that we might no longer be in slavery to sin. For a

---

[34] *Ibid.*, 1316.
[35] *Ibid.*, 1672.

dead person has been absolved from sin. If, then, we have died with Christ, we believe that we shall also live with him. We know that Christ, raised from the dead, dies no more; death no longer has power over him. ... Consequently, you too must think of yourselves as [being] dead to sin and living for God in Christ Jesus (Rom 6: 2-11).

To die definitively to sin: The first and most fundamental demand of baptism is our definitive death to sin. Any Christian aware of the exalted dignity of his state as an adopted child of God should consider the prospect of committing one mortal sin as a non-negotiable.

Who would trade his life for a nickel? There's no possible comparison between what sin offers us and what God offers us through grace. Nonetheless, we are continually tempted by the world, the flesh, and the devil.

There is nothing in the physical order that can be compared to what happens spiritually to a soul in mortal sin. St. Teresa of Avila, who through the mercy of God saw the effects of mortal sin, affirms that,

"There is no darkness as black as that." She goes on to say, "I know of a person of whom our Lord wished to show what a soul was like when it committed mortal sin. That person says that, if people can understand this, she thinks they would find it impossible to sin at all, and, to avoid putting itself in occasion of sin, it would go to the greatest lengths imaginable."[36]

Fortunately, as long as the sinner is alive in this life his tragedy, regardless of how abominable, is not irreparable. Everything can be repaired by the hands of him knows how to

---

[36] First Mansions, c, n. 2.

create. For sure, the justification of the sinner is a greater act than the creation of the entire universe; and it is nonetheless not beyond the power, and much less, beyond the infinite mercy of God.

To die definitively to sin is the foremost and most fundamental demand which baptism brings with it. But this is in no way the ideal of a Christian. The final goal is far beyond that and to reach it one must lead a new life, completely handed over to Jesus Christ in God.

To live with Christ in God: After reminding us that by baptism we have died to sin, St. Paul exhorts us to live for God in Christ Jesus (Rom 6:11). Referring to the exigencies which baptism, that is our resurrection Christ brings with it, he writes: *If then you were raised with Christ, seek what is above, where Christ is seated at the right hand of God. Think of what is above, not of what is on earth. For you have died, and your life is hidden with Christ in God* (Col 3:1-3).

Unfortunately, there are legions of Christians who are so in name only. They are absorbed by the concerns of this world, enchanted by the things it promises, rarely lifting their eyes, much less their hearts, to heaven. They may live good lives on a natural plane but without supernatural horizons or ideals of perfection, they do not long for sanctity. For such as them physical health is more important than spiritual health; earning money is more important than winning grace; comfort is more important than penance. For some, unfortunately, they will only discover their folly at the moment of the definitive divorce of their body and soul.

The demands of Christianity seem unbearable to worldlings – effete spirits who shrink at the idea of sacrifice. And nonetheless for those who have tasted the goodness of the Lord the demands are more than reasonable, they are a source of tremendous joy – even when lived imperfectly, because they are immersed in the great mystery of Christ and the sublime elevation of their Christian vocation, and their greatness of spirit is revealed supported by the many blessings of God.

The true great ones of this world are those hidden in cloisters, those who carry out their duty according to their state in life – lay or consecrated - in a quiet humble fashion, not concerned for fame or what this world has to offer but rejoicing in doing the will of God precisely because it is the will of God. For them the words of St. Paul always ring true: "For the wisdom of this world is foolishness in the eyes of God" (1 Cor 3:19).

The Christian who is aware of his divine greatness and of the sublime nature of his eternal destiny passes through this brief life as a pilgrim and a stranger to the things of this world, fulfilling with joy and a profound sense of freedom the demands and obligations proper to his temporal state. He reminds himself constantly that *here we have no lasting city, but we seek the one that is to come* (Heb 13:14).

In similar terms St. Peter says, *Beloved, I urge you as aliens and sojourners to keep away from worldly desires that wage war against the soul* (1 Pet 2:11).

Our foremost concern must be to center ourselves effectively on this one task of intensely living our baptismal grace, living the new life of Christ hidden in Christ, walking from virtue to virtue until we see God on the holy Mount Zion (*cf.* Ps 83:8), until we are perfectly transformed into Christ.

-8-

Utter Disaster: The Loss of Grace

The treasure of divine sanctifying grace can be culpably lost through sin. This sad reality is present in the lives of most men, even those who profess faith in Christ. To better understand our enemy, we will consider its nature in the following pages.

Sin: our mortal enemy

Sin is enemy number one of the Christian lives, and in fact, it is our singular enemy; since the world, the flesh, and the devil can only provoke temptation but never compel us to sin.

Sin is a voluntary transgression of the law of God. It supposes three essential elements: prohibited matter (or at least considered as such by the sinner); knowledge on part of the intellect, and consent on part of the will. If the matter is grave and the knowledge and consent are full, and sin committed, it is considered mortal – it kills the supernatural life of the soul. If the matter is not grave or the full knowledge lacks, or the will has not given full consent, the sin is venial – called as such because it is easier to obtain pardon (*venia*) for it.

Sin, even the most light or venial, constitutes a great disgrace for the person who commits it. Whatever purely natural calamity that can befall the body or one's life can never compare with the disaster of sin. The disaster is exponentially incremented if the sin is committed frequently and directed deliberately, since a habit of venial sins prepares us for the ultimate disaster of mortal sin, bringing about our own spiritual death, the loss of the life of grace. When committed with full deliberation, a mortal sin rips out the life of grace from the soul and the person becomes a cadaver, walking dead, in the spiritual and supernatural order. Such a person becomes a separated limb, cut off from Jesus Christ, the Head of the Mystical Body. He is a twig cut off from the branch with no life of his own, good for nothing except to be thrown into the fire to be burnt.

Classifications of sin

Not everyone who lives habitually in the state of sin has contracted the same degree of responsibility before God. Distinguishing the degrees of gravity, we find four categories of sin:

Sins of ignorance: Here we are not referring to total or invincible ignorance which would cancel out responsibility, rather the results of a faulty religious education or indifference joined to limited intelligence, hostile environment or education or distance from authentic religious influence. People who live in such circumstances still have access to the demands of natural law and therefore understand some things are sinful and some things are not. Such people understand that certain actions that they commit are not morally correct. At times they even experience remote remorse of conscience. As a result, they have some sufficient capacity to commit gravely immoral acts with sufficient knowledge and will to make it mortal, thus jeopardizing their eternal salvation.

Nonetheless, all of this is important to recognize that their responsibility is somewhat mitigated before God, and the collection of circumstances is considered by divine justice and mercy. If Christ has said, *Much will be required of the person entrusted with much* (Lk 12:48), it makes sense that for him who has received little, little will be expected.

Someone who has conserved a healthy horror for sin, and in the depths of his heart, in spite of his own weakness, has followed his conscience, who has tried to be faithful to the little that he has learned in the order of faith, and in the face of death lifts up his repentant heart and mind to God asking for mercy, such a one can be assured of experiencing Divine Mercy.

Generally, people who have not received very good spiritual or religious instruction and nonetheless have sought to be faithful to the dictates of their conscience and the demands of natural law, once they are confronted with the truth of the faith through grace, receive it wholly and without obstacle. Because the disorder in their life is not engendered by malice but rather through ignorance they are open to the action of grace. It is often the case that through a difficult or traumatic experience such as the death of a loved one or something of similar pain, it is enough for such people to be exposed to the truth for them to accept it. Having received this actual grace, it is important for this person to learn the faith and live according to it, as well as to take advantage of the means of ongoing formation offered by his parish (provided the formation offered there is solid and true to Catholic teaching – which sadly, is not always the case).

Sins of weakness: Many people have received enough formation in the Faith that they must also bear its contingent responsibility. Like the former category, their sins are not the result of calculated malice or a cold heart. They are simply weak and have little energy and less willpower. Strongly inclined to the pleasures of the flesh, they suffer the effects of having given in to their carnal desires: a compromised will.

These people admire virtue in others and bemoan their own faults. They would like to be better, but they lack the fortitude and the courage to actually be better. Certainly, these dispositions do not excuse their sin; on the contrary, they are more culpable than those who sin in ignorance because of their increased awareness. Rather than malice, the root of the problem is weakness.

Confessors and spiritual directors should seek to fortify these people, encourage them, give them sound counsel, and invite them to frequent the sacraments. The weak-willed person will only triumph if he builds his spiritual life on the foundation of grace and mental prayer (more about that later).

Sins of coldness and indifference: There is a third category of the sinners who do not sin out of ignorance, as in the case of the first group; nor, as in the second category, are they ashamed at their own conduct. They sin knowing they sin, not precisely because they want evil since it is evil – that is, a desire to offend God – rather because they refuse to renounce the pleasures sin brings with it and are not concerned with the fact that their sins are offensive in God's sight. These unfortunate ones sin with coldness, with indifference, without remorse of conscience, attempting to quiet whatever voice of their consciences left in order to continue in their sinful way with as little obstruction as possible.

From this category conversions are rare. The continual infidelity to the inspiration of grace, the cold indifference with which these people live before the Face of God, going against reason, the natural order, their natural and supernatural ends close their minds to whatever good counsels come their way. They end up not only with a cold heart but a hardened heart. It would require a true miracle of grace for them to be converted. If they are caught by death in this state their eternal life will be the horrible result of their free choices.

For somebody in this state the most helpful means to come out of their torpor would be to do Ignatian spiritual exercises (provided the retreat is in accord with Catholic teaching and authentic Ignatian spirituality).

Although it may seem strange, it is not unheard of that from among this category of sinner, miracles of grace can occur. For somebody like this to do the spiritual exercises it is often necessary that a friend or a peer make the personal invitation. What an honor it is to be the agent of grace in making the invitation! *The love of Christ compels us* (cfr. 2 Cor 5:14) to share the treasure that has brought us so much joy.

Obstinate and malicious sinner: Finally, the fourth category of sinners is the most horrible and culpable of all. These people do not sin out of ignorance, weakness, or indifference, rather have achieved a certain refined malice and a diabolical stubbornness. Amongst these people the most common sin is that of blasphemy, uttered out of hatred for God. Such an attitude as this is not achieved overnight.

It could be that these people in this category began as solid Christians who followed the slippery slope of the disordered passions, and once made slaves to their disorder they consciously and willfully opt for it, embracing their own disaster. Once in the grip of desperation, whether tacit or manifest, they formulate a fundamental option against God. These people become enemies of God and his Church and their words and works prove it. The conversion of one of such of these would require a grace greater than the resurrection of the dead in the natural order.

It would be useless to attempt to convert an obstinate sinner by means of argumentation. There is no other way than the strictly supernatural: prayer, fasting, tears, and incessant recourse to the Blessed Virgin Mary – the Refuge of Sinners. God hears such prayers but does not always respond to them in the way we would prefer. He respects our free will, but he also respects the free will of the obstinate and malicious sinner. Although Divine Mercy is infinite, it is also conditional – dependent upon the repentance of the sinner and his willingness to accept it. God's justice is perfect and awaits the unrepentant.

The return to grace for people of this ilk would require a true miracle of grace. On the other hand, many of the great masses of people who continue in sin out of weakness or ignorance, and nonetheless have maintained supernatural faith, practice certain devotions, albeit on a superficial level, and as a result consider eternity and the life of their souls occasionally. It seems they put off their conversion by immersing themselves in work, hobbies, distractions of politics and news, entertainment. Limiting one's following of Christ to simply going to Mass on Sundays and confessing once a year certainly puts one's eternal life at risk. What can be done to open these people to the truth of their situation? If the love of Christ is not enough to inspire them to change their ways, perhaps a catechesis on the nature and consequences of mortal sin would help.

Developing a horror for mortal sin

To attain a healthy horror for mortal sin and its disastrous consequences, dedication to a life of prayer and other supernatural means is necessary. The great spiritual theologian Abbot Carlos Grimaud offers us an impressive and graphic image of what the catastrophe of mortal sin means for the member cut off from Christ, The Head of the Mystical Body, resulting in death for the severed member:

To better understand the evil consequences of this rupture with Christ we can compare it to the situation in which the hand is severed from the body in an accident.

Just as my wrist constitutes a strong union between my hand and my arm so too in the Mystical Body the member maintains its union with the Divine Head through grace, as St. Paul says, *and not holding closely to the head, from whom the whole body, supported and held together by its ligaments and bonds, achieves the growth that comes from God* (Col 2:19). More particularly, the unifying principles are those that assure solidity between the member and the Head and the Mystical Body such as faith, hope, and charity.

Being born again *of water and the Holy Spirit* (Jn 3:5), the soul is re–created. To its natural being are aggregated supernatural powers, rendering it capable of union with Christ and attaching it to him. These new faculties permit the soul, as it were, to touch God: faith, which permits us to be united to Christ, the eternal truth and the Blessed Trinity; hope, which gives us the power to be bound to the supreme good which it will possess in heaven; charity, which grants us the possibility of being fed by divine love. By way of these three bonds the member is solidly united to the head, attached to the Mystical Body as a hand is to an integral human body – it is one solid individual.[37]

After describing charity as the nerve center in the arteries which conduct the regenerating divine blood in the spiritual organism, our author compares faith and hope to the tendons that strengthen the union between the hand and the arm:

It could be that after a certain accident my hand is not completely separated from the arm. The artery and the nerves – that is charity – has been severed. The tendons of faith and hope keep the hand from falling off completely, albeit in a disastrous state. Mortal sin, the worst of spiritual disasters possible, works in an identical way cutting off the vital connection to the mystical body. Rarely are the contingent ligaments of faith and hope cut completely. Charity is always cut off and with it the spiritual arteries and nerves. But faith and hope – the tendons – remain. As a result, the sinner who has just consented to temptation preserves his faith in Christ and his desire for heaven, saying to himself "God is so good he will forgive me." Some people reason along the following lines: I might as well enjoy the sin because later I can ask pardon in confession. Such calculation reveals broken friendship not necessarily broken faith and hope. From this moment, just as in the case of the severed hand hanging on by a few tendons, this poor sinner – severed from the Body – has the possibility of being reunited to the Body of Christ. He is the withered branch, lifeless and separated from the vine: *The branch which does not produce fruit will be cut off, taken and thrown in the fire.* (Jn 15:5,6)

Before such a threat as this, that is, divine justice, the separated member has no other recourse than to call upon the

---

37 *El y nosotros: un solo Cristo* (Buenos Aires, 1944) p. 62. My translation.

merciful help from the head of the Mystical Body to be re-integrated to its proper place in the body.

How many members of Christ have foolishly separated themselves from him and refused to call upon his mercy! If nobody were to take care of that hand it would remain lifeless and hanging by its tendons - what a horrible image! In the same way, stubborn in their sin, many sinners, that is lifeless members, remain dangling from the side of the Mystical Body without any concern for the reintegration. Much like the hand, which is lifeless, they begin to rot.

Once putrefaction has taken over the tendons which kept the hand suspended and connected to the arm are slowly eaten away. Such is the fate of the spiritual tendons which kept the sinners subject to the mystical body: first hope goes, then faith. Once this occurs the disgrace is complete: an absolute separation from the Mystical Body of Christ.

Indeed, this dynamic sadly repeats itself in the lives of many sinners who lose hope for eternal rewards: "Heaven is not for me," they say. The same sinner ends up not believing in God: "If there were a God why would he be so demanding?" or pablum such as "I'm spiritual not religious" as an excuse to disbelieve what God has revealed. Once this was a member of the glorious Body of Christ. It now has been reduced to a severed limb in the spiritual order.[38]

Grace lost through mortal sin can be recovered

In human terms it is impossible for a sinner who has voluntarily separated himself from God by way of mortal sin to be reintegrated. If God does not grant him the gratuitous grace

---

[38] Op. cit.

of repentance, he will eternally remain in his sin. It is not unlike the situation of someone who has voluntarily thrown himself down a well only to find it impossible for him to get out without assistance. If God does not throw him a rope - the actual grace of efficacious repentance: a prevenient grace – something to which no sinner has a right, given his voluntary situation, his disgrace will be absolutely irreparable. He will be eternally lost.

Let everyone then abhor sin, which defiles the mystical members of our Redeemer; but if anyone unhappily falls and his obstinacy has not made him unworthy of communion with the faithful, let him be received with great love, and let eager charity see in him a weak member of Jesus Christ. For, as the Bishop of Hippo remarks, it is better "to be cured within the Church's community than to be cut off from its body as incurable members." As long as a member still forms part of the body there is no reason to despair of its cure; once it has been cut off, it can be neither cured nor healed."[39]

God, however, in his ineffable mercy does not normally deny the grace of pardon to the person who asks with true contrition. As such he instituted the sacrament of reconciliation, confession, which any baptized Catholic may receive. God can also give the grace of perfect contrition to those who are not baptized, that is, an impulse of actual grace to ask for pardon.

Abbot Grimaud goes on to say:

Imagine the excitement produced if a saint with the gift of miracles such as Vincent Ferrer, Jean Marie Vianney, or Don Bosco were to find somebody hurt in an accident and at the

---

[39] Mystici Corporis, 24.

poor injured man's bidding, were to make a sign of the Cross and miraculously rejoin an already purified hand to the arm making the man completely well – and all of this to the glory of the Holy Trinity!

Crowds from all over would rush to see the man who has been miraculously healed to his previous strength and active life, made once again a productive member of society. In order not to be carried off in triumph the humble miracle worker would have to escape the crowds.

History offers us a few cases of miraculous healing such as this. On a Sabbath Day our Lord enjoined the man with the withered hand, *"Put out your hand," He put out his hand and it was healed* (Lk 6: 6-10). St. John Damascene, falsely accused by the caliph, was condemned to have his right hand cut off. "But the blessed virgin, Defender of the Innocent, came to the aid of her faithful servant and his hand was reintegrated to the arm as if it had never been separated from his body" (*Breviarium Romanum*).

Such miracles certainly are extraordinary and nonetheless count as very little in comparison with what it means to be restored to one's place in the Mystical Body of Christ, from which one had been separated. This is a miracle our Lord is willing to repeat for thousands each day through sacramental confession.

St. Augustine says: "To justify an unrighteous man is a greater work then the creation of the heavens and the earth."[40] When God created the world he drew things out of nothing and called them good; when God re-integrates a corrupt member to

---

[40] In Io. 72.

the Mystical Body he elevates an evil being to a participation in Divinity. Divine Mercy, which is infinite, is extended to its maximum power assuring such results. And nonetheless it is enough to simply invoke the Head of the Mystical Body with sincerity and submit oneself to him to be truly integrated into him. His mercy is granted to us with such ease that it almost seems as if it were owed to us when all along it springs from his pure generosity. What insanity! If we understood the horror of our crimes and the immensity of his parting with what delicacy of conscience we, like the saints, run from the smallest of faults! With what contrition would we seek absolution if we were to consider that of our own will we became putrefying members, absolutely powerless to revive ourselves, and that God has no obligation to reconstitute us as members, with what gratitude towards God for having made us pleasing in his sight and returning us to the life which we enjoyed in Christ before our fall!

One may ask himself with wonder why divine justice abandons its rights against such members who voluntarily ripped themselves away from the Mystical Body, as if it were impotent in executing itself against the sinner, but rather calls him back to union. Regardless of the repugnance that such corruption in the severed member causes God, he superimposes his love and pardon.

This attitude of the Father is rooted in the contract signed with his Son on Golgotha, *By canceling the record of debt that stood against us with its legal demands. Thus he removed it from our midst, nailing it to the cross* (Col 2:14). The Passion of his divine Son rendered the Father disarmed. The Son of Man with the price of his death acquired an absolute right over sinners. They make up his capital, they belong to him. From that moment onwards the saved can find refuge in the shadow of the Cross. Christ will refuse no one who comes to him, regardless of how repugnant they made themselves.

With what gratitude should we approach the Head of the Mystical Body, who when we were dead in our sins and in the uncircumcision of our flesh were made alive in Christ and forgave us all our sins (*cf.* Col 2:13). Let us never forget that the greatest disgrace that can befall us is to be separated from him: *Let us never be parted from you* (*Roman Missal*).[41]

To what degree can grace be recovered?

We are to keep in mind that sanctifying grace, infused virtues, and the supernatural merits slain by one mortal sin are not always recovered through penance to the same degree of intensity of their previous state, rather sometimes to an equal degree, other times to a lesser or greater degree according to the actual dispositions of the penitent upon his repentance of his sin and at the moment of the reception of sacramental absolution.

As a result, according to the official teaching of the Church:

> Justification itself follows this disposition or preparation, which is not merely remission of sins, but also the sanctification and renewal of the interior man through the voluntary reception of the grace and gifts, whereby an unjust man becomes a just man, and from being an enemy becomes a friend, that he may be an heir to life everlasting.[42]

This means that the justification of the sinner – however this

---

[41] Grimaud, *op. cit.* pp. 68-70.
[42] Denzinger, 1528.

may be produced: the baptism of an adult, perfect contrition, or through the sacrament of reconciliation admits to different degrees of intensity. The minimum degree of sanctifying grace indispensable for the destruction of sin is received in each of these cases since, if it were not the case, true justification would not result.

But the greater or lesser degree of intensity or the degree of the grace recovered depends on the Holy Spirit who distributes his gifts to the measure of his own desiring and is dependent upon the dispositions and the cooperation of the sinner who receives this justification – with an infinite amount of the variances according to the greater or lesser intensity of the actual grace which has impelled the sinner to repentance. Afterwards the degree of sanctifying grace which the sinner achieves upon being justified will be greater or lesser according to his dispositions upon receiving it.

Theology teaches us that the degree of sanctifying grace coincides exactly with the degree of intensity of the infused virtues and the supernatural merits which proceed from it. As a result, there is no doubt that the degree of virtues and of the merits which are recovered by the sinner upon receiving grace once again will be greater or lesser than that which he had before his fall into sin, according to the measure of his actual dispositions upon receiving justification. Thomas explains this doctrine:

The movement of the free will, in the justification of the ungodly, is the ultimate disposition to grace; so that in the same instant there is infusion of grace together with the movement of the free will, which movement includes an active penance.... According to the degree of intensity for remissness in the movement of the free will, the penitent receives greater or lesser grace.

Now the intensity of the penitent's movement may be proportionate sometimes to a greater grace than that from which man fell by sinning, sometimes to an equal grace, sometimes to a lesser. Wherefore the penitent sometimes arises to a greater grace than that which he had before, sometimes to equal, sometimes to a lesser grace: and the same applies to the virtues, which flow from grace."[43]

Note the importance of this doctrine. It is not only illusory, it is of gravest imprudence for a sinner to calmly sin, thinking to himself that he can just as easily recover all that he has lost through confession. Aside from the fact that God might not offer him the grace of repentance – without which it will be absolutely impossible for him to leave his sinful way, much like the man who has thrown himself down into a deep well from which he cannot leave of his own power - it is almost certain that he will rise up from his sin to a lesser degree of sanctifying grace than that which he had before he decided to sin. The reason for this is that the damage wrought by mortal sin does such a great degree of harm that one will scarcely summons the required intensity sufficient for such an act of repentance. The ensuing damage of mortal sin is incalculable.

---

[43] *S Th* III, 89,2.

Part Two:
Cultivation of Grace

Introduction

The follower of Christ can and ought to grow continuously in grace as long as he has life in this world. Once received in seed form through baptism grace needs to grow and develop so that it reaches its fullness in us according to Christ's plan for each individual (*cf.* Eph 4:13). This is the foremost and fundamental goal of the life of a Christian; it is for this that we have been given this life on earth. All the other activities of life are senseless and empty if they are not lived out in function of the supreme finality. The life of man on earth is nothing more than of preparation for eternal life, a sort of novitiate for eternity.

There are three supernatural means which dispose the followers of Christ to grow and develop baptismal grace until such a moment that he achieved the degree of perfection to which he is called according to the gift of Christ: the sacraments, the practice of the infused virtues, and prayer. Sacraments produce grace in the soul (or increase it) by their own intrinsic power (*ex opere operato*). The practice of virtues develops grace in our souls by the way of supernatural merit. Prayer increases grace through its own impetration before the mercy and goodness of God.

-1-

Growth Through the Sacraments

Holiness begins from Christ; and Christ is its cause. For no act conducive to salvation can be performed unless it proceeds from Him as from its supernatural source. "Without me," He says, "you can do nothing." If we grieve and do penance for our sins, if - with filial fear and hope - we turn again to God, it is because he is leading us. Grace and glory flow from His inexhaustible fullness. Our Savior is continually pouring out His gifts of counsel, fortitude, fear and piety, especially on the leading members of His Body, so that the whole Body may grow ever more and more in holiness and integrity of life.

When the Sacraments of the Church are administered by external rite, it is He who produces their effect in souls. He nourishes the redeemed with His own flesh and blood and thus calms the turbulent passions of the soul;

He gives increase of grace and prepares future glory for souls and bodies. All these treasures of His divine goodness He is said to bestow on the members of His Mystical Body, not merely because He, as the Eucharistic Victim on earth and the glorified Victim in heaven, through His wounds and His prayers pleads our cause before the Eternal Father, but because He selects, He determines, He distributes every single grace to every single person "according to the measure of the giving of Christ." Hence it follows that from our Divine Redeemer as from a fountainhead "the whole body, being compacted and fitly joined together, by what every joint supplies according to the operation in the measure of every part, makes increase of the body, into the edifying of itself in charity.[44]

After some brief notions on sacraments in general we shall discuss the fundamental dispositions to obtain the maximum sanctifying efficacy of penance and of the Eucharist, which are the two sacraments we receive continuously and constitute the principal nutrition for our supernatural life.

Sacraments in general

As has often been repeated, the sacraments are external signs instituted by our Lord Jesus Christ to signify and produce sanctifying grace in those who receive them worthily. More about this definition:

External: They are perceived by the senses: The water of baptism, the bread and wine of the Eucharist, the oil of confirmation or the unction of the sick, and the words of the formula proper to each.

Signs: A significance represented by something else, such as a flag representing a country or smoke is the sign of fire.

Instituted by Our Lord Jesus Christ: Only he can do this, not the Church, since sanctifying grace springs from his pierced Heart

---

[44] Mystici Corporis, 51.

as its only source.

Signify and produce sanctifying grace: The water of baptism washes the body of the baptized to signify the ablution of the soul, which remains cleansed of all sin; the Eucharist is given to us in the form of corporal nourishment – under the species of bread and wine – to signify spiritual food for the soul which receives the Eucharistic grace, etc.

In those who receive them worthily: That is to say, in those in whom there is no *obex* or voluntary and, therefore, insurmountable obstacle. As a result, the minimum indispensable exigency is to possess the state of grace in order to receive the sacraments of the living (confirmation, Eucharist, anointing of the sick, holy orders, and matrimony) and to be repentant, at least with a supernatural attrition, upon receiving the absolution in the sacrament of penance, or baptism in the case of adults (of course children who have not attained the age of reason do not require any necessary disposition for baptism to produce in their souls its sacramental effect).

Each sacrament confers sacramental grace, with a distinctive modality proper to it. Sanctifying grace is specifically *one.* That means that there is no more than one unique species of grace that springs – as we have said – from the Heart of Christ as its only source. But this unique grace ordinarily comes to us channeled, as it were, through seven different venues which are the seven sacraments. Passing through each one of the seven channels it acquires a special modality, that is a proper characteristic of each sacrament; just as one light can shine through the many colors in the stained glass producing the same light in different modalities. Let us look at each sacrament specifically.

Baptism: In baptism the regenerative grace which completely renews the whole person, erases original sin and all actual sins that one may have, including whatever temporal or eternal punishment is contingent upon them. It grants the person the faculty to receive the other sacraments. It is, as it were, the gateway to the other sacraments and adds a special aid to overcome the cloudiness of the intellect and the hardness of heart to believe and overcome obstacles to faith.

Confirmation: "By the chrism of Confirmation, the faithful are given added strength to protect and defend the Church, their Mother, and the faith she has given them."[45] Proper to the sacrament of confirmation is the corroborative grace that augments the life of faith, conducting it along the lines of spiritual progress and granting the soul special vigor, as well as the helping graces to bravely confess the faith even under pain of martyrdom.

Eucharist: The sacrament of the Eucharist brings with it a nutritive and unitive grace inasmuch as it nourishes and transforms the man in Christ through charity, with special helps against disordered self-love that impedes man's perseverance in the love of God. "…[F]or in the Holy Eucharist the faithful are nourished and strengthened at the same banquet and by a divine, ineffable bond are united with each other and with the Divine Head of the whole Body."[46]

Penance: "In the Sacrament of Penance a saving medicine is offered for the members of the Church who have fallen into sin, not only to provide for their own health, but to remove from other members of the Mystical Body all danger of contagion, or rather to afford them an incentive to virtue, and the example of

---

[45] Mystici Corporis, 18.
[46] Idem.

a virtuous act."[47] The sacrament of penance brings with it a properly healing grace which destroys actual sins and converts the person to God, granting it special help to not repeat those confessed sins.

The anointing of the sick: "Like a devoted mother, the Church is at the bedside of those who are sick unto death; and if it be not always God's will that by the holy anointing she restore health to the mortal body, nevertheless she administers spiritual medicine to the wounded soul and sends new citizens to heaven - to be her new advocates - who will enjoy forever the happiness of God."[48] This grace is a fully reparative grace which erases the last vestiges of sin, strengthening the spirit of the sick against the assaults of the enemy and prepares it for a holy death and an immediate entry into glory.

Holy orders: "Through Holy Orders men are set aside and consecrated to God, to offer the Sacrifice of the Eucharistic Victim, to nourish the flock of the faithful with the Bread of Angels and the food of doctrine, to guide them in the way of God's commandments and counsels and to strengthen them with all other supernatural helps."[49] The sacrament contains a consecrating grace of the minister of God's special helps to carry out the sacred ministry in a holy way.

Matrimony: The conjugal grace proper to those who are married sacramentally affords the recipient the ability to be perfectly faithful and carry out the responsibilities proper to the married state in a Christian way. "Through Matrimony, in which the contracting parties are ministers of grace to each

---

[47] Idem.

[48] Idem.

[49] Idem.

other, provision is made for the external and duly regulated increase of Christian society, and, what is of greater importance, for the correct religious education of the children, without which this Mystical Body would be in grave danger."[50]

One must keep in mind that, with equal subjective dispositions on the part of those who receive the sacraments, the more excellent sacraments – especially the Eucharist – confers greater grace than the less excellent sacraments. But if the dispositions of the one receiving a lesser sacrament (such as confession) were more perfect than those of somebody else receiving the more excellent sacraments, the former could receive grace in a higher degree than the latter.

Further, regarding the effects of the degree of grace that is communicated to us through the sacrament, proper preparation is of utmost importance. Each sacrament infuses grace in the moment it is received – not afterwards – and in proportion to our dispositions, that is our fervor and devotion upon receiving. It is impossible to insist too much on the great importance of preparation and personal devotion at the moment of the reception of the sacrament.

Sacrament of Reconciliation

To receive the maximum effects of the sacrament of penance, and to cooperate with that grace and make it develop in our souls we must insist on the following dispositions.

Contrition: A confession without true contrition would be a sacrilege. Absolution would be invalid, since the sacrament would be lacking the proper matter.

Repentance: The intensity of repentance, born above all perfect

---

[50] Idem.

contrition. With a very intense contrition one may attain not only the full remission of its faults and of the temporal pain due to them – meted out in purgatory - but as well considerable increase in sanctifying grace which would make us advance with great strides along the ways of perfection.

The purpose of amendment: Lacking this necessary aspect of the sacrament, that is, the firm desire to not repeat one's confessed sins, the sacrament is invalid. This is often the case with people who are routine in their confessions. As a result, we cannot be satisfied with a general purpose to not sin again, which is too imprecise to be efficacious. Without excluding this general purpose of amendment, we also need a very concrete, energetic resolution which includes applying the means to avoid confessed faults and sins and the desire to increase our practice of a determined virtue. To make this a reality, daily examination of conscience is necessary. It is also helpful to keep our confessor apprised of our fidelity or lack of it. How many confessions are sterile for lack of these essential elements!

Regarding our sincerity and firmness in our purpose of amendment we ought to note that one thing is to foresee a desired falling back into our faults which is quite distinct from a fall back into one's confessed sins, having confessed them with a sincere desire to not commit them again. One who knows his own weakness and fears falling back into sin, who also recognizes that he will most likely fall back into sin but he does not desire this fall, but rather maintains a sincere rejection of them before God at the time of his confession, such a confession is therefore valid and grace giving, inspired by one's own recognized weakness.

Quite a different situation is the person who confesses his sin while foreseeing a fall back into it because he still desires it. In the latter case a sacrilege is committed, and, despite the priest's words of absolution, no forgiveness is granted.

The same can be said for somebody who commits sins against the sixth commandment with another person, confesses those sins, and nonetheless has no desire of avoiding occasions of sin in the future with that person. Similar to that too is the person who has confessed to having stolen property and has no desire or purpose of amendment to restore it to its proper owner.

Profound humility: The penitent must recognize his own misery and begin to make reparation accepting voluntarily his own abject state before the confessor.

Those who fall into a humiliating sin and therefore seek out a different confessor than their normal confessor out of embarrassment or human respect, receive a valid and licit sacrament but impede their own spiritual project on account of their own pride and naturalist thinking. Bound up in disordered self-love they diminish the virtue of true humility.

How different are those who truly want to work on their own spiritual progress. Without faulting against the truth by exaggerating the quality or the number of the person's sins – something that would be a true profanation of the sacrament they accuse themselves of their sins in the most humbling way possible. Unlike those about whom John of the Cross laments, "They confess their sins in the most favorable light so as to appear better than they actually are, and thus they approach the confessional to excuse themselves rather than accuse themselves,"[51] But rather, "They are more eager to speak of their faults and sins, and reveal these to others, than other

---

[51] *Dark Night of the Soul,* I, ch.2, n.4 (henceforth cited as D).

96

virtues. They are inclined to seek direction from one who will have less esteem for their spirit and deeds."[52] Without these profound and sincere sentiments of humility, one hardly achieves the fruits of sacramental confession in the order of growth and development of grace in Christian perfection.

The Sacrament of the Eucharist

The Eucharist is not only the most excellent of all the sacraments rather it is the summit and consummation of them all: "The sacrament of the Eucharist is the greatest of all the sacraments: first of all because it contains Christ himself substantially:... Secondly, all the other sacraments are ordered to this one as to their end."[53] St. Thomas Aquinas also says,

Before receiving the sacrament, the reality of the sacrament can be had for the very desire of receiving the sacrament. Accordingly, before actual reception of the sacrament, a man can obtain salvation through the desire of receiving it, just as he can before baptism to the desired baptism.[54]

Its sanctifying efficacy is remarkable, since it not only confers grace unto a degree far superior to that of any other sacrament but also it gives us and unites us intimately to the very Person of Christ, the source and summit of grace. Just one Holy Communion received with great fervor would be enough, without a doubt, to elevate us to the heights of sanctity.

But to obtain graces to their highest degree from the

---

[52] Op cit. n. 7.
[53] *S Th* III, 65, 3.
[54] *S Th* III, 73,3.

Eucharist, it is necessary to receive Holy Communion with the most perfect dispositions. The most important of which correspond to the three theological virtues and humility of heart.

Living faith: Christ demanded it as an indispensable condition in order to confirm grace (*cf.* Mk 9:22-23). An antonomasia for the Eucharist is *mysterium fidei*, since neither reason nor the senses perceive Christ's true presence. St. Thomas Aquinas reminds us that in the cross Christ's divinity was hidden, but on the altar even his humanity disappears *latet simul et humanitas.* This fact demands from us a living faith, exercised and perfected in Eucharistic adoration.

But not only in the sense – a lively ascent to the Eucharistic mystery – faith is absolutely indispensable for every sort of contact with Jesus. We are to consider our souls as leprous through sin and repeat with living faith the prayer of the leper in the Gospel: *Lord, if you wish, you can make me clean* (Mt 8:2).

Profound humility: Before instituting the Eucharist, Christ gave his apostles an example of humility by washing their feet (Jn 13:15). If the Blessed Virgin Mary prepared herself to receive the eternal Body of Christ with the deepest of humility, so much so that she could say *Behold, I am the handmaid of the Lord* (Lk 1:38), how much more must we humble ourselves?

It doesn't matter that we have perfectly repented of our sins and are living in a state of grace. The guilt was pardoned; the criminal forgiven, but have we done enough penance? Regardless of the degree of holiness that we may possess, we should never forget that we have been forgiven. If we have committed one mortal sin, we have merited hell for ourselves. Approaching Communion, we should say with the most profound humility and sincere repentance the same sublime words of the centurion, *Lord, I am not worthy....* (Mt 8:8).

Boundless confidence: It is important to keep in mind that the remembrance of our sins should bring us humility and not discouragement - a sort of disguised but disordered self-love. Jesus Christ is the great forgiver who receives all repentant sinners into his infinite and tender embrace. He will never change.

Therefore, we must approach him with profound humility and reverence but also with immense confidence in his goodness and mercy. He is Shepherd, Healer of souls, the divine Friend who opens his Sacred Heart of love to us. Our trust in him is his weakness. He can never resist it.

Hunger for Communion: This is the disposition that most directly affects the sanctifying efficacy of Holy Communion. This hunger and thirst for receiving Jesus Christ sacramentally, which proceeds from love and is almost identical with it, equips us to receive sacramental grace in giant proportions.

How much water is taken from a fountain is determined by the size of the bucket. If we concerned ourselves with ardently asking our Lord for this hunger and thirst for the Eucharist we can be assured that we will foment it with all the means at our disposal and soon we would truly be saints.

St. Catherine of Siena, St. Teresa of Jesus, St. Michaela of the Blessed Sacrament, and many other saints had a hunger and thirst for the Eucharist which, in a certain sense, consumed them. This prepared them to suffer so many pains and dangers with the sole desire of receiving their Lord one more day. In these dispositions not only do we see in them the effects but also as well one of the most efficacious causes of such high sanctity. The Eucharist received with such ardent desire augments grace in souls in an incalculable way, carrying them along the ways of holiness at a quick pace.

In truth, each one of our Holy Communions ought to be more fervent than the previous one, augmenting our hunger and thirst for the Eucharist. Since each new Communion augments the degree of sanctifying grace in us and further disposes us to receive the Lord with greater devotion the next time. In other words, our spiritual capital increases and, as a result, so too our desire. Here, just as in the entire process of the spiritual life, one ought to advance with uniformly accelerated movement; much like the rock rolling down the hill picks up speed the longer it rolls.

About this, Thomas says, "Someone might say: 'Why should we make progress in faith?' Because a natural movement, the closer it gets to his goal, the more intense it becomes, whereas the opposite is true of forced movement. But grace inclines in the matter of nature; ... *The path of the just, as a shining light, goes forward and increases even to perfect day* (Prov 4:18)."[55]

Thanksgiving: It is obvious that the thanksgiving after having received Holy Communion has a particular sanctifying efficacy. The moments following the reception of the Eucharist are among the most precious in the life of a Christian.

We must take advantage of this true presence of our Lord in our soul ardently asking that he bring us the fullness of grace so that we may glorify the Blessed Trinity with all our strength and better cooperate in the work of saving the greatest amount of souls redeemed by his Precious Blood.

We should ask to forget our own selfish old interests and occupy ourselves with his, trusting that he will take care of us. The conversation we carry with our Lord ought to be filled with

---

[55] In epist. ad Heb. I, 25.

sentiments of adoration, reparation, petition, and thanksgiving – the Holy Sacrifice of the Mass – all characterized by a burning love for him and a boundless confidence in his infinite goodness and mercy.

We should prolong our thanksgiving as long as possible according to our obligations determined by our state in life. It is irreverent and indelicate of us to cut off our Communion too quickly. Just as we do not walk away from somebody in the middle of a conversation so too should we allow our Lord to communicate to us everything he wants to say and do in us. Some spiritual writers maintain that since the sacramental presence remains within us for about 15 minutes, we should remain in thanksgiving for as long as that, unless particular extraordinary circumstances such as work demand that we abbreviate this. In such a case we should ask our Lord in his goodness and mercy, that he accept our abbreviated thanksgiving as we continue to give him glory throughout the day lifting our hearts and minds to him with sentiments of gratitude.

-2-

Growth Through Virtue

The second means in the process which disposes us for growth and development of grace consists of the ever increasingly perfect practice of the infused virtues. To achieve their maximum sanctifying effect, we must practice them with a strictly supernatural motive and with the greatest intensity possible. With some care we shall now consider these two aspects.

Supernatural motive

As mentioned before when discussing virtues in general, we saw that there exists a doubled series of them: natural virtues – that is, those acquired through repeated action, and the supernatural or the infused virtues.

Both types of virtue have the same material object, since they involve the same matter. Thus, for example, the virtue of patience, whether acquired or infused, has as its object to bear without sadness of spirit or discouragement of heart those physical and moral sufferings that life serves us; the virtue of justice, whether natural or supernatural, has as its object to give to each one what is his due; the virtue of temperance has as its object to moderate one's inclination to sensible pleasures, etc. Whether the virtue be natural or supernatural, the material object is the same.

Nonetheless, since both classes of virtue have the same material object in what way do we distinguish their actions? What is the criterion we use to know when the acquired virtue is acting, or the infused virtue is acting? In other words, how can we know in a determined case whether we have acted naturally or supernaturally?

This is not a superfluous question above all regarding supernatural merit for actions and its contingent sanctifying efficacy in the exercise of virtues. The Church has always taught that purely natural actions can merit absolutely nothing in the supernatural order. To affirm the contrary is tantamount to falling into the Pelagian heresy, or the semi-Pelagian heresy, both of which have been condemned by the Church:

If anyone asserts that without the grace of God mercy is divinely given to us when we believe, will, desire, try, labor, pray, watch, study, seek, ask, urge, but does not confess that through the infusion and the inspiration of the Holy Spirit in us it is brought about that we believe, wish, or are able to do all these things as we ought; or if anyone subordinates the help of grace to humility or human obedience and does not agree that it is by the gift of his grace that we are obedient and humble, opposes the apostle who says, *What have you, that you have not received?* (1 Cor 4:7), and, *By the grace of God I am that which I am* (1 Cor 15:10).

If anyone affirms that without the illumination and the

inspiration of the Holy Spirit, - who gives to all sweetness in consenting to and believing in the truth - through the strength of nature he can think anything good which pertains to the salvation of eternal life, as he should, or choose, or consent to salvation, that is to the evangelical proclamation, he is deceived by that radical spirit, not understanding the voice of God speaking in the Gospel: *Without me you can do nothing* (Jn 15:5), And that of the Apostle, *Not that we are sufficient of ourselves to claim anything as coming from us; our sufficiency is from God* (2 Cor 3:5).

That grace is preceded by no merits. A reward is due to good works if they are performed; but grace, which is not due, precedes, that they may be done.

No one is saved except by God's mercy. Even if human nature remained in that integrity in which it was formed, it would in no way save itself without the help of its Creator; therefore, since without the grace of God it cannot guard the health that it received, how without the grace of God will it be able to recover what it has lost?[56]

As the word suggests, what is supernatural is a thousand times above that which is purely natural. It is still illogical and absurd that a purely natural act should produce supernatural effect.

Thus, if the material object is indistinguishable where is the difference? If someone, even in a state of grace, were to carry out an act of mercy towards his neighbor moved by a sentiment

---

[56] *Denzinger*, 376-77, 388-89.

of purely natural compassion that person has carried out a good action. But this merciful action proceeded from the natural virtue of mercy and, as a result, praiseworthy and good as it may be in the purely natural order, it lacks supernatural value in an absolute way. On the other hand, if the motivation is supernatural – that is, for the love for God or love of neighbor for the sake of God because he is our brother in Christ, etc. – the infused virtue of mercy is at work and that person has acted under the impulse of supernatural charity. As a result, this supernatural act is meritorious in the supernatural order.

In the lives of the saints we see this ideal: with great simplicity and even greater spontaneity they act on a supernatural instinct proceeding from inspiration of the Holy Spirit by way of his gifts. Such perfection of life is not within the grasp of most people simply in virtue of being in a state of grace.

Before approaching these sublime heights of the mystical life – which elevates us to perfection of supernatural merit through good works, there certainly can be supernatural merit but to a lesser degree. It is enough to persevere in virtual intention of doing all things for the love of God. This virtual intention is necessary at the beginning of the divine project or good work and must be carried out throughout the entire execution of that act or project without any express retraction of it through some sort of incompatible act such as venial sin.

The supernatural intention placed at the beginning of the act continues influencing the person throughout the entire process even if he is not necessarily aware of this supernatural influence. It is enough that he has this virtual intention at the beginning and then simply does nothing to counter-act it throughout.

Because of this beautiful doctrine we can appreciate the importance and the necessity of frequently renewing one's supernatural intention for the good one does for God and for one's neighbor in Christ. In other words, we ought not be content with a general offering of the intention but should second it time and time again. This is a useful practice to increase merit and intensity of grace. It was to this that St. Paul referred when he said the following: *So whether you eat or drink, or whatever you do, do everything for the glory of God* (1 Cor 10:31) and again, *And whatever you do, in word or in deed, do everything in the name of the Lord Jesus, giving thanks to God the Father through him* (Col 3:17).

The intensity of human acts

Along with the supernatural motivation another element for the perfect development of grace by means of the practice of infused virtues is that of the intensity with which they are carried out.

The theological key to understand this process is that the infused virtues – which are supernatural habits – cannot grow by addition, rather only through a greater establishment in the acting subject as we shall see presently.

Material things or quantitative things grow by addition. A pile of wheat grows by adding more wheat to it, even if only a little. A few pennies make a treasure grow. This is growth by addition and has nothing to do with the growth of infused habits, such as the supernatural virtues because they are not quantitative realities but qualitative whose very essence consists in accidentally modifying the subject in which they are established, giving him the capacity to act supernaturally and granting him a greater or lesser degree of the rootedness established in the subject. This brings about a greater participation of the supernatural in the subject – again not by additional quantity since this is a spiritual and qualitative reality. To claim that infused virtue can grow by addition is illogical and absurd since it confuses spirit with matter, quality with quantity.

Growth and development of infused virtues in the subject is transformative. As a result, growth and development through a deeper rootedness of infused virtues in the subject demands a more intense act compared to its previous acts. Lacking this greater intensity, the infused virtue would not root itself more deeply in the subject. Therefore, to be more deeply rooted in the subject the actions must increasingly be more intense. The mere multiplication of weak actions does not bring about this transformation.

If water in a tub is measured at 72° merely adding more water of the same temperature will not make it hotter or colder. To increase the temperature, increasingly hotter water must be introduced to the tub. Something similar happens with the infused virtues. Many virtuous actions of lesser degree do not increase the degree of the infused virtue in the subject, regardless of how many of those mediocre acts there are. The only way to increase, that is, to grow infused virtue is to increase the intensity of virtuous actions.

This raises the question, though: are all of those many less intense actions good for nothing? In terms of development they bring about no effect. Nonetheless, they have a remote contribution to a greater development inasmuch as they can prepare a well-disposed person to act with greater intensity in the future and thus, indirectly help towards a greater development. They can contribute to a greater disposition, a promptness to carry out in a certain moment a more fervent and intensely virtuous action that may not have been possible if these many less fervent actions had not been executed. Although imperfect, these actions will have their corresponding reward in heaven.

What follows are some of the important practical consequences of this teaching. Frist, one fervent act is worth more than a thousand mediocre actions. With only one intensely virtuous action we can achieve true growth in the corresponding infused virtue, something that never would have happened with less fervent actions. For example, one Hail Mary prayed with fervent devotion is worth more than an entire Rosary prayed with distraction or little intensity.

Second, given the fact that it is impossible to maintain maximum intensity in all our actions, it is helpful to at least consecrate certain moments of the day to carry out intense actions of virtue – especially those actions requiring supernatural charity for God, by way of fervent acts of love for Him. In those brief moments of intensity, we merit more than in the rest of our day.

Third, since one singularly intense act can make us scale the heights of supernatural merit before God, it follows that each one of these actions is more valuable than all the previous ones during the day. Likewise, we see in the lives of the saints that the last chapter of their life is the time of greatest growth and development in the infused virtues, bringing with it a proportionate supernatural merit before God.

Fourth, it is not necessarily true that the more fervent the action, the more difficult it is for us to carry it out. Much to the contrary; as the infused virtues are more deeply rooted in the soul proportionately more fervent actions are easier to carry out.

Saints carry out the most intense acts of virtue with ever-greater spontaneity and natural reality, without much effort. Here we are not discussing physical effort but rather the spiritual dispositions, the more intense the disposition, the easier the act.

Finally, as it is impossible to carry out a more intense act without a previous impulse of actual grace proportionate to it, and since that actual grace does not depend upon us but rather upon God, as we have seen in our study of actual grace, we have to ask for this from God with faith, humility, confidence, and perseverance to obtain it from him. Without this actual grace of God, we can do nothing in the supernatural order.[57] As a result, in this sense we can say that the process of our sanctification is reduced to two things: prayer and humility; prayer to ask God for these actual and efficient graces, and humility to attract them.

---

[57] Cf. Denzinger, 375.

-3-

Growth Through Prayer

The third element at our disposal to augment sanctifying grace in our souls, and along with it the ever more perfect expansion of our Christian lives, consists in the efficacy of prayer. By way of prayer we can obtain from God gratuitously, that is to our begging, many things that we otherwise would never achieve by way of justice or strict retribution.

Fundamental notions

St. Thomas Aquinas says prayer brings together four great values: satisfaction, merit, impetration, and produces in the soul a sort of spiritual refreshment. He says:

> Prayer is twofold, common and individual. Common prayer is that which is offered to God by the ministers of the Church representing the body of the faithful: wherefore such like prayer should come to the knowledge of the whole people for whom it is offered: and this would not be possible unless it were vocal prayer.

Therefore, it is reasonable that an ordained minister in the church should say these prayers in a loud voice, so that they may come to the knowledge of all.

On the other hand, an individual prayer is that which is offered by any single person, whether he pray for himself or for others; and it is not essential that such a prayer be vocal. And yet the voice is employed in such like prayers for three reasons.

First, to excite interior devotion, whereby the mind of the person praying is raised to God, because by means of external signs, whether of words and deeds, the human mind is moved as regards apprehension, and consequently, involves the affections. As Augustine says, 'By means of words and other signs we arouse ourselves more effectively to an increase of holy desires.' Hence, when alone we should use words, and suchlike signs that help to excite the mind internally. But if they distract or in any way impede the mind, we should abstain from them; and this happens chiefly to those whose mind is sufficiently prepared for devotion without having recourse to those signs.

Secondly, the voice is used in praying as though to pay a debt, so that man may serve God with all that he has from God not only with his mind, but also with his body: and this applies to prayer considered especially as satisfactory. Hence it is written, *Take away all iniquity, and receive the good: and we will render the calves* (sacrifice) *of our lips* (Hos 14:3).

Thirdly, we have recourse to vocal prayer, through a certain overflow from the soul into the body, through excess of feeling, according to Psalm 16:9, *My heart is glad and my tongue has rejoiced.*[58]

Although we are most interested in the element of impetration, we will say a few words about the other three elements.

Satisfactory value

That prayer has a satisfactory value (in the order of a debt paid) should be obvious simply by considering that we humble ourselves and approach God whom we have offended with our sins, all of which are rooted in our pride and excessive self-love. It springs from charity, that is, the source of all satisfaction. And finally, when prayer is well-done, it is experienced as costly to the nature of the novice in the spiritual life given the effort of attention and the exercise of the will that is demanded. Consequently, it is satisfactory for the debt contracted by our sins before God. The Council of Trent speaks clearly about the satisfactory value of prayer:

> The priests of the Lord ought, therefore, so far as the spirit of prudence suggests, to enjoin salutary and suitable satisfactions, in keeping with the nature of the crimes and the ability of the penitent, lest, if they should connive at sins and deal too leniently with penitents, by the imposition of certain very light works for grave offenses, they might become participators in the crimes of others. Moreover, let them keep before their eyes that the satisfaction imposed be not only for the safeguarding of a new life and as a remedy against infirmity, but also for the retribution and chastisement of former sins. . . . When the Innovators wish to observe this, they teach that the best penance is a new life, in order to take

---

[58] *S Th* II-II, 83, 12.

away all force and practice of satisfaction.[59]

If anyone says that for sins, as far as temporal punishment is concerned, there is very little satisfaction made to God through the merits of Christ by the punishments inflicted by him and patiently born, or by those enjoined by the priest, but voluntarily undertaken, as by fasts, prayers, alms-giving or also by other works of piety, and that therefore the best penance is only a new life: let him be anathema.[60]

Meritorious value

As in any other act of supernatural virtue, prayer receives its meritorious value from charity, the source from which springs the virtue of religion which is its proper act. As a meritorious act, prayer is submitted to the same conditions of the other virtuous works directed by the very same laws that govern religion. St. Thomas lays out the proper conditions for such merit: "Prayer, besides causing spiritual consolation at the time of praying, has a twofold efficacy in respect of a future effect, namely, efficacy in meriting and efficacy in attaining.

Meriting: Now prayer like any other virtuous act, is efficacious in meriting, because it proceeds from charity as its root, the proper object of which is the eternal good that we merit to enjoy.

Prayer proceeds from charity through the medium of religion, of which prayer is an act, and with the concurrence of other virtues requisite for the goodness of prayer, viz. humility

---

[59] Denzinger, 1692.
[60] Ibid., 1713.

and faith. For the offering of prayer itself to God belongs to religion, while the desire for the thing that we pray to be accomplished belongs to charity. Faith is necessary in reference to God to whom we pray; that is, we need to believe that we can obtain from him what we seek. Humility is necessary on the part of the person praying, because he recognizes his neediness. Devotion too is necessary: but this belongs to religion, for it is its first act and a necessary condition of all secondary acts.

Attaining: As to its efficacy and impetrating, prayer derives this from the grace of God to whom we pray, and instigates us to pray. Thus, Augustine says, 'He would not urge us to ask, unless he were willing to give'.[61]

Spiritual refreshment

The third effect of prayer well-done is that of producing a sort of spiritual refreshment. This is the effect as produced by prayer, by its very presence: *praesentaliter efficit*. "The third effect of prayer is that which it produces at once; this is the spiritual refreshment of the mind, and for this effect attention is a necessary condition.[62]

For this spiritual refreshment to be produced within us, keen attention is absolutely necessary because spiritual refreshment is incompatible with voluntary distraction of the mind.

As a result, mystical prayer – above all when it reaches the heights of ecstasy – is the maximum expression of concentration of all of one's psychological energy in the object contemplated. This brings with it the maximum delight possible, in fact, even in the corporal order. In comparison all the delights and

---

[61] *S Th* II-II, 83, 12.
[62] *Ibid.*, 13

pleasures of this world are repulsive and like so much chattel, as St. Teresa of Avila says about this conversion of affections from creatures to Creator:

> The better he gets to know the greatness of God, the better he comes to realize the misery of his own condition; having now tasted the consolations of God, he sees that earthly things are mere refuse; so, little by little, he withdraws from them and in this way becomes more and more his own master.[63]

Everything that takes place now in this state brings the very greatest consolation; and the labor is so slight, that prayer, even if persevered in for some time, is never wearisome. The reason is, that the understanding is now working very gently, and is drawing very much more water than it drew out of the well. The tears, which God now sends, flow with joy; do we feel them, they are not the result of any efforts of her own.[64]

Impetration

Regarding growth and development of sanctifying grace this is the element that most interests us. Thomas teaches us:

> God hears the sinner's prayer if it proceeds from a good natural desire, not out of justice, because the sinner does not merit to be heard, but out of pure mercy, provided however he fulfill the four conditions given: namely, that he beg for himself those things necessary for salvation, piously and persevering.[65]

---

[63] Fourth Mansions, 3, n. 9.
[64] Life, 14, n.5.
[65] S Th II-II, 83, 16.

In the first place let us consider the principle differences between the meritorious value and that of impetration in prayer:

Prayer as a matter of meritorious act speaks of a relationship of justice and the recompense; on the other hand with regard to impetration, it speaks singularly of the mercy of God. This is a gratuitous offering. As meritorious it has an intrinsic efficacy to obtain its end; as impetration its efficacy is based solely in the promise of God: *Whatever you ask for in prayer with faith, you will receive* (Mt 21:22). Its meritorious efficacy is based above all in charity; whereas impetration is founded in faith: *Whatever you ask for in prayer with faith you will receive* (Mt 21:22).

Merit and impetration do not always share the same object although at times they can coincide. The just merit but do not always obtain; the sinner can obtain it without having merited.

What prayer achieves

According to these notions, we can obtain by the way of prayer a growth in the infused virtues and the gifts of the Holy Spirit which accompany them. This results in an increase or a development of our Christian life as well as the actual efficient grace. Above all, it can attain the sovereign grace of final perseverance - which absolutely no one can merit, not even the greatest of saints - given its totally and absolutely gratuitous nature. Only prayer can achieve these graces that escape the limits of merit.

The Church gives us the example of this type of petition when in the liturgy it continually begs the grace of final perseverance or the increase of infused virtues: "Almighty ever living God, increase our faith, hope and charity, and make us love what you command, so that we may merit what you promise."[66]

About this, St. Thomas Aquinas says:

We impetrate in prayer things that we do not merit, since God hears sinners who beseech the pardon of their sins, which they do not merit as Augustine claims, 'Now we know that God does not hear sinners,' (Jn 9:31) otherwise it would have been useless for the publican to say: *O God, be merciful to me a sinner* (Lk 18:13). So too may we impetrate of God in prayer the grace of perseverance either for ourselves or for others, although it does not fall under merit.[67]

Explaining in what way prayer can achieve what merit cannot, Father Garrigou-Lagrange says:

We should recall here the difference between the prayer of petition and merit. The sinner who has lost sanctifying grace cannot merit in this state, for sanctifying grace is the radical principle of all supernatural merit.

Yet, by an actual transitory grace, the sinner can pray; he can ask for the grace of conversion; and, if he asks for it with humility, confidence, and perseverance, he will obtain it. Whereas merit, which is a right to a reward, is related to divine justice, prayer is addressed to the mercy of God, which often restores fallen souls and hears their prayers without any merit on their part.

From the depths of the abyss into which it is falling and where it can no longer merit, the most wretched soul may

---

[66] Collect from *The Roman Missal* for the 30th Sunday in Ordinary Time.
[67] *S Th* I-II, 114, 9 ad 1.

utter the cry to the divine mercy, which is prayer. The abyss of wretchedness calls to that of mercy, *Deep calls unto deep*, and if the sinner puts his whole heart into this appeal, he will be heard. The soul will be lifted up, and God will be glorified, as was the case with Magdalen. The impetrating power of prayer does not presuppose the state of grace, whereas merit does."[68]

With respect to the person in sin, stripped of sanctifying grace prayer is the only recourse at his disposition to leave this sorry state, given that God will not deny a person the necessary actual grace to pray. We now shall consider the impetrative efficacy of the prayer of the just.

After conversion or justification, we can obtain the increase of life of grace both by merit and by prayer. When prayer is humble, trusting, and persevering, it obtains for us a more lively faith, a firmer hope, more ardent charity, all of which we ask for in the first three petitions of Our Father. Thereby we see how fruitful mental prayer can be; how it draws God strongly toward us that he may give himself intimately to us and that we may give ourselves to him.

We should often recite the beautiful prayer of blessing by Nicholas of Flue: 'Lord Jesus, take me from myself, and give me to thyself.' It is a fervent meritorious act which immediately obtains the grace of charity that it merits, and a supplication which obtains even more than it merits. Then one's heart dilates more and more to receive divine grace more abundantly; the soul empties itself of every creature and becomes more eager for God, in whom it finds in an eminent degree all that is worthy of

---

[68] Garrigou-Lagrange, The Three Ages of the Interior Life, pt. 1, c. 7.

being loved.

It would be impossible to live too deeply by these things in recollection; sometimes it is given to us all to leave our family in the absolute silence of the night when everything is quiet, and the soul is completely alone with its God, with the Savior, Jesus Christ. It then experiences his immense goodness and, by its mental prayer, which at once is meritorious and salvific, it offers itself entirely to him and receives them in a prolonged spiritual communion that has a taste of eternal life. This is eternal life already begun, as St. Thomas says. Often, therefore the impetrating force of prayer is united to merit to obtain an increase of charity, a purer and stronger love of God.

Moreover, the just man may by prayer obtain certain graces which he could not merit, the gift of final perseverance. This gift cannot be merited, for it does nothing other than the continuation until death of the state of grace, which is the principal of merit.

Obviously, it would be impossible to merit the very principle of merit. However, final perseverance or the grace of a happy death can be obtained by humble, trusting, daily prayer. For this reason, the Church invites us to say daily with fervor in the second part of the Hail Mary: 'Holy Mary, mother of God, pray for us sinners, now and at the hour of our death. Amen.' Here prayer goes farther than merit, addressing itself, not to divine justice but to infinite mercy.

We can also ask God for the grace to know him in an ever more loving and intimate manner, by that knowledge which is called infused contemplation, and which results in a closer and more fruitful union with God.

By addressing infinite mercy, prayer manifestly exceeds

merit. The sinner who is still incapable of meriting, may by prayer obtain the grace of conversion. By prayer, the just man often obtains graces which could not be merited, such as final perseverance and the efficacious graces which lead to it. [69]

And with this we conclude this chapter about the growth of grace. Sacraments of themselves confer a growth *ex opere operato*; the practice of the infused virtues brings about growth by the way of merit; the efficacy of prayer produces the same results by way of impetration

---

[69] *Ibid.* See also *S Th* II-II, 83, 9; 83, 15, ad 2; 83, 15; 83, 16; II-II, 24, 3 ad 2; 69, 2; *De veritate*, 14, 2; *S Th* I-II, 114, 9.

-4-

Fidelity to Grace

We have just examined the three methods at our disposal for the growth and development of sanctifying grace in our spiritual lives: sacraments, virtue, prayer. The reason most people do not attain the perfection that God wills for them is precisely on account of their infidelity to grace in these three areas.

But to obtain their maximum sanctifying efficacy fidelity to grace is absolutely indispensable; that is, seconding the action of grace with an ever-increasing docility through obedience to the internal inspirations of the Holy Spirit and the varied external influences he uses as his agents in the work of our sanctification. Without this constant and ever-growing fidelity to grace, these three great means of growth remain sterile.

There are a few general notions about fidelity to grace worth mentioning. First, since we owe God this fidelity it is a work of justice. Second, since fidelity to grace is a work of love demanded of us, it fulfills the duty of charity to God. Third, it is a work of prudence since the Holy Spirit is the one who inspires us and he knows perfectly the proper means to an end. Fourth, fidelity to grace is proper to the virtue of *honestia* – the habit of always looking for the right thing to do in all circumstances, regardless of how one feels. Fifth, true grace arouses us to good resolutions and virtues. And finally, it can affect the emotions, but this is not the norm. We ought to be cautious in the world of the emotions as an indicator of God's will. In fact, as we grow in grace through prayer, sacraments, and exercise of virtue, the emotions play less and less of a role in our lives. In other words, grace tends to calm emotions, not incite them.

Fidelity to Grace

In general, fidelity is nothing other than loyalty, perfect adhesion, the exact observance of the trust one owes another. In medieval usage fidelity meant the obligation that a vassal had to present himself to his lord and render him homage, offering himself as his subject, even going so far as taking his masters name in absolute obedience. Most certainly all of this has its own application – in its maximum expression – when concerning fidelity to grace which is nothing less than loyalty or docility in following the inspirations of the Holy Spirit in whatever form they are manifest.

In other words, fidelity to grace implies interior attention. By inspirations I mean being drawn, those feelings, interior reproaches, lights and intuitions, with which God moves us, presenting our hearts to his fatherly love and care, and then awakening, exciting, urging, and attracting them to goodness, to heavenly love, to good resolutions, in short, to whatever tends to our eternal welfare.

This is what we read in the *Canticle of Canticles,* when the bridegroom knocks at the door, awakens his love, calls upon her, seeks her, bids her to eat of his honey, gather the fruit and flowers of his garden, and let him hear her voice, which is sweet to him."[70]

These divine inspirations are produced in many ways. Even sinners receive them in the form of impulses to conversion; but for the just in whom the Blessed Trinity dwells it is perfectly connatural to receive them in every moment. By way of them the Holy Spirit enlightens our mind so that we can see what we have to do and moves our will so that we can desire to fulfill it, as St. Paul says: *For God is the one who, for his good purpose, works in you both to desire and to work* (Phil 2:13).

The Holy Spirit blows where he wills in the soul of the just. Therefore, he acts when and in whatever manner he desires. Sometimes his action is limited to illumination, for example, in doubtful cases in which one does not see with clarity; other times he merely moves us, that is, inviting us to carry out a good action which it was considering on its own; finally, in other moments - and this is what is most frequent - he illumines and moves concurrently.

At times he produces an inspiration amid one's work, in a completely unexpected way, when one is completely distracted or forgetful of the object of the inspiration; other times he produces this grace during prayer, after Holy Communion, in moments of particular recollection or fervor.

The Holy Spirit directs and governs the adoptive child of God in the ordinary things of daily life as well as in the business of utmost importance. St. Antony of the Desert entered a church and, upon hearing the preacher repeat the words of the Gospel: *If you wish to be perfect, go, sell what you have* (Mt 19:21), was moved to act immediately, selling all that he had, and retired to

---

[70] St. Francis de Sales, *Introduction to the Devout Life*, Pt. 2, ch. 18

the desert. It is important to notice that the inspiration of grace works on the intellect and the will, and not the feelings. True consolations are the effect of following grace, not its motor.

The Holy Spirit does not always directly inspire us of himself. Sometimes he makes use of our guardian angel, a preacher, a good book, or a friend. Behind all these agents is the same Holy Spirit, the principal Author of each authentically divine inspiration.

The importance and necessity of fidelity to grace

It is difficult to exaggerate the importance and necessity of the exceptional importance and the absolute necessity of fidelity to grace in order to advance on the path of supernatural perfection.

In a certain sense this is the fundamental problem of the Christian life, since on this depends whether one makes incessant progress to reach the heights of perfection or merely remains paralyzed in the spiritual life. The principal concern of every spiritual director must be that of bringing the directee to the most delicate and constant fidelity to grace. Without this all the other methods and procedures which he may attempt are condemned to failure. The profoundly theological reason for this is found in the divine economy of actual grace.

As theology teaches us, actual grace is necessary for every salvific act. In the supernatural order actual grace is a previous divine motion, which is indispensable for the most minor of supernatural actions – even if one were to be in a state of grace, possessing infused virtues and the gifts of the Holy Spirit. Actual grace is something akin to divine air that the Holy Spirit breathes into our souls allowing us to live in a supernatural atmosphere.

Actual grace is constantly offered to us for the accomplishment of the duty of the present moment, just as air comes constantly into our lungs to get us to breathe. As we must inhale in order to draw into our lungs the air that renews our blood, so we must will to receive with docility the grace that renews our spiritual energies in the journey toward God.

A person who does not inhale will die of asphyxiation; he who does not receive grace with docility will eventually die of spiritual asphyxiation. Therefore St. Paul says: *And we exhort you that you not receive the grace of God in vain* (2 Cor 6:1). We must correspond with it and cooperate generously with it. Were this elementary truth put into practice daily, it would lead to sanctity.[71]

And nonetheless there is still more. In the ordinary and normal economy of his providence, God has subordinated posterior graces he has in mind to grant to a person dependent upon the use of anterior graces. Therefore, a simple infidelity to grace can frustrate the entire chain of graces that God had intended to successively grant to that person. And this loss is irreparable. Only in heaven will we appreciate how the sanctity of so many has been frustrated through infidelity to grace, although only venial in and of themselves, these persons willfully – albeit not with full knowledge - paralyzed or stunted the action of the Holy Spirit ordered toward bringing them to the heights of perfection. Thus Fr. Garrigou-Lagrange further teaches us:

The first grace of light, which efficaciously produces a good thought in us, is sufficient in relation to a voluntary good

---

[71] Garrigou-Lagrange, *The Three Ages of the Interior Life*, Pt. 1, c. 3, a.5.

consent, in the sense that it gives us, not the act, but the power to produce it. However, if we resist this good thought, we deprive ourselves of the actual grace that would have efficaciously led us to a good consent.

Resistance falls on sufficient grace like hail on the tree in bloom that promised much fruit; flowers are destroyed, and the fruit will not form. Efficacious grace is offered us within sufficient grace, as the fruit is in the flower; moreover, the flower must not be destroyed if the fruit is to be given to us. If we do not resist sufficient grace, actual efficacious grace is given to us, and by it we advance surely in the way of salvation. Sufficient grace thus leaves us without excuse before God, and efficacious grace does not allow us to glory in ourselves; with it we advance humbly and generously.[72]

Fidelity to grace is, therefore, not only of great importance but necessary and indispensable to make progress on the path towards union with God. The Christian and his spiritual director should have no other obsession than that of a continuous loving and exquisite fidelity to grace.

Sanctifying efficacy of fidelity to grace

First, a word about what fidelity to grace is not. Fidelity to grace can never be contrary to divine law, to natural law, to authentic Catholic Tradition and teaching, nor contrary to the authority of sound spiritual principles.

The reason so few people advance in the ways of grace is because they are ignorant of the basic spiritual mechanisms and those principles that direct them. In other words, if so many

---

[72] Ibid.

people are not aware of the principles of human nature, how many more are unaware of how grace functions?

Father Lallemant, that spiritual master from the early years of the Society of Jesus, says:

> The two elements of the spiritual life are the cleansing of the heart in the direction of the Holy Spirit. These are the two poles of all spirituality. By these two ways we arrive at perfection according to the degree of purity we have attained, and in proportion to the fidelity with which we have cooperated with movements of the Holy Spirit and followed his guidance.
>
> Our perfection depends wholly on this fidelity, and we may say that the sum of the spiritual life consists in observing the ways and the movements of the Spirit of God in our soul, and in fortifying our will in the resolution of following them, employing for this purpose all the exercises of prayer, spiritual reading, sacraments, the practice of virtues and works.
>
> The end to which we ought to aspire, after having for a long time exercised ourselves in purity of heart, is to be self-possessed and governed by the Holy Spirit that he alone shall direct all our powers and all her senses, and regulate all our movements, interior and exterior, while we, on our part, make a complete surrender of ourselves, by a spiritual renunciation of our own will and her own satisfaction. We shall thus no longer live in ourselves, but in Jesus Christ, by a faithful correspondence with the operations of his divine spirit, and by a perfect subjection of all the rebellious inclinations to the power

of his grace.

Few persons attain the graces which God has destined for them; or when they have lost them, succeed afterwards in repairing the loss. The majority lack the necessary courage to conquer themselves, and the fidelity to trade with advantage in the gifts of God.

And yet the principal point in the spiritual life so entirely consists in disposing ourselves to grace by purity of life, that if two persons were to consecrate themselves to the service of God at the same time and one were to avail himself wholly to good works, and the other to apply himself altogether to the purifying of his heart and rooting out whatever ought not be there with minimal support to grace, the latter would attain perfection twice as quickly as the former.

Thus, our greatest care should be, not so much to read spiritual books, as to pay great attention to divine inspirations, which are sufficient along with a little reading; and to be faithfully exact in corresponding with the graces which are offered to us.

We should also frequently beg God to enable us to repair before we die all our past losses of grace, and to reach that height of merit, which in his first intention he desired to lead us; that intention we have hitherto frustrated by our infidelities. Finally, we ought to beg that he forgive us those sins of which we have been the cause in others, and that he also repair in them those losses of grace which they have incurred through our fault.

It sometimes happens that after receiving some good inspiration from God, we immediately find ourselves assailed by repugnance, doubts, perplexities, and difficulties, which proceed from our own corrupt interior, and from our passions, which are opposed to the divine inspiration. Were we to receive it with an absolute docility of heart, it would fill us with that peace and consolation which the Spirit of God bears when he communicates to souls in which he meets with no resistance.

The reason why we are so slow in arriving at perfection, or never arrive at it at all, is that in almost everything we are led by natural and human views. We follow but little, if at all, the guidance of the Holy Spirit, to whom it belongs to enlighten, direct, and animate.

The majority of religious, even from among the good and virtuous, use reason and good sense as their guide; and in this way many of them excel. The rule is a good one, but it is not sufficient in order to arrive at Christian perfection.

Such persons are guided ordinarily by the general opinion of those amongst whom they live; and as the latter are imperfect, although their life not be irregular or disordered, seeing that the number of the perfect is very small, they never attain to the sublime ways of the Spirit; they live like the majority, and, as a result, their method of directing others is imperfect.

We may say with truth that there are but very few who persevere constantly in the ways of God. Many wander from them perpetually; the Holy Spirit calls them back by his inspirations; but as they are intractable, full of themselves, attached to their own opinions, puffed up with their own wisdom, they do not really let themselves be guided. They may make a little progress, and are ultimately surprised by death, after having taken only twenty steps of progress where they might have taken 10,000, had they abandoned themselves to the guidance of the Holy Spirit.

On the other hand, truly interior persons who are guided by the light of the Spirit of God, for which they dispose themselves by purity of heart, in which they follow with perfect submission, proceed with giant steps and even fly, so to say, in the ways of grace.

One of our greatest evils is that we are so sensual, and so delighted with exterior things, that we esteem, we admire, we have a taste for nothing but what attracts attention and flatters our senses. Nevertheless, it is a matter of faith that the least inspiration of God is a thing more precious and more excellent than the whole world, seeing that it is of supernatural order, bought at the price of his Precious Blood.

Occupations of distinction, the esteem of men, our own little conveniences and satisfactions. Monstrous illusion! Of which, nevertheless, many are undeceived only at the hour of death."[73]

How to remain faithful

Since fidelity to grace is of such capital importance – for upon it depends whether we will arrive at the heights of Christian perfection or not - we ought to have some clear ideas of how to exercise it.

We will consider fidelity to grace from the side of God and from the side of the generous person who attempts to cooperate with Grace.

The inspiration of the Holy Spirit: Commenting on St. Paul's words: *For those who are led by the Spirit of God are children of God* (Rom 8:14), St. Thomas Aquinas says:

This can be understood in the following way: *For whomsoever are led by the Spirit of God* (Rom 8:14), i.e., ruled as by a leader and director, which the spirit does in us, inasmuch as he

---

[73] Louis Lallemant, SJ, *Spiritual Doctrine,* Principle IV, Ch. II, Art. 1-3.

enlightens us inwardly about what we ought to do... Whereas the spiritual man is not only instructed by the Holy Spirit regarding what he ought to do, but his heart is also moved by the Holy Spirit. ... For those are led who are moved by a higher instinct. Hence we say that animals do not act but are led, because they are moved to perform their actions by nature and not from their own impulse. Similarly, the spiritual man is inclined to do something not as though by the movement of his own will chiefly, but by the prompting of the Holy Spirit. ... However, this does not mean that spiritual men do act without will or free choice, because the Holy Spirit supports the very movement of the will and the free choice and then, as it says in Philippians: *God is at work in you both to will and to work* (2:13).[74]

Inspiration of the Holy Spirit is to the act of virtue what temptation is to the act of sin. Man descends into sin by way of a three-step ladder: temptation, delight, and then voluntary consent.

Regarding divine inspirations the Holy Spirit proposes the act of virtue to the intellect, and then he excites the will to fulfill it; the recipient of this grace first approves and then fulfills it under the influence of divine grace.

The acts of virtue produced are under the impulse and direction of Holy Spirit; and in the measure to which the recipient is faithful to this impulse, he acquires the facility and the delight in the exercise of the virtue - and these acts are called fruits of the Holy Spirit. Some of them spring from within with such perfection and con-naturality that they bring such

---

[74] Ad Romanos c. 8, lect. 3.

tremendous delight as a sort of anticipated love of the blessedness of the souls in heaven. As a result, these are called the evangelical beatitudes.

Possessing these precious gifts by the loving infusion of the Holy Spirit – and we have them by the way for the precise purpose of making us docile to divine inspirations - we have a certain right to ask for them and to expect them. We should make no other petition with as much frequency as this:

Come Holy Spirit, fill the hearts of your faithful and enkindle in them the fire of your love. Send forth your Spirit and they shall be created. And you shall renew the face of the earth. O God, who by the light of your Holy Spirit, did instruct the hearts of the faithful, grant that by the same Holy Spirit we may be truly wise and ever enjoy his consolations. Through Christ our Lord. Amen.[75]

And in all of this we are responsible for three things: *attentiveness* to the inspirations of the Holy Spirit; *discernment* in order to distinguish the source of the movements within us – whether they be from the Holy Spirit, our human spirit, or the devil; and *docility* in order to carry out those inspirations. What follows is a brief explanation of these three aspects.

Attentiveness: The fact that the Holy Spirit dwells within our souls through grace ought to be the subject of continual consideration (1 Cor 6:19). If we could but manage to empty ourselves of our attachments to those created things that surround us and often fill us, and if we were to live in a recollected way with interior and exterior silence we would

---

[75] Ancient prayer to the Holy Spirit.

doubtlessly perceive the sweet insinuations transmitted by the Holy Spirit. This is by no means an extraordinary grace but rather the normal and ordinary way of the Christian life.

If the Holy Spirit is continually communicating with us why are we unaware of his presence and his inspirations? The three most common reasons are dissipation, sensuality, and disordered attachment, which we will discuss.

Our own eventual dissipation: God is within us yet we live outside of him. "A spiritual man quickly recollects himself because he never wasted his attention upon externals."[76] The Holy Spirit himself reminds us of our need for solitude and interior recollection: *Therefore, I will allure her now; I will lead her into the wilderness and speak persuasively to her* (Hos 2:16).

Fr. Raul Plus, the great 20th-century spiritual writer, says "God is discreet; but not out of timidity or impotence. If he so desired he could impose himself; but he does not do that, rather out of delicacy towards us, and to open the way for our own initiative in range of action.

Further, we cannot imagine that the Lord is not the master; God does not communicate through noise. When he discovers the interior of the soul hindered by a thousand things, he is not in a rush into the soul to appropriate it, nor will he seek to accommodate himself amongst all the clutter. God is not satisfied to be one more item amongst a collection of cheap things. Sometimes, nonetheless, he takes the initiative and, despite our inattentiveness he grabs our attention. Perhaps we were not open to his voice and nonetheless he enters and speaks. But this is not the norm. He usually avoids an audience that was not sought. If the soul is in grace it is evident that God

---

[76] Imitation of Christ, 2, 1.

dwells there, but he doesn't reveal himself. Since the soul does not deign to receive him formally he remains there ignored, and the soul continues to distract itself with cheap substitutes. The more a soul pours itself out to created goods, the less capable is the soul of giving attention to the Supreme Good for whom the soul has been created.

If, on the other hand, the soul ceases to give such absolute value to created things and seeks God in silence, God allows himself to be found.[77]

Our own sensuality: Now the natural person does not accept what pertains to the Spirit of God, for to him it is foolishness, and he cannot understand it, because it is judged spiritually (1 Cor 2:14). St. Paul is saying that the carnal man does not know how to appreciate or even enjoy spiritual realities because of his inordinate attachment to created goods. As a result, mortification and penance are indispensable to renounce our carnal attachments and inordinate appetites.

Our disordered attachments: "And who is more free than the man who desires nothing on earth? It is well, then, to pass over all creation, perfectly to abandon self, and to see in ecstasy of mind that you, the Creator of all, have no likeness among all your creatures, and that unless a man be freed from all creatures, he cannot attend freely to the divine. The reason why so few contemplative persons are to be found, is that so few know how to separate themselves entirely from what is transitory and created."[78] We need think only of our addictions to technology such as texting, emails, immediate information, etc. Such disorders make attentiveness to the Holy Spirit nearly

---

[77] *La fidelidad a la gracia* (Barcelona 1951), Edicion Circulo, pp. 59-60
[78] *Imitation of Christ*, 3, 36.

impossible.

Two things, therefore, are necessary to practice in order to perceive the voice of God: To detach oneself from every disordered earthly affection and to practice docility to the Holy Spirit in our souls. For this we require a permanent attitude of humble expectation: *Speak, for your servant is listening* (1 Sam 3:10).

As a result, one who desires to advance along the road of the Cross of Christ requires serious penance and mortification. What is the difference between these two? The distinction between mortification (synonymous in most spiritual writers with self-denial, abnegation, self-renunciation, dying to self) and penance (synonymous with penitence, sacrifice or self-sacrifice, and reparation) has to do with the interior motive behind the action. In other words, the exterior action (fasting, for example, or taking a cold shower on a cold morning) can be exactly the same but depending on the reason why one carries out the action (my intention), the spiritual nature of the act can be either mortification or penance.

The intentionality of an act of mortification is to *drive* [i.e., discipline] *my body* [i.e., self-seeking tendencies] *and train it, for fear that, after having preached to others, I myself should be disqualified* (1 Cor 9:27). In other words, one freely denies oneself the satisfaction of a normal and healthy desire in order to grow in spiritual maturity, to learn to govern the self-seeking tendencies built into my fallen nature; for example, purposefully mortifying one's perfectly legitimate desire for meat and dessert on Wednesdays and Fridays, in order to better able control an illegitimate desire to get drunk whenever that desire happens to surface. Mortification is spiritual training, tempering of the willpower to be able to better govern our passions and instincts, starving the weeds in the garden (vices and selfish tendencies) so the flowers (virtues) can flourish.

The intentionality of an act of penance is *[to fill] up what is lacking in the afflictions of Christ* (Col 1:24). In that case, one does penance for sin, making up for an evil, destructive deed, just as Christ did by dying on the cross. He offered his obedience as "payment" (or atonement) for our disobedience. This is how he repaired (made "reparation" for) the breach between God and man created by original sin. He sacrificed himself (made himself into an offering to God) on our behalf. Penance, therefore, is done to tell God we are sorry for our sins, or for the sins of others, and to make up for them. For example, should someone's spouse refuse to go to Mass on Sunday, one may attempt to to make up for this ungrateful offense against the majesty and goodness of God by doing penance on the offender's behalf – perhaps making a Holy Hour on Monday evening instead of watching a favorite television show, or not listening to music during the morning commute this week. When we do penance, we are repairing for sin, reversing the self-indulgent act of sin by replacing it with a self-giving sacrificial act.

Two other points remain on this issue. First, the only way that mortification and penance really help advance Christ's Kingdom is if we are united to Christ. We must be living the life of grace – Christ must be alive in us – for us to unite our actions to his, so that they share in his merits. Similar to having a bank account with co-signers, the check only draws from the vault of merit if it is signed both by the penitent (junior partner) and by Christ (senior partner). We cannot save ourselves by ourselves; we cannot grow in holiness apart from the source of holiness: *without me you can do nothing* (John 15:5).

136

Second, the concept of sacrifice also includes an element of intercession and petition. Offering God a sacrifice can be a way of intensifying a prayer of intercession. Thus, when St. Therese of the Child Jesus was interceding for the conversion of a criminal condemned to death, she and her sisters joined sacrifices (acts of self-denial) to their prayers. In the same way, a generous person can offer sacrifices (acts of self-denial, obedience, patience...) to God to benefit other members of the Body of Christ who may be in need – those in temptation or sorrow, those in prison or suffering persecution. Christians are connected to them through our membership in Christ.

Discernment: Discernment is necessary in this spiritual life to understand who is speaking: The Holy Spirit, the human spirit, or the devil. What follows are some important criteria to recognize divine inspirations which ought to be subjected to objective criteria of discernment, avoiding the subjective at all costs.

The holiness of the object – evil spirits will not invite us to virtue; our own human spirit does not tend towards the discomforts and the difficulties that virtue requires of us. On the other hand, the devil will lead us to cheap imitations of virtue above all in the order of excess or defect, avoiding the mean. The devil will never spur us on to moderation in the virtues, except for theological virtues; these last ones permit no moderation.

Conformity with our true state in life – The Holy Spirit will not call a Carthusian to be a preacher, nor a contemplative to work in a hospital.

Peace of heart: The peace with which grace is received is the seal of its authenticity because peace is the cessation of emotions. *Quies* (the result of conformity with the will of God) is not emotional or rooted in the sentiments, since emotions blind the intellect, and the work of grace is to enlighten the intellect while strengthening the will.

Now one of the best marks of the goodness of all inspirations in general, and particularly of extraordinary ones, is the peace and tranquility of the heart that receives them: for though indeed the Holy Spirit is powerful, yet his might is gentle, sweet and peaceful. He comes as a mighty wind (Acts 2:2), and as a heavenly thunder, but he does not overthrow the apostles, nor does he perturb them; any fear which they had in hearing the sound was not continual, but was immediately followed by a sweet assurance.[79] The devil, on the other hand, usually fills our minds with disquiet.

Tranqullitas ordinis, that peace of soul which makes us more open to grace is not to be confused with the Buddhist notion of "peace". The peace they speak of is produced, not from grace or conformity with God's will, but from distancing themselves naturally from objects of emotion. That is a natural occurrence. Here we speak of something supernatural: the peace of order established by God and cooperated with by the Christian.

Humble obedience: "In obedience all is secure; outside of it all is to be suspected... Whosoever says he is inspired, and yet refuses to obey superiors and follow their counsel, is an imposter."[80] Examples of this are the great number of heretics and apostates who claim to be inspired by the Holy Spirit throughout Church history.

The judgment of the spiritual: the small daily decisions that fill up our day do not require much deliberation, but rather it is

---

[79] St. Francis de Sales, *Treatise on the Love of God,* 8, 12.
[80] Ibid. 8, 13.

enough to simply choose what seems to be, to the best of our knowledge, in conformity with divine will, without scruples or disquiet of conscience; but in doubtful cases of greater importance, the Holy Spirit will often work in our consciences with the assistance of a spiritual director. St. Teresa of Avila said that when she consulted even the most obvious things with her spiritual director, a renewed sense of peace came back to her soul.

What follows are some red flags along the way of discernment: since our very fallible judgment is at work and we all have the experience of having been easy prey for the Evil One. It ought to interest us not a little to recognize some patterns of behavior that are definitely from the Holy Spirit and those that clearly are not.

Ordinarily, *God does not call someone to contradict his own state in life.* For example, a mother of a large family, regardless of how much consolation she may feel when visiting chapels, especially convents, is not called to the consecrated life as long as she has a family to take care of.

God does not act with violence, rather with sweetness – when dealing with a person in grace who truly seeks God's will. Quite another story is a person who lives in sin and experiences the Holy Spirit: often it is not pleasant since the Holy Spirit wants to rouse the person from his deplorable state.

Since grace enlightens the intellect and fortifies the will, *the work of the Holy Spirit is not primarily in the area of the emotions* since piqued emotions tend to blind the intellect and sway the will in a disordered fashion.

A "call" to exotic things in the spiritual life is always doubtful. The desire for singularity and creativeness – calling attention to oneself – is of the devil. St. Thomas Aquinas calls this sin *admiratio* - a sort of immature "look at me" attention seeking attitude not proper to adults. The appropriating of what is divine for human purposes is one instance of this behavior.

Longing for extraordinary gifts is also spurious. St Teresa of Avila tells us that the devil can easily inspire such a longing and if we ask for it, he is more than willing to stimulate it in us, since the vast majority of so-called "extra-ordinary gifts" attributed to God in people are not of him.

Longing for the extraordinary in virtue is also doubtful. Virtue is in the mean. The devil will never counsel us to moderation except in the order of theological virtues, which do not permit limits given their divine nature.

Although we are all called to do penance, the desire to do extra-ordinary penance is also suspect. Constancy and regularity in moderate penance is much more fruitful than sporadic "heroic" acts.

Constant consolation is not from God (unless, of course, you are in heaven). A true follower of Christ must also pass through darkness and desolation. St. Ignatius of Loyola counsels us to remember that our times of desolation will be soon followed by consolation, and vice-versa.

Docility: This consists in following the inspirations of grace in the very moment in which it is produced, without making the Holy Spirit to wait even a second. He knows better than we what is good for us; therefore, let us accept what is good for us, that is whatever he inspires, and we ought to carry it out with joy. For this one requires a habitual state of openness to whatever the will of God is in each moment: *Teach me to do your will, for you are my God. May your kind spirit guide me on ground that is level* (Ps 143:10).

Such are the principal characteristics of our response to the inspirations of the Holy Spirit. Cardinal Mercier was strongly convinced of the high importance of fidelity to the interior motions of the Holy Spirit in the order of our full justification. Once, he said:

> I'm going to reveal to you the secret of holiness and joy. If you learn to quiet yourselves for five minutes every day, still in your imagination, closing your eyes to sensible things, and your ears to the noises of this life in order to penetrate into your own interior, there, in the sanctuary of your baptized soul is the temple of the Holy Spirit. Say to him: *Oh Holy Spirit, Soul of my soul. I adore you. Illumine me, guide me, strengthen me, console me. Tell me what I ought to do. Give me your orders. I promise to submit myself to everything you say and desire of me. I promise to accept everything that you allow to occur. Only let me know your most holy will.*

If you make this your own prayer you will find joy, serenity, and consolation amid your struggles; because grace will be granted for each trial, granting you the strength to bear it, bringing you to the gates of paradise covered in merit. Such submission to the Holy Spirit is the secret of holiness.[81]

St. Francis de Sales' teaching on fidelity to grace

As a summary or a compendium of this most important chapter about fidelity to grace we will now consider Francis de Sales' doctrine on this matter as found in his book, *The Introduction to the Devout Life.*

---

[81] Quoted by Joseph Becaud in *L'action, instrument d'evangelisation* (Paris, 1955), p. 432.

The bridegroom of the *Canticles* says that the bride has ravished his heart with *one of her eyes, one lock of her hair* (Song 4:9). And so the divine bridegroom makes us to know that he accepts not only the great works of devout people, but every poor and lowly offering too; be ready then, my child, to bear great afflictions for your Lord, even to martyrdom itself; resolved to give up to him all that you hold most precious, if he should require of you; – father, mother, brother, husband, wife, or child; the light of your eyes; your very life; for all such offering your heart should be ready.

But so long as God's providence does not send you these great and heavy afflictions by means of these little matters, lovingly and freely accepted, you will give him your whole heart, and win his.

I mean the acts of daily forbearance, the headache, or toothache, or heavy cold; these tiresome peculiarities of husband or wife, the broken glass, the loss of a ring, ... they offer us fertile soil for gathering in spiritual riches, if only we will use them rightly.

When I read in the life of St. Catherine of Siena, of her ecstasies and visions, her wise sayings and teaching, I do not doubt but that she was "ravished" by her bridegroom's heart with the eye of contemplation; but I must recognize that I behold her with no less light in her father's kitchen, channeling the fire, turning the spit, baking the bread, cooking the dinner, and doing all the most menial offices in a loving spirit which looked through all things straight to God. Nor do I prize the low meditations she was wont to make while so humbly employed less than the ecstasies with which she was favored at other times, probably as a reward for this very humility and loneliness.

142

Her meditations would take the shape of imagining that all she prepares for her father was an act of loving service to our Lord; her mother was a symbol of Our Lady, her brothers of the apostles, and that she mentally ministered to all the heavenly courts, the filling of our humble ministrations with an exceeding sweetness, because she saw God's will in it all. Let this example, my daughter, teach you how important it is to dedicate all we do, however trifling, to his service.

Seek higher things, such as prayer and meditation, the sacraments, leading souls to God. In a word, by all manner of good works according to your vocation; but meanwhile do not neglect your daily chores… and amid all these things cultivate such spiritual thoughts as Saint Catherine intermingled with her work.

Great occasions for serving God come seldom, but little ones surround us daily; and the Lord himself has told us that *He that is faithful in that which is least is faithful also in much* (Lk 16:10). If you do all in God's name, all you do will be well done, whether you eat, drink, sleep, enjoy yourself, so long as you do all wisely, you will gain greatly as in God's sight, doing all because he would have you do it.[82]

There are signs of the Holy Spirit's promptings. First, He grants clarity regarding the truths of the Faith and the spiritual life. Second, He calls us to greater surrender and a deeper spirit of prayer. And third, He inclines us to root out our vices and disordered attachments, since attachments are the root of all evil within us.

However, there are also hindrances to fidelity to grace, and these are more numerous. First, our attachments and affections

---

[82] Introduction to the Devout Life, pt. 3, chpt. 35.

are not held in check. Second, we allow emotions to guide our spiritual life rather than sound doctrinal principles. Third, there is disorder in pleasure and sensuality. Fourth, we make ourselves our own reference point rather than an authority outside of ourselves, and this is called immanentism. Fifth, we choose to follow unapproved "revelations" rather than sound spiritual/doctrinal principles. Sixth, there is lack mortification of the intellect, will, and passions. Seventh, we are attached to vice. Eighth, there is willful permission of venial sin and imperfection. Ninth, there is ignorance of God and authentic Church teaching. And tenth, there is lack of humility leading us to presumption.

Part Three:
Development of Grace in its
Three Stages

Introduction

In the first part of this work we concerned ourselves with the fundamental principles of the theology of grace according to Tradition; in the second part we considered the means and procedures for growth in grace; and now in this third part we will discuss the different stages or degrees of development of grace in the soul of the Christian.

Before embarking upon this we ought to keep in mind that each person on the path of holiness responds to singular – that is, unrepeatable - impulses and directives from the Holy Spirit. As a result, there are no two spiritual physiognomies exactly alike.

Nonetheless, the masters of the spiritual life in Catholic Tradition have attempted to classify the predominant symptoms and dispositions proper to the various stages of spiritual growth. These serve as solid points of reference to gauge one's spiritual place and growth. This content is of utmost importance for spiritual directors, confessors, or indeed anyone interested in spiritual growth.

At times, this notion of the three ways runs into opposition. For some reason, certain spiritual directors and writers eschew the categorical divisions of the stages. While we do not pretend to know what their motives may be, we can affirm that Scripture and Magisterial Teaching of the Church lay down the foundations for the spiritual itinerary.

Already in St. Paul's writings we see the notion of spiritual development: *I fed you milk, not solid food, because you were unable to take it. Indeed, you are still not able, even now* (1 Cor 3:2).

In our own time, St. John Paul II, when speaking about the difference between being good and perfect does so in the context of the encounter between Christ and the so-called rich young man. This young man experiences a longing from deep within. This passing grace, Christ's entry into his life, leaves him unsettled and with not a little disquiet.

He is a good man. He has faithfully kept all the commandments. If he is not satisfied with simply being good, how much more must our Lord desire his spiritual perfection? Our Lord shares some of his own longing with this young man, which stirs up within him the following question:

"I have kept all these; what do I still lack? " (Mt 19:20). It is not easy to say with a clear conscience "I have kept all these", if one has any understanding of the real meaning of the demands contained in God's Law. And yet, even though he can make this reply, even though he has followed the moral ideal seriously and generously from childhood, the rich young man knows that he is still far from the goal: before the person of Jesus he realizes that he is still lacking something. It is his awareness of this insufficiency that Jesus addresses in his final answer. Conscious of the young man's yearning for something greater, which would transcend a legalistic interpretation of the commandments, the Good Teacher invites him to enter upon the path of perfection: "If you wish to be perfect, go, sell your possessions and give the money to the poor, and you will have treasure in heaven; then come, follow me" (Mt 19:21).

We do not know how clearly the young man in the Gospel understood the profound and challenging import of Jesus' first reply: "If you wish to enter into life, keep the commandments".

But it is certain that the young man's commitment to respect all the moral demands of the commandments represents the essential ground in which the desire for perfection can take root and mature, the desire, that is, for the meaning of the commandments to be completely fulfilled in following Christ. Jesus' conversation with the young man helps us to grasp the conditions for the moral growth of man, who has been called to perfection: the young man, having observed all the commandments, shows that he is incapable of taking the next step by himself alone. To do so requires mature human freedom ("If you wish to be perfect") and God's gift of grace ("Come, follow me").[83]

St. John Paul II is telling us that spiritual perfection is to be understood as a given for the follower of Christ. Love does this to us. When we have made a decision for Christ, the Holy Spirit begins a new sort of work within the soul, impelling, inviting, moving the person to greater surrender.

Under the influence of the Holy Spirit this inner, "spiritual," man matures and grows strong. Thanks to the divine self-communication, the human spirit which "knows the secrets of man" meets the "Spirit who searches everything, even the depths of God." In this Spirit, who is the eternal gift, the Triune God opens himself to man, to the human spirit. The hidden breath of the divine Spirit enables the human spirit to open in its turn before the saving and sanctifying self-opening of God.

---

[83] *Veritatis Splendor*, 16, 17. John Paul II.

Through the gift of grace, which comes from the Holy Spirit, man enters a "new life," is brought into the supernatural reality of the divine life itself and becomes a "dwelling-place of the Holy Spirit," a living temple of God. For through the Holy Spirit, the Father and the Son come to him and take up their abode with him. In the communion of grace with the Trinity, man's "living area" is broadened and raised up to the supernatural level of divine life. Man lives in God and by God: he lives "according to the Spirit," and "sets his mind on the things of the Spirit."[84]

The history of spiritual theology has consistently presented us with the three stages of the spiritual life. Pseudo-Dionysius, St. Augustine, Evagrius, Diadochos of Photike, St. Thomas Aquinas, St. Catherine of Sienna, St. John of the Cross, all coincide on this. Although their respective terminology may differ for these stages, they all agree on the substance. For our purposes, we will use St. John of the Cross' terminology: purgative, illuminative, and unitive.

Synthesizing these three stages in the context of St. Teresa of Avila's seven mansions within a massive circular castle, divided into concentric circles, each containing many rooms. It could be summarized in this fashion.

---

[84] *Dominum et Vivificantem*, 58. John Paul II.

Sinners	No Christian Life – no grace: outside the castle
	Cultural Christians: Near the castle wall
Purgative Stage	Novices – First Mansion
	The Good – Second Mansion
Illuminative Stage	The Pious – Third Mansion
	The Fervent – Fourth Mansion
Unitive Stage	The Relatively Perfect – Fifth Mansion
	The Heroic – Sixth Mansion
	Great Saints – Seventh Mansion

-1-

The Sinful

Before studying the upward trajectory towards perfection, we ought to briefly consider the stages of sin. Just as those who are constantly faithful ascend the mountain of perfection, so too the rebellious, on the contrary, can debase himself to such an extent that he plunges himself into the abyss of evil. This chapter is divided into two parts: the absence of Christian life and cultural Christians.

The Absence of Christian Life

For sure, there are many pagans and decidedly Godless people. In their case, the Evil One barely concerns himself with them since, with his help, they have made their own self-destructive choices long ago. They follow the logical trajectory of their choices in this world into the next.

Some of those people were never afforded an introduction to Christ and the truth about grace. Others, on the other hand, ended up rejecting the truth they received. Such people do not necessarily renounce their faith immediately, either because of a particular grace of God, an attachment to the religion in which they were raised, or the good example of their Christian families and friends. Their intellectual acceptance of the faith is not put in doubt.

In the first instances of their spiritual descent their contrition is real. This person, at first, would like to take leave of his sins but he lacks courage. He suffers the tyranny of his passions before becoming a slave to them. Perhaps it is shame that keeps him from confession and, as a result, keeps him bound to his sins. Perhaps this person goes to Communion in the state of sin because of embarrassment and further aggravates his spiritual situation. Sooner or later he must make a choice. He either chooses conversion or allows sin to define him. Nonetheless this person has not arrived at the point of obstinacy or hardness of heart yet. His conversion is still possible, above all, if he still has a habit of prayer - even if it consists of little more than a daily Our Father or Hail Mary. It is rare, however, that a person remains in this malaise for long.

The resistance to goodness and the continual infidelity, conspire to make the work of prevenient grace less efficacious. Ignoring the voice of God in the sanctuary of one's conscience – something that caused pain earlier - now becomes quite easy. Contrition wanes. Faith, though not completely extinguished, is obscured. On the other hand, the passions, which have been coddled until now, become more and more demanding and in control. This is the step toward hardness of heart.

This is a deplorable spiritual state, offensive to God, and extremely dangerous for the spiritual life. This person sets his face like flint before good influences, graces of conversion, sound counsel, interior calls to prayer and repentance. None of this penetrates the soul anymore. The spirit becomes ossified, not because the person lacks judgment, but rather this hardness resides in the obstinate will that *a priori* rejects that which would bring about its good.

Some Christians get angry when they see their undertakings failing, misfortunes overwhelming them, or death snatching from them those whom they love, and then lay blame on divine providence. 'What have I done to God,' say these poor creatures in their madness, 'that you should treat me so harshly?' And then, as a kind of revenge, they neglect their religious duties more and more, and plunge deliberately into sin.

Others are vexed that they cannot indulge their passions in peace; they fall into a kind of rage against themselves and against God. As they cannot get rid of faith, and are keenly susceptible to the sting of conscience, they enter a struggle with God and, drown all their remorse in sin.[85] Such are those who may eventually commit the intellectually dishonest act of calling sin innocuous.

Vast numbers have a natural goodness and merely follow the established norms of a post-Christian society. In their inability to recognize Christ and all he is and offers, they become equally incapable of recognizing sin for what it is. The insidious mantra "I'm spiritual, not religious" acts as a sort of placebo to inoculate their consciences against the demands of the natural law. Often, social activism acts as their ersatz religion, and the dogmas of their man-made causes are quite inflexible, demanding an assent of faith that defies reason, rather than suppose and supersede it.

Cultural Christians

St. Teresa of Avila says,

---

[85] Abbe A. Saudreau, *The Degrees of the Spiritual Life,* vol. 1, ch1, nn.6 and 15.

Many souls remain in the outer court of the castle, which is the place occupied by the guards; they are not interested in entering it and have no idea what there is in that wonderful place, or who dwells in it, or even how many rooms it has.

Let us say no more, then, of these paralyzed souls, who, unless the Lord himself comes and commands them to rise, like the man who had lain beside the pool for 30 years: poor unfortunate creatures who live in great peril.[86]

The ordinary thoughts of the souls, their actual desires, their concerns, their dreams are purely natural, never or almost never do they reflect on serious things inspired by faith and its demands. There is no desire to conform themselves to the content much less the norms of Revelation. If they do practice virtue and even deny themselves for the good of others such as for parents or friends in need, it is not because they follow the inspirations of grace: they are obeying the natural instinct proper to natural law in all people. If they fight to overcome their defects, it is for merely human, that is, natural motives rather than those inspired by God. Fear of offending God is not what moves them to overcome sin but rather the natural abhorrence to evil. They consider sin as having little importance and, at best, something easily forgivable, thus placing themselves in the greatest of danger, succumbing to temptations without the help of Grace.

From time to time a supernatural grace may come to their souls and awaken in them notions of faith: the funeral for a loved one, suffering in their own life, the exceptional circumstances, such things that awaken in them good

---

[86] Interior Castle, 1, 5 and 8.

sentiments. If they are conscious of having fallen into certain sins they may even have a certain healthy remorse. But outside of these particular circumstances these people do not live on a supernatural plane and are not motivated by supernatural inspiration, deaf to the intimate still voice of God whose sweet murmurs demand recollection and calm in order to be heard: *but the Lord was not in the wind . . . but the Lord was not in the earthquake* (1 Kg 19:11). These people, completely given over to distraction, are hardly capable of recognizing the voice of the Divine:

These people only observe what is strictly necessary regarding Christian practice: Mass on Sundays, and that at rare intervals. And when they do go they are filled with many distractions, few if any vocal prayers.

Spiritual reading, devotional exercises, only fill them with weariness, and, indeed, they rarely think of them, so absorbed are they in material occupations. Their minds are not concerned with these things, and if some external influence should happen to bring them into the region of the spiritual world, they find themselves uneasy in the surroundings, and do not stay long.

These unhappy ones can hardly, then, be said to lead a Christian life; faith still lives in the depth of their hearts, but it is, as it were, torpid; their days are empty of God, and their salvation is in great danger. They may be kept in this state by external circumstances; if they are surrounded by Christian influences, and shy away from contact with bad company and dangerous locations, they will not commit grave errors. But if these external helps should happen to fail them – if they should, for instance, move to new surroundings and lack the good example that carries them along, they will quickly lose their good habits, grow weary of their good practices, and soon become like those who surround them.

The state which we have just described is that of many young people who belong to careless families, and whose religious education is not yet completed. They hear the things of faith rarely mentioned, and how are they likely to be able to avoid a life of vice and sensuality?"[87]

---

[87] Degrees of the Spiritual Life, Vol 1, book 1, 2, nn.25-26.

-2-

The Purgative Way

Those who live "by the flesh" experience God's law as a burden, and indeed as a denial or at least a restriction of their own freedom. On the other hand, those who are impelled by love and "walk by the Spirit" (Gal 5:16), and who desire to serve others, find in God's Law the fundamental and necessary way in which to practice love as something freely chosen and freely lived out. Indeed, they feel an interior urge — a genuine "necessity" and no longer a form of coercion — not to stop at the minimum demands of the Law, but to live them in their "fullness". This is a still uncertain and fragile journey as long as we are on earth, but it is one made possible by grace, which enables us to possess the full freedom of the children of God (cf. Rom 8:21) and thus to live our moral life in a way worthy of our sublime vocation as "sons in the Son".[88]

When someone sincerely desires to follow Christ, he enters the purgative way; that is the first stage of charity. "For at first it is incumbent on man to occupy himself chiefly with avoiding

---

[88] Veritatis Splendor, 18.

sin and resisting his concupiscence, which moves him in opposition to charity: this concerns beginners, in whom charity has to be fed or fostered lest it be destroyed."[89]

Relating this fundamental division with the magisterial descriptions of St. Teresa in her *Interior Castle*, we can distinguish in the first phase of the spiritual life; that is, the development of grace, two degrees, or categories, of people. We can call them "beginners" (that is, those in the first mansion of St. Teresa) and "good people" (who are found in the second mansion).

Beginners

When the person begins to enter himself, running from all sorts of dangers and seductions offered by the world, the flesh, and the devil, he enters the first mansion of the castle. Here, with greater or lesser constancy, one finds himself at last within the castle. We consider now St. Teresa's masterful description of this moment:

> As far as I can understand, the door of entry into this castle is prayer and meditation: I did not say mental prayer rather than vocal, for, if it is prayer at all, it must be accompanied by meditation. If a person does not think whom he is addressing, and what he is asking for, and who it is that is asking and of whom he is asking it, I did not consider that he is praying at all even though he move his lips...
>
> Let us say no more, then, of these paralyzed souls, who, unless the Lord himself come and command them to rise, like

---

[89] *S Th* II-IIae, 24,9.

the man lying beside the pool for 30 years (Jn 5:5): They are unfortunate creatures and live in great peril. Let us rather think of certain other souls, who do eventually enter the castle.

These are very much absorbed by worldly affairs; but their desires are good; sometimes, though infrequently, they commend themselves to our Lord; and they think about the state of their souls, though not very carefully. Full of a thousand preoccupations as they are, they pray only a few times a month, and as a rule they are thinking all the time of their preoccupations, for they are very much attached to them, and, *where your treasure is, there also will your heart be* (Mt 6:21).

It is for this reason, daughters, that I said we must set our eyes on Christ our good, from whom we shall learn true humility, and also upon his saints. Our understanding, as I have said, will then be ennobled, and self-knowledge will not make us timorous and fearful; for, although this is only the first mansion, it contains riches of great price and any who can elude the reptiles which are to be found in it will not fail to go farther. Terrible are the crafts and wiles used to prevent souls from learning to know themselves understanding his ways.

With regard to these first mansions I can give some very useful information out of my own experience. I must tell you, for example, to think of them as comprising not just a few rooms, but a very large number. There are many ways in which souls enter into them, always with good intentions;

but as the devil's intentions are always very bad, he has many legions of evil spirits in each room to prevent souls from passing from one to another, and as we, poor souls, fail to realize this, we are tricked by all kinds of deceptions…

You must note that the light which comes from the palace occupied by the King hardly reaches these first mansions at all; for, although they are not dark and black, as when the soul is in a state of sin, they are to some extent darkened, so that they cannot be seen (I mean by anyone who is in them); and this is not because of anything that is wrong with the room, but rather (I hardly know how to explain myself) because there are so many bad things – snakes and vipers and poisonous creatures – which have come in with the soul that prevent it from seeing the light.

It is as if one were to enter a place flooded by sunlight with his eyes so full of dust that he could hardly open them. The room itself is light enough, but he cannot enjoy the light because he is prevented from doing so by these wild beasts and animals, which force him to close his eyes to everything but himself. This seems to me to be the condition of the soul which, though not in a bad state, is so completely absorbed in things of the world and so deeply immersed, as I have said, in possessions or honors or business, that, although as a matter of fact it would like to gaze at the castle and enjoy its beauty, it is prevented from doing so, it seems quite unable to free itself from all these impediments.

Everyone, however, who wishes to enter the second mansion, will be well advised, as far as the state of life permits, to try to put aside all unnecessary affairs and business. For those who hoped to reach the principal mansion, this is so important that unless they begin in this way I do not believe they will ever be able to get there. For, indeed, even though it has entered the castle, the soul is not free from great peril in the mansion which it actually inhabits; for, being among such poisonous things, it cannot at some time or another, escape being bitten by them."[90]

Despite a radical change of habits and an alteration of external behavior, all is not well in their interior. In their external conduct we at once notice that these souls know nothing of Christian abnegation; they may make some efforts at distant intervals, but they have little fidelity, and dissipation of mind soon makes an end of their weak resolutions. These souls have natural rather than supernatural virtues.

If they have been preserved from grave faults and have received a Christian education, they may be able to continue to avoid mortal sin and keep their horror of evil, and thus remain all their lives without either great faults or great virtues. In this category are a great number of souls who have been but little enlightened by the inspirations of grace. Either because they are not very intelligent, or because, they have not received much education about piety. Having no very fierce temptations, they lead a quiet and correct life, but they do not seem destined for very high reward. We are sometimes astonished at the little delicacy of conscience that is found in souls who, in the best possible faith, imagine that their lives are almost blameless.

This comes from their taking scarcely any heed except as to

---

[90] *Interior Castles*, First Mansion, 2, nn. 12-14.

external acts of sin, and not making much of the evil motions of the soul, of the ill-restrained desires, or those interior feelings which are more or less opposed to the law of God. Such souls are indeed very frail, and some particularly dangerous occasion would be exceedingly formidable for them. If, on the other hand, they have known evil, they easily succumb to the least temptations, and may thus fall into a state of indifference for eventual sin. As to venial sin, they, like the last named, trouble little about it; they take no pain to combat the defects of character, temper, laziness, vanity, greediness, avarice, etc.; they often have an affection for one or other of these defects, and therefore do not repent of it. Sometimes they recognize their faults, and, when the occasion is over, regret their weakness; but with regard to these of the venial sins their purpose of amendment is feeble enough, and there is little hope of improvement.[91]

Such is the spiritual and moral state of the inhabitants of the first mansion: Inconstant in grace, they fall and get up. They lack a firm foundation and their purpose of amendment is weak. This is the lot of the beginner.

The Good

"Good souls" are how St. Teresa describes the inhabitants of the second mansion. These people do everything in their power to avoid grave sin. With a certain facility, they recognize and run from occasions of grave sin and, nonetheless, they have yet to treat venial sin in the same way, and, as a result, lack adequate reparation. As such, they live habitually in the state of grace but only with struggle and a degree of violence in

---

[91] Degrees of the Spiritual Life, 1,1,1, n. 35.

combating temptation.

More and more they sense divine inspiration and they see the will of God with ever greater clarity, and nonetheless they have little fortitude to carry it out with perfection or even with adequate regard for fulfillment. The inhabitants of the second mansion have not given themselves over to Christ completely. As a result, what is required here is a renewed determination to surrender themselves to prayer, and this way they will achieve the fortitude they need to live out God's will. People in this stage of the spiritual life need to meditate on the passion of the Lord, his sufferings, his death. They will benefit much by allowing themselves to undergo the influence of truly spiritual people so that they are ever more awake to the life of the soul in the attractive truth of Jesus Christ.

Because of the growth in the spiritual life, they begin to experience the spiritual joys they never knew before. Peace and tranquility are their new treasure. About them St. Teresa of Avila says:

> This chapter has to do with those who have already begun to practice prayer and to realize the importance of not remaining in the first mansions, but too often are not yet resolute enough to leave those mansions, and will not avoid occasions of sin, which is a very perilous condition. But it is a very great mercy that they should contrive to escape from the snakes and other poisonous creatures, if only for short periods and should realize that it is good to flee from them.

> In some ways, these souls have a much harder time than those in the first mansions; but they are in less peril, for they seem now to understand their position and there is great

hope that they will proceed further into the castle still. I say that they have a harder time because the souls in the first mansions are, as it were, not only dumb, but can hear nothing, and so it is not such a trial to them to be unable to speak; the others, who can hear and not speak, would find a trial much harder to bear. But that is no reason for envying those do not hear, for after all it is a great thing to be able to understand what is said to one.

The souls, then, can understand the Lord when he calls them; for, as they gradually get nearer to the place where his Majesty dwells, he becomes a very good neighbor to them. And such are his mercy and goodness that, even when we are engaged in our worldly pastimes and businesses and pleasures and hagglings, when we are falling into sins and rising from them again (because these creatures are at once so venomous and so active and it is so dangerous for us to be among them that it will be a miracle if we escape stumbling over them and falling) – in spite of all that, this Lord of ours is so anxious that we should desire him and strive after his companionship that he calls us ceaselessly, time after time, to approach him; and this voice of his is so sweet that the poor soul is consumed with grief and being unable to do his bidding immediately, and thus, as I say, it suffers more than if they could not hear him.[92]

As is apparent from this text, even in the most ordinary and imperfect life, the occupants of the second mansion not infrequently, and often without realizing it, receive very

---

[92] Second Mansions, n 2.

164

special divine inspirations in certain rays of a divine illumination which helps them understand what God wants from them and for them. And, if they are faithful to these divine invitations, they will soon be enveloped by divine light and the splendors of God himself who will transform them and put them firmly on the path to divinization.

Ah, My Lord! It is here that we have need of your aid, without which we can do nothing. Of your mercy, allow not this soul to be deluded and led astray when his journey is but begun. Give it light so that it may see how all its welfare consists in this and may flee from evil companionship. It is no small matter for a person to associate with others who are walking in the right way: to mix, not only with those who he sees in the rooms where he himself is, but with those whom he knows dwell in the rooms closer to the center, for they will be of great assistance to him.

Let him have a fixed determination not to allow himself to be beaten, for, if the devil sees that he is firmly resolved to lose his life and his peace and everything that he can offer him rather than to return to the first room, he will very soon cease troubling him. Let him play the man and not be like those went down on their knees to drink when they went to battle – but let him be resolute, for he is going forth to fight with all the devils and there is no better weapon than the cross…

All that the beginner in prayer has to do – and you must not forget this, for it is very important – is to labor and be resolute and prepare himself with all possible diligence to bring his will into conformity with the will of God.

And I shall tell you later, you may be quite sure that this comprises the very greatest perfection which can be attained on the spiritual road. The more perfectly a person practices it, the more you will receive of the Lord and the greater the progress you will make on this road; do not think we have to use strange jargon or dabble in things of which we have no knowledge or understanding, our entire welfare is to be found in what I have described.

Let this war now cease. By the Blood that Christ shed for us, I beg this of those who have not begun to enter within themselves; and those who have begun to do so must not allow such warfare to turn them back. They must realize that to fall a second time is worse than to fall once. They can see that will lead them to ruin: let them place their trust, not in themselves, but in the mercy of God, and they will see how his Majesty can lead them on from one group of mansions to another and set them on safe ground where these beasts cannot harass or hurt them, for he will place the beasts in their power and laugh them to scorn; and then they themselves – even in this life, I mean – will enjoy many more good things than they could ever desire."[93]

In summary, if the first mansion is the place of those who run from worldly noise and have entered the life of grace, to love of God, then the second is inhabited by those who, with all their strength, struggle to avoid what is truly dangerous – grave sin and its occasions. They renounce unnecessary hobbies, they

---

[93] *Ibid.* nn. 6,8,9.

adopt a life of greater recollection, they have fixed times for mental prayer, and from time to time experience lights, inspirations, and movements of the Holy Spirit who disposes them to carry out the content of those inspirations and moves them to be alone with him in an ever greater solitude where he speaks to their hearts (*cf.* Hos 2:14).

It is advantageous to discuss with greater detail the interior dispositions corresponding to the second mansions.

Practices of devotion: Those in the second mansion are ones who, besides their ordinary prayers, have recourse, willingly, indeed, but without great fervor, to practices of devotion beyond the essentials, such as the Rosary and daily Mass. We said, "without great fervor." Sometimes, however, you will see them pray with all their hearts. Is it the breathings of divine grace that moves them? This recollected demeanor, these burning aspirations, these heart yearnings – are they the effects of a lively and sudden devotion? We must take knowledge that nature has a great share in all this. When we inquire the object of these fervent prayers, we shall find that it is some temporal favor earnestly desired, or to be saved from some trial, but never, or very seldom, purely spiritual blessings.

Such souls communicate often; not that they experience much sweetness in their Communions, but they understand the greatness of the act, and they are readily induced to make a serious preparation for it. But if they are easily led to practice some devotional exercises they also very easily give them up again, and if they are not kept up to the mark become extremely negligent.

Interior dispositions: Although the dwellers in this mansion are for the most part preoccupied with natural cares, yet ideas connected with religion are more frequent with them than with those in the first mansion. However, even here they do not, as a rule, arise spontaneously. 'They come,' says St. Teresa, 'by discourses heard from good people, or from sermons or by reading pious books, or many other ways which are well-known, such as by sickness and adversity; and he causes certain truths to shine into the soul in times of prayer.'

It is, so to speak, a state of intermittent piety. We say piety because the soul desires not only to correct its faults but also progress in virtue; but these desires are intermittent. It experiences them, for instance, in confession or Holy Communion, or when hearing a sermon; in a word, on the various occasions mentioned by St. Teresa; but apart from this, the desire for progress is seldom manifested. The soul is more determined to remain faithful to God. Such souls, however, are far less constant in this respect than one would imagine, or than they themselves suppose, but they are often ignorant of their own weakness.

External conduct: Christian self-denial is beginning to appear. From time to time this all tries to overcome itself, and is even capable of serious mortification, but without much perseverance. Grave sin is rare, except when some dangerous occasion presents itself, for then even the good, but frail, soon succumb. Another exception, in the case of those who have already had acquaintance with the evil, is any violent temptation against holy purity, for then these people, imperfectly mortified, are not strong enough to overcome them.

In the first mansion the soul still had but little horror of venial sin. It too easily committed deliberate venial sins even without any violent excitement of the passions. 'What I am doing is not right, but it does not signify a grave transgression.' In the second mansion the soul avoids venial sins with more care; but when it is a case of self-interest, when the passions are aroused, when susceptibility, self-love, vanity, or sensuality assail it, or, again, when it is afraid of some worry or annoyance, it sins with open eyes and full consent. 'After all,' it says to itself, 'it is not so very serious.' It is true that when the occasion is past, and the passions abate, it sincerely regrets having yielded, but a relapse is still much to be feared. These persons are not attached to their faults, but they have not really at heart the work of struggling against them all.

Christians who have arrived at this degree of the spiritual life have, then, the appearances of piety without any true devotion. As we have just said, they sometimes fall into lamentable errors, and even from time to time indulge in most unedifying language. For these reasons they are sometimes very severely criticized, they reveal a certain hypocrisy and insincerity, while, as a matter of fact, their faith is still genuine and their good dispositions real. A director must be aware of such severe judgments and remember that these people are unstable but not hypocritical.

It is likewise because of their inconstancy, the rapid alterations of their good and evil moments, the mixture of the religious sentiments and a worldly spirit which is found in them – it is because of all this that certain Christians do not give God's cause the support that one would expect of them.

Such are the general characteristics of the second mansion. There are from time to time real aspirations after spiritual progress, but virtue still seems a very difficult thing to acquire, and, as a rule, there are still weary struggles to be endured.

Some, however, have not advanced beyond this degree, and yet they do not undergo any violent assaults. A great number who style themselves "practicing Catholics" are in the state.

Without having frequented the sacraments much, or long cultivated mental prayer, which begins the process of the active purification of the intellect, they are yet firmly established in natural goodness. They keep themselves apart from the dangers of the world and are also preserved from its perils by their horror of the wicked - even shunning worldly things. On the other hand, the good education which they have received, the habitual association with virtuous people, the profit that they have derived from sermons and other external aids of religion, their fidelity to the duties of their state in life – all this has developed their good dispositions. We notice in them a supernatural life of faith, a sincere love of the Church, and a true zeal for her interests. Some of them are valuable assets in their parishes; they are very dedicated to God's cause, and they bring to the service of religion natural qualities that are sometimes remarkable. These souls only need a more complete spiritual training to make great progress in the spiritual life.[94]

Challenges encountered in this stage

This is a stage of spiritual infancy. God treats them in the same way the best of mothers treats her child,[95] and does not expect much more from them than the virtue proper to children,[96] weak and imperfect,[97] operating, not out of true conviction but because of the spiritual joy they receive[98] and the consolations resulting from their good choices.[99] With that in mind, it makes

---

[94] Degrees of the Spiritual Life, pp. 32-36.
[95] D 1, chpt. 1, 2.
[96] "Ignorant children" says our author. A 1, chpt. 4, 5.
[97] D 1, chpt. 1, 3.
98 D 1, chpt. 6, 6.
[99] D 1, chpt. 1, 3.

sense that the evil one will take advantage of these imperfect dispositions in order to tempt them.[100]

People in the purgative stage are tempted to pride upon experiencing sensible fervor resulting from their exercise of new-found piety and prayer. Often, they experience a hidden self-esteem and self-satisfaction when considering their own good works.

Diabolical attacks are to be expected. In fact, the devil can give increase to the sensible fervor experienced by the novice, fomenting a strong desire to multiply his good works. As this desire increases, so does the danger of falling into presumption – precisely what the Evil One has in mind. In other words, his goal is to transform such works, desires, and feelings into vice.[101]

St. John of the Cross says that the devil will even create false ecstasies in these people – albeit, often in public, than in private[102] - because he is well aware of their vain self-complacency and longing to be "caught" by others in such a state.[103]

Regarding lust, novices undergo many trials of the flesh, even when recollected, in prayer, going to Communion or confession.[104] It seems that their sensible fervor has been so piqued and their habit of self-dominion so new, that they have a difficult time knowing what to do with this whirlwind of feelings.

To bring disquietude and disturbance during prayer, or when attempting to pray, he endeavors to excite impure

---

[100] This is a common theme with our author: A 2, chpt. 27, 6; A 3, chpt. 6, 2; A 3, chpt. 29, 1; D 1, chpt. 14, 1; *Spiritual Canticle* 3, 8 (henceforth cited as C).; C 3,9, etc.

[101] Loc. Cit. 2.

[102] Loc. Cit. 3.

[103] Ibid.

[104] D 1, chpt. 4, 1.

feelings in the sensory part. And if people pay any attention to these, the devil does them great harm. Through fear, some grow slack in their prayer - which is what the devil wants - to struggle against these movements, and others give it up entirely, for they think these feelings come while they are engaged in prayer rather than at other times. And this is true because the devil excites these feelings while people are at prayer, instead of when they are engaged in other works, so that they might abandon prayer. And that is not all; to make them cowardly and afraid, he brings vividly to their minds foul and impure thoughts. And sometimes the thoughts will concern spiritually helpful things and persons. Those who attribute any importance to such thoughts, therefore, do not even dare look at anything or think about anything lest they thereupon stumble into them.

These impure thoughts so affect people who are afflicted with melancholia that one should have great pity for them; indeed, these people suffer a sad life. In some who are troubled by this, the trial reaches such a point that they clearly feel that the devil has access to them without their having the freedom to prevent it. Yet some of these melancholics are able through intense effort and struggle to forestall this power of the devil.

If these impure thoughts and feelings arise from melancholia, individuals are not ordinarily freed from them until they are cured of that humor - unless they enter the dark night, which in time deprives them of everything.[105]

Spiritual gluttony is common among novices in the spiritual life. A great deal can be said on spiritual gluttony. There are hardly any persons among these beginners, no matter how excellent their conduct, who do not fall into some of the many

---

[105] D 1, chpt. 3.

imperfections of this vice. These imperfections arise because of the delight beginners find in their spiritual exercises.[106]

As contradictory as it might seem, these beginners in the spiritual life sometimes experience such spiritual delight in their corporal penance which, when unchecked, can sink into carnal pleasure. For St. John of the Cross, the key to a healthy life of *askesis* is its intention and submissiveness in obedience to one's spiritual director. The danger here for the novice, is his own self-assurance that he is pleasing God so much with his pious and penitential indiscretions (he must be, he is pleasing himself to no end!) that he will outwardly accept what his spiritual director says, but legalistically modify his own behavior in order to continue doing what he was already doing.[107] When called to account again by his spiritual director, this person gets angry, defensive, complains of being misunderstood.[108]

Exercise of Virtue

While we labor toward the acquisition of virtues, our spiritual foes are not idle. They return stealthily to take the offensive, either by causing in us a reawakening, in a subtler form, of the seven capital sins and, or by leading us to complacency and luke-warmness.

Capital sins

St. John of the Cross gives an excellent description of these capital sins as they exist in those we call beginners, in those who are on the threshold of contemplation through the night of the

---

[106] D 1, chpt. 6, 1.
[107] Ibid.
[108] Loc. Cit. 2

senses.[109]

This inclination is manifested in six principal ways: pride, envy, sensuality (gluttony), spiritual lust, sloth, and spiritual avarice.

Pride: While aiming at fervor and remaining faithful to their spiritual exercises, these beginners take complacency in their works and hold themselves in high esteem. They presumptuously plan too many projects and carryout scarcely any.

They speak of the things of the spiritual life rather to give lessons to others than to put these lessons into practice themselves, and harshly condemn those who do not approve of their type of spirituality. Some of them cannot stand rivalry. If a rival happens to appear, they condemn him and belittle him.

They seek the good graces in the intimacy of their spiritual director, and if the latter does not approve of their ways, they look for another who will be more accommodating. The better to succeed in this, they tone down their faults, and if they happen to fall into a grave sin, they accuse it to another confessor and not to the regular director. Should they commit a grievous sin, they act out of sorts with themselves and lose heart, peeved in not having reached sanctity as yet. They love to attract notice by outward manifestations of their piety, and readily speak to others of their good works and the success.

Envy: From pride springs envy, revealing itself by displeasure at the sight of the spiritual good of others. These people experience pain at hearing others praised, are saddened at their manifest virtue, and when the occasion presents itself, they do not fail to speak ill of those who are spiritually superior

---

[109] D 1, chpt. 2-7.

174

to them and, as a result, threatening to their egos.

Sensuality: Spiritual gluttony manifests itself in two ways First, there can be an excessive craving for consolations. These are to be found even in the practice of austerities, having recourse to corporal mortification. At times one finds in novices of the spiritual life, a still unpurified and complex self-love that, while they seek to impress their spiritual directors with their regimen of penance, they can find a secret satisfaction in carrying them out, resulting in sensual consolations.

For the same reason, some persons make forced efforts during meditation or the time of communion, in order to procure a feeling of devotion, or they wish to go frequently to confession with a view of finding some comfort in this exercise. Often these efforts and longings remain sterile, and then discouragement takes hold of these people who are more attached to consolations than to God himself.

Spiritual lust: Spiritual lust appears especially under two forms. One seeks sentimental or sensual friendships, under the pretext of devotion, and one is hesitant to give them up, pretending that such relations are an aid to piety.

At times, the sensible consolations experienced in prayer or Communion produce in persons of a tender and affectionate nature pleasures of another sort, which may prove to them a source of temptation or anxiety. St. Teresa of Avila speaks of this in a letter to her brother, Lorenzo de Cepeda, saying,

About the distress about which you complain, in no instance must it be concerning to you. Although I do not claim to be able to speak from experience, since God has always preserved me from such passions, I understand what occurs. It is the very intensity of the light produced in the soul that brings about such reactions in our nature. With God's grace that shall pass away, if you will not be disturbed by it.[110]

Sloth: Sloth leads to numerous faults. First, there is a weariness in the performance of spiritual exercises when one does not find any relish in them, and prompts either to shorten or omit them. It also leads to dejection of spirit, when one receives from a superior or spiritual director orders or counsels which seem too difficult. One would prefer a more congenial sort of spirituality that does not interfere with one's petty schemes, a sort of do-it-yourself tailor version of following Christ.

Spiritual avarice: There are beginners who do not cease to cram their souls with spiritual counsels and precepts; they must possess and read numerous spiritual treatises on which they spend all their time, and have none left for the fulfillment of their first duty: namely, mortification and perfect interior detachment.

Besides, they load themselves with holy pictures, rosaries, crucifixes, and expensive and curious objects of devotion. Then they quit one thing for another, change and exchange, arrange and rearrange, and the final choice centers upon that which is singular or expensive.[111]

All this is clearly against the spirit of poverty, and it shows at the same time that one attaches undue importance to accidentals and neglects the essentials of true devotion.

Evidently these imperfections are a great hindrance to spiritual progress. St. John of the Cross holds that God, to correct them, conducts them into the dark night, of which we shall soon speak. As to those who do not enter this phase of the

---

[110] Letter 138.
[111] St. John of the Cross, D bk 1, ch 3, § 1.

spiritual life, they must strive to disentangle themselves from these dangers by practicing the counsels for behavior regarding consolations and desolations with obedience, fortitude, temperance, humility, and meekness.

Luke-warmness

Unless we react against the aforementioned faults, it will not be long before we fall into luke-warmness, a most dangerous spiritual disease. This is a spiritual malady that may attack beginners, proficients and the perfect. Nonetheless, it manifests itself especially during the illuminative way. It presupposes, in fact, that the person has already reached a certain degree of fervor, and that it gradually allows itself to become lax.

Luke-warmness consists in the sort of spiritual laziness which saps the energies of the will, inspires one with the horror for effort and thus leads to the decline of the Christian life. It is a kind of sluggishness, a sort of torpor which though not qualified yet as "death" yet, insensibly leads to it through a gradual weakening of our moral fortitude. One may compare it to those slow working diseases, such as consumption, which little by little prey upon some vital organ.

Luke-warmness causes defective spiritual nourishment. To live and grow, we need wholesome spiritual food. For this to happen, we must be nourished by the necessary spiritual exercises, that is, meditation, devout reading, prayer, examination of conscience, the fulfillment of the duties of state, exercise and the practice of the virtues – all of which keep it in communion with God, the source of spiritual life. Therefore, if these exercises are performed with negligence, with voluntary distractions, without effort to react against routine or sluggishness, then we, deprived of many graces and poorly nourished, become weak and incapable of practicing the virtues of the Christian life in face of even minor difficulties.

We ought to note in passing that this condition is altogether different from that dryness or spiritual affliction permitted by God to try us. In these, instead of welcoming distractions, one experiences pain and humiliation in having them, and one earnestly seeks to avoid them. The luke-warm man, on the contrary, lets himself be carried along by useless thoughts, takes pleasure in them, hardly makes any effort to be rid of them, and soon distractions overrun his prayers. Then, seeing how little profit he derives from his exercise of piety, he begins to shorten them, and in time suppresses them entirely. Thus, his examination of conscience becomes wearisome, irksome, a mere matter of routine, and finally ends up being omitted; he is no longer aware of his faults, of his defects, and he allows them to gain the upper hand. He no longer strives to grow in virtue, and soon has vices. His inordinate inclinations tend find new vigor.

Luke-warmness also causes entry of some noxious germ into the spiritual life. The outcome of spiritual apathy is the gradual decline of the soul – a species of spiritual anemia – that paves the way for entrance of some destructive germ one of the three concupiscences, or perhaps all of them at once.

The avenues of the soul being poorly guarded, the exterior and interior leave themselves open to unwholesome suggestions of curiosity and sensuality, and frequent temptations arise only to be half repulsed. At times the heart yields itself to the current of disturbing affections: one commits an imprudence and courts danger; venial sins are multiplied and hardly regretted; as one slides downwards the peril is great. Should he avoid a mortal fall he ought to count himself fortunate.

Pride, which was never completely subdued (as is apparent from the above), renews its onslaughts. One begins to indulge in self-complacency. To achieve a better opinion of self, this person begins to compare himself to others, seeing them as scrupulous for their fulfillment of duty, ending up despising them for their virtue. This pride brings in its wake envy, jealousy, impatience, anger and harshness in his relations with others.

Avarice is rekindled in the heart. One feels the need of money to secure more pleasures, to make a greater impression; and to provide more of it one has recourse to questionable means, which border on injustice.

Hence, numerable deliberate venial sins are committed for which one feels scarcely any compunction, since the light of judgment and the delicacy of conscience have gradually weakened. This person lives in habitual dissipation of mind and performs the examination of conscience carelessly. Thus, horror for sin diminishes, God's graces are spurned, and whatever there is of them becomes rarer, and the profit derived from them smaller. In a word, there is a weakening of the spiritual organism, which prepares the way to shameful surrenders.

From what we have said it is evident that there are many degrees in luke-warmness. However, it is enough to distinguish incipient from extreme luke-warmness. In the first instance, one yet preserves horror for mortal sin, though committing influences that may lead to there too. One easily commits deliberate venial sins, notably, such as correspond to one's predominant fault. Besides, one brings little earnestness to the performance of spiritual exercises, and often performs them through mere routine.

Because of allowing oneself to drift into such culpable negligence, one ceases to harbor the old instinctive horror for mortal sin. On the other hand, the love of pleasure so increases that one comes to regret the fact that such or such pleasure is forbidden under the pain of loss of grace. One repels temptations but feebly, and the moment arrives when one asks, and not without reason, whether one is still in the state of grace. This is extreme luke-warmness.

The special danger of the state consists in the gradual weakening of the soul's energies, a condition fraught with more danger than the commission of some isolated moral sin. This is the sense in which our Lord speaks to the luke-warm: *I know your works, that you are neither cold nor hot. I wish you were either cold or hot. So, because you are lukewarm, neither cold or hot, I will spit you out of my mouth. For you say, 'I am rich and affluent and have no need of anything,' and yet do not realize that you are wretched, pitiable, poor, blind, and naked* (Rev 3:15-17). It is just like the difference existing between chronic and acute diseases. The latter, once cured, leave no bad effect; the former, having slowly sapped the strength of the body, leave it for a long time in a state of great weakness.

The first effect of luke-warmness is a kind of blinding of conscience. After habitually excusing one's own faults, the judgment becomes warped, and sins, in themselves grave, come to be considered as slight. Thus, a lax conscience begins to form, which can no longer discern the gravity of the sins committed: *Sometimes a way seems right, but the end of it leads to death* (Prov 16:25). Thinking himself rich, because of such pride, this one is impoverished before God.

Along with this comes the gradual weakening of the will. Because of making concessions to sensuality and pride in small things one ends up yielding to pleasures and things of greater importance; for all the elements of the spiritual life hold together. As sacred scripture says: *The person who is trustworthy in very small matters is also trustworthy in great ones; and the person who is dishonest in very small matters is also dishonest in great ones* (Lk 16:10), which means that the earnestness or carelessness with which we perform certain tasks transfers itself to other actions.

Soon one reaches the point of loathing all effort. The will feels run down, one lets oneself go the way of natural desires, indifference, of pleasure. In this there is great danger and unless one reacts, great faults are bound to ensue. Indeed, in so acting, one abuses grace and offers frequent resistance to the inspirations of the Holy Spirit, thus preparing the way for a grave fall.

Such falls are more difficult to repair since they occur almost insensibly. One lets oneself slide, so to speak, to the depth of the abyss without any great shock. Then one tries to practice self-deception, convincing oneself that the fault is only venial; that, if the matter were in fact grave, there was no full consent; so, blame it on "surprise" so it cannot be considered mortally sinful.

In this manner a false conscience is formed which, in regular confession, continues to reveal only trivial matters. So, begins the long chain of sacrilegious confessions and Communions. When the rubber ball falls from a great height, it rebounds; when it rolls down to the bottom of the abyss, it merely settles there. Such is the sad story of the lukewarm heart: it remains in the depths into which it has gradually and almost insensibly slid.

Luke-warmness can be remedied. Our Lord himself pointed out the remedies: *I advise you to buy from me gold refined by fire, so that you may be rich* (Rev 3:18). One must, therefore, never despair. Jesus is ever ready to give us his friendship, his intimate friendship, if we would simply be converted.

To be converted, one must have frequent recourse to a wise confessor, frankly open one's soul to him and sincerely beg his help to overcome tepidity. One must follow his counsels energetically and with constancy. Under his guidance, one will return to the fervent practice of the exercises of piety, especially of those that secured the fulfillment of the others; namely, mental prayer, examination of conscience and the frequent renewal of the intention of doing all for God. This fervor is not rooted in feeling, but in generous will that strives to refuse God nothing.

One will also take up once more the practice of the virtues and the fulfillment of one's duties of state in all earnestness, making one's particular examination of conscience successfully upon the chief points and giving an account thereupon in confession.

By these means we once again attain fervor and the past lessons serve as a reminder of the reparation and atonement we owe God out of justice.

The Practice of Prayer

Above all, the attacks a novice experiences in prayer are indirect, usually regarding the senses. Satan excites disordered movements in the senses to "disquiet and bother the soul at prayer or preparing to pray."[112]

St. John of the Cross says that this is a fight the enemy often wins. The person who wants to pray well or, indeed, is already at prayer, experiences rebellions of the flesh and, fulfilling

---

[112] Ibid.

exactly what the devil intended, interrupts his prayer to fight against the temptation, instead of calmly continuing his prayer and not paying attention to the temptation. These people often fall into discouragement because of such experiences and hesitate to advance along the way of perfection. They do not make the connection that the enemy is at work, sowing these temptations more often during prayer than outside of it. They wonder if they will ever make progress.[113]

In the prayer of the novice there is a predominance of accentuated activity in the interior senses, so much so that the purgative stage has as one of its goals to bring the person from imaginative prayer and sensory meditation to a more spiritual prayer – contemplation.[114]

When the Lord decides to elevate the person and free him from the lowly prayer of senses and imagined discourses, then begins the crisis of the passive night of the senses.[115] Such persons are at a loss, so much so that they do not know how to pray in this new place of darkness. Their imaginative sense is confounded.[116]

The period of transition is visited by dryness and temptations of all sorts[117] with differing lengths of trial in different people, according to the heights to which our Lord wills to elevate them.[118]

St. John identifies three possible trials during this phase of prayer. First, there can be attacks by the spirit of fornication. An

---

[113] D 1, chpt. 4, 3.
[114] *Ascent of Mount Carmel*, book 2, chpt. 14.1 (henceforth cited as A).
[115] D 1, chpt. 8, 3.
[116] Ibid.
[117] D 1, chpt. 14, 6.
[118] D 1, chpt. 13, 1; loc. Cit. 4.

angel of Satan (2 Cor. 12:7), which is the spirit of fornication, is given to some to buffet their senses with strong and abominable temptations and afflict their spirit with foul thoughts and very vivid images, which sometimes is a pain worse than death for them.[119]

Second, there can be attacks by the spirit of blasphemy: At other times a blasphemous spirit is added; it commingles intolerable blasphemies with all one's thoughts and ideas. Sometimes these blasphemies are so strongly suggested to the imagination that the soul is almost made to pronounce them, which is a grave torment to it.[120]

And third, there can be attacks by a spirit of loathing: sometimes another loathsome spirit, which Isaiah calls *spiritus vertiginis* (Is. 19:14), is sent to these souls, not for their downfall but to try them. This spirit so darkens the senses that such souls are filled with a thousand scruples and perplexities, so intricate that such persons can never be content with anything, nor can their judgment receive the support of any counsel or idea. This is one of the most burdensome goads and horrors of this night - very similar to what occurs in the spiritual night.[121]

Teresian Doctrine of Prayer for Those in this Stage (The First Mansion)

It is important to know that *The Interior Castle* is St. Teresa's best synthesis of her spiritual doctrine and prayer experience. The nine grades of prayer and the seven mansions mentioned there are regarded by St. Teresa as intrinsically inseparable from

---

[119] D 1, chpt. 14, 1.
[120] Lc. Cit. 2.
[121] Loc. Cit. 3.

each other.

Accordingly, on the eve of Trinity Sunday, 1577, God showed her in a vision the infrastructure of our soul. It is like a crystal castle in which there are seven mansions, The Most Holy Trinity lives in the center of the seventh mansion in the greatest splendor. These different mansions represent, therefore, various stages in spiritual growth or journey of prayer. Outside the castle all was darkness, with toads, vipers and other poisonous vermin. As we consider the various mansions we will also discover the types of prayer possible to people in those mansions – degrees of prayer that also reveal the state and maturity of one's spiritual life.

Vocal Prayer: Even at the height of sanctity, one cannot omit altogether vocal prayer. The words spoken or sung aloud have immense power to purify or cleanse one's spirit, soul, and body of all unwanted human and spiritual energies.

They have also great power to ignite or re-ignite one's docility to the action of the Holy Spirit, too often muffled deep within one's self and environment. Normally it works slowly in those filled with sins or sinful energies, while more assiduously in purer hearts. Just as in Mass, it is always necessary to begin our prayer with an intense prayer of humility or humble repentance. In varying degrees we are all subject to the ensuing disorder wrought by our past sins.

It is sad to see that many Christians stop at this grade of prayer after a long vocal prayer or hymn singing. Even worse, many who lapsed have never known or experienced other grades. They fall without a good fight, a growth in grace, or a proper nourishment of their souls. To let the Holy Spirit lead us to a higher grade in prayer, it seems better if we can do our vocal prayer at the beginning of our prayer time.

Meditation (Discursive Mental Prayer): Meditation can be defined as a reasoned application of the mind to some supernatural truth in order to penetrate its meaning, love it, and carry it into practice with the assistance of grace."[122] "Regardless of method, all mediation can be reduced ultimately to a basic framework containing all the essential parts of meditation: consideration of some supernatural truth, application of that truth to one's life, and the resolution to do something about it.[123]

Through our misuse of our internal and external senses we gather lots of clutter. Meditation begins the process of re-appropriating one's interior and claiming it for Christ. It's difficult if one has not yet achieved the habit – hence the need to persevere. Indeed, meditation can help us penetrate certain spiritual truths, know ourselves, repent of our sins, correct our faults, discern God's will, understand others, realize the situation, refocus our life, and make a firm resolution to spend our time, energy and resources fruitfully for our love for God and others. As St. Teresa points out, meditation consists not so much in thinking a great deal but in loving much. Yet love cannot be idle. It constantly urges us to action.

Affective Prayer: Although St. Teresa of Avila does not use the expression *affective prayer* in any of her writings, she does refer to this grade of prayer, and it has been accepted by all schools of spirituality. Affective prayer may be defined as a type of prayer in which the operations of the will predominate over discourses of the intellect. It is merely a simplified meditation in which love predominates. This is made possible after sufficient purification of the intellect carried out by means of mental

---

[122] Jordan Auman, OP, *Spiritual Theology,* p. 318.
[123] *Ibid,* p. 322.

prayer. What follows on the heels of the purification of the intellect is the purification of the will.

The will is a blind faculty that needs direction and enlightenment before it can love and desire the good. For that reason, discursive meditation and spiritual reading play an important part in the practice of affective prayer; they supply the material that stimulates the activity of the will.

Hence, we must be careful not to terminate discursive meditation before the affections have been stimulated. This would be a waste of time and could also be the source of illusion. Neither should we force the affections; when they do not come forth spontaneously, or when they have run their course, we should return to discursive or vocal prayer and not try to prolong the affection by our own efforts... As soon as some thought has stimulated and aroused a movement of the will, we should stop reading and allow the will to perform its operation."[124]

Without doubt, meditation and affective prayer can move us to a deeper consolation of love, joy, peace and inner freedom, etc. But the true fruits should be a more transformed will to will as God wills; a more intense virtuous life, a greater self-denial and detachment, a purer love for God and others, etc. Focusing on our feelings is a spiritual gluttony. It may also lead us to spiritual laziness in which we would not return to the practice of meditation. However, we should not suppress such gifts of consolation when they come from God. Yet, God may at times allow us to enter spiritual desolation as He wants us to accord the intensity of grace to our daily living, rather than to its sentimental wonders. Our focus should always be on God, his

---

[124] *Ibid.* pp. 324-325.

holiness, and his will for us.

Ultimately, what God is seeking is our union with God in love, beginning on earth. A good meditation and affective prayer oftentimes ends with newfound conviction for a certain truth, situation, experience, trial, consolation, or discernment, etc., in life. It may also save us a lot of time and energies struggling in confusion and bitterness, etc.

Points of Discernment for this stage according to St. Ignatius of Loyola

First, in the persons who go from mortal sin to mortal sin, the enemy is commonly used to propose to them apparent pleasures, making them imagine sensual delights and pleasures to hold them more and make them grow in their vices and sins. In these persons the good spirit uses the opposite method, pricking them and biting their consciences through the process of reason.

Second, in the persons who are going on intensely cleansing their sins and rising from good to better in the service of God, it is the method contrary to that in the first Rule, for then it is the way of the evil spirit to bite, sadden and put obstacles, disquieting with false reasons, that one may not go on; and it is proper to the good to give courage and strength, consolations, tears, inspirations and quiet, easing, and putting away all obstacles, that one may go on in well doing.

Third, regarding spiritual consolation. I call it consolation when some interior movement in the soul is caused, through which the soul comes to be inflamed with love of its Creator and Lord; and when it can in consequence love no created thing on the face of the earth, but in the Creator of them all.

Likewise, when it sheds tears that move to love of its Lord, whether out of sorrow for one's sins, or for the Passion of Christ our Lord, or because of other things directly connected with His service and praise. Finally, I call consolation every increase of hope, faith and charity, and all interior joy which calls and attracts to heavenly things and to the salvation of one's soul, quieting it and giving it peace in its Creator and Lord.

Fourth, regarding spiritual desolation. I call desolation all the contrary of the third rule, such as darkness of soul, disturbance in it, movement to things low and earthly, the unquiet of different agitations and temptations, moving to want of confidence, without hope, without love, when one finds oneself all lazy, tepid, sad, and as if separated from his Creator and Lord. Because, as consolation is contrary to desolation, in the same way the thoughts which come from consolation are contrary to the thoughts which come from desolation.

Fifth, in time of desolation never make a change; but be firm and constant in the resolutions and determination in which one was the day preceding such desolation, or in the determination in which he was in the preceding consolation. Because, as in consolation it is rather the good spirit who guides and counsels us, so in desolation it is the bad, with whose counsels we cannot take a course to decide rightly.

Sixth, although in desolation we ought not to change our first resolutions, it is very helpful intensely to change ourselves against the same desolation, as by insisting more on prayer, meditation, on much examination, and by giving ourselves more scope in some suitable way of doing penance.

Seventh, let him who is in desolation consider how the Lord has left him in trial in his natural powers, in order to resist the different agitations and temptations of the enemy; since he can with the Divine help, which always remains to him, though he does not clearly perceive it: because the Lord has taken from him his great fervor, great love and intense grace, leaving him, however, grace enough for eternal salvation.

Eighth, let him who is in desolation labor to be in patience, which is contrary to the vexations which come to him: and let him think that he will soon be consoled, employing against the desolation the devices, as is said in the sixth Rule.

Ninth, there are three principal reasons why we find ourselves desolate. The first is, because of our being tepid, lazy or negligent in our spiritual exercises; and so through our faults, spiritual consolation withdraws from us. The second, to try us and see how much we are and how much we let ourselves out in His service and praise without such great pay of consolation and great graces. The third, to give us true acquaintance and knowledge, that we may interiorly feel that it is not ours to get or keep great devotion, intense love, tears, or any other spiritual consolation, but that all is the gift and grace of God our Lord, and that we may not build a nest in a thing not ours, raising our intellect into some pride or vainglory, attributing to us devotion or the other things of the spiritual consolation.

Tenth, let him who is in consolation think how he will be in the desolation which will come after, taking new strength for then.

Eleventh, let him who is consoled see to humbling himself and lowering himself as much as he can, thinking how little he is able for in the time of desolation without such grace or consolation. On the contrary, let him who is in desolation think that he can do much with the grace sufficient to resist all his enemies, taking strength in his Creator and Lord.

Twelfth, the enemy acts like a woman, in being weak against vigor and strong of will. Because, as it is the way of the woman when she is quarrelling with some man to lose heart, taking flight when the man shows her much courage: and on the contrary, if the man, losing heart, begins to fly, the wrath, revenge, and ferocity of the woman is very great, and so without bounds; in the same manner, it is the way of the enemy to weaken and lose heart, his temptations taking flight, when the person who is exercising himself in spiritual things opposes a bold front against the temptations of the enemy, doing diametrically the opposite. And on the contrary, if the person who is exercising himself commences to be afraid and lose heart in suffering the temptations, there is no beast so wild on the face of the earth as the enemy of human nature in following out his damnable intention with so great malice.

Thirteenth, likewise, he acts as a licentious lover in wanting to be secret and not revealed. For, as the licentious man who, speaking for an evil purpose, solicits a daughter of a good father or a wife of a good husband, wants his words and persuasions to be secret, and the contrary displeases him much, when the daughter reveals to her father or the wife to her husband his licentious words and depraved intention, because he easily gathers that he will not be able to succeed with the undertaking begun: in the same way, when the enemy of human nature brings his wiles and persuasions to the just soul, he wants and desires that they be received and kept in secret; but when one reveals them to his good Confessor or to another spiritual person that knows his deceits and evil ends, it is very grievous to him, because he gathers, from his manifest deceits being discovered, that he will not be able to succeed with his wickedness begun.

Fourteenth, likewise, he behaves as a chief bent on conquering and robbing what he desires: for, as a captain and chief of the army, pitching his camp, and looking at the forces or defenses of a stronghold, attacks it on the weakest side, in like manner the enemy of human nature, roaming about, looks in turn at all our virtues, theological, cardinal and moral; and where he finds us weakest and most in need for our eternal salvation, there he attacks us and aims at taking us.

-3-

The Illuminative Way

Following Christ is not an outward imitation, since it touches man at the very depths of his being. Being a follower of Christ means becoming conformed to him who became a servant even to giving himself on the Cross (cf. Phil 2:5-8). Christ dwells by faith in the heart of the believer (cf. Eph 3:17), and thus the disciple is conformed to the Lord. This is the effect of grace, of the active presence of the Holy Spirit in us.

Having become one with Christ, the Christian becomes a member of his Body, which is the Church (cf. Cor 12:13, 27). By the work of the Spirit, Baptism radically configures the faithful to Christ in the Paschal Mystery of death and resurrection; it "clothes him" in Christ (cf. Gal 3:27): "Let us rejoice and give thanks", exclaims Saint Augustine speaking to the baptized, "for we have become not only Christians, but Christ (...). Marvel and rejoice: we have become Christ! ".

Having died to sin, those who are baptized receive new life (cf. Rom 6:3-11): alive for God in Christ Jesus, they are called to walk by the Spirit and to manifest the Spirit's fruits in their lives (cf. Gal 5:16-25). Sharing in the Eucharist, the sacrament of the

New Covenant (cf. 1 Cor 11:23-29), is the culmination of our assimilation to Christ, the source of "eternal life" (cf. Jn 6:51-58), the source and power of that complete gift of self, which Jesus — according to the testimony handed on by Paul — commands us to commemorate in liturgy and in life: "As often as you eat this bread and drink the cup, you proclaim the Lord's death until he comes" (1 Cor 11:26).[125]

When one has firmly decided to take to a solidly pious life and progresses along the ways of virtue, he enters upon the illuminative way. According to St. Thomas Aquinas, this person's principal concern is to grow and advance in the Christian life, increasing his charity and cooperating with grace.

Thus we speak of a man being an infant until he has the use of reason, after which we distinguish another state of man wherein he begins to speak and uses reason, while there is again a third state, that of puberty when he begins to acquire the power of generation, and so on until he arrives at perfection.

In like manner the diverse degrees of charity are distinguished according to the different pursuits to which man is brought by the increase of charity. For at first it is incumbent on man to occupy himself chiefly with avoiding sin and resisting concupiscence, which moves him in opposition to charity: this concerns beginners, in whom charity must be fed or fostered lest it be destroyed. In the second place man's chief pursuit is to aim at progress in good, and this is the pursuit of the proficient, whose chief aim is to strengthen their charity by adding to it: well man's third pursuit is to aim chiefly at union with and enjoyment of God: this belongs to the perfect who *desired to be dissolved and to be with Christ.*[126]

---

[125] Veritatis Splendor, 21.

In the context of Teresa's vision of the mansions we can distinguish two classes or categories of people within the illuminative way: *The Pious* (the third mansion) and *The Fervent* (the fourth mansion).

Nonetheless, we should be clear that the three fundamental ways of the spiritual life, that is, the purgative way, the illuminative way, and the unitive way, do not constitute static departments with clear and defined limits and boundaries. This would be a mistake. In each of the stages one may find, in fact, aspects of purification, illumination, and union. Further, St. Teresa emphasizes that there are many mansions – that is, the spectrum of each phase is varied and broad. What is also clear in her presentation is that in each of the three stages mentioned there is a certain predominance of attitudes and phenomena corresponding to that stage. For example, proper to the purgative stage is the purification of sins and imperfections; in the second, the reception of vivid lights in order to advance in virtue; and in the third, the fundamental aspiration to intimately unite oneself to God and the most elevated heights of Christian perfection.

The Pious

We call them so because they possess the spiritual dispositions that St. Teresa of Jesus describes in the third mansion:

To those who by the mercy of God overcome in these combats, and as a result of perseverance have entered the third mansion, what shall we say about *blessed is the man that*

---

[126] S Th II-II24,9.

fears the Lord? As I am so stupid in these matters, it has been no small thing that his Majesty should have enabled me to understand the meaning of this verse in the vernacular. We shall certainly be right in calling such a man blessed, for, unless he turns back, he is, so far as we can tell, on the straight road to salvation.[127]

Soon after this affirmation the great Carmelite reformer goes on to say:

I believe that, through his goodness, there are many such souls in the world: they are most desirous not to offend his Majesty; they avoid committing even venial sin; they love doing penance, they spend hours in recollection; they use their time well; they practice works of charity toward their neighbors; and they are very careful in their speech and dress and in the government of their household if they have one. This is certainly a desirable state and there seems no reason why they should be denied entrance to the very last of the mansions if they desired, for their disposition is such that he will grant them any favor.[128]

Nonetheless, as good as the dispositions are of these devoted people they are still not perfect, above all in the order of perfect self-denial and the spirit of penance that the more advanced possess. St. Teresa says:

The penances done by these persons are as carefully ordered

---

[127] Third Mansion, 1,1.
[128] Ibid., 1,5

as their lives. They have a great desire for penance, so that by means of it they may serve our Lord – and there is nothing wrong in that – and for this reason they observe great discretion in their penances, lest they should injure their health. You need never fear that they will kill themselves: they are eminently reasonable folk! Their love is not yet ardent enough to overwhelm the reason. How we wished ours would make us dissatisfied with this habit of always serving God at a snails pace! As long as we do that we shall never get to the end of the road. And as we seem to be walking along and getting fatigued all the time – for, believe me, it is an exhausting road – we shall be very lucky if we escape   getting   lost.

Do you think, daughters, if we could get from one country to another in a week, it would be advisable, with all the winds and snow and floods and bad roads, to take a year over it? Would it not be better to get the journey over and done with? For there are all these obstacles for us to meet and there is also the danger of serpents.[129]

However determined such persons may be not to offend the Lord, they will do well not to run any risk offending him; for they are so close to the first mansions that they might easily return to them, since their fortitude is not built on solid ground like that of souls who are already practiced in suffering. These last are familiar with the storms of the world and realize how little is necessary for them to once again desire worldly pleasures. If those of whom I am speaking, however, have to

---

[129] Ibid., 2,7.

suffer great persecutions, they might well return to such pleasures and the devil well knows how to contrive such persecutions in order to do us harm; they might be pressing onward with great zeal, and trying to preserve others from sin, and yet be unable to resist any temptations which came to them.[130]

Those who have managed to penetrate this deeply into the third mansion live a life of greater conformity to the evangelical norms than those in the previous mansions. With greater frequency they begin to experience an increasing influence of the gifts of fear of the Lord and of piety, that moves us to a deeper prayer which is more often affective than discursive, as well as acquiring a deeper horror for sin – regardless of how light the matter may be – and an increased love for the imitation of Christ; all the while they enjoy the first fruits of victory. From there they may continue to pass into the other mansions receiving copious amounts of divine lights and intimate communications.

For this to occur they must undergo very difficult trials, dryness, and all sorts of purifications which our Lord in his mercy has prepared for them to make them capable of perceiving his mysterious influences and enjoying those divine and intimate communications. This will only happen once they have entered into the full exercise of the so-called "spiritual senses," which are awakened in proportion to the degree to which the person has died to the satisfaction of corporal senses.

As a result, the Lord begins to blind them to those things and into the merely natural way of seeing reality in preparation for them to savor supernatural and divine realities. This is when, so says St. Teresa, they enter into "great dry spells in prayer…. and

---

[130] Ibid., 2,12.

interior trials, which attacks many good souls to an intolerable degree, and through no fault of their own, but from which the Lord always rescues them, to their great profit."[131]

During this time our Lord excites in these people a great longing to be totally his and to enjoy him more than anything. "These souls know that nothing would induce them to commit sin – many of them would not intentionally commit even a venial sin – and they make good use of their lives and their possessions. So they cannot be patient when the door is closed to them and they are unable to enter the presence of the King, whose vassals they consider themselves, and in fact are."[132] In this way these people manage to live in such a detached way from everything that is not of the Lord or does not lead to him, renouncing everything except their longing to be with him: suffering great dryness, darkness, difficulties, penances and all sorts of rigors.

This is meant to be a transitory phase. Those who do not pass to the next mansion do so because of their own weakness and their infidelity to grace, not persevering amid the trials. About this St. Teresa says,

> There is no doubt that, persevering in this detachment and abandonment of everything, we shall attain our object. But it must be on this condition – and note that I am warning you of this – that we consider ourselves unprofitable servants. ... The Lord will make them clear to you, so that these periods of aridity may teach you to be humble, and not make you restless, which is the aim of the devil. Be sure that, where

---

[131] *Ibid.*, 1, 5.
[132] *Ibid.*

there is true humility, even if God never grants the soul favors, he will give it peace and resignation to do his will, with which it may be more content than others are with favors.[133]

As is becoming increasingly obvious, these ascetical exigencies reveal that the night of the senses has begun, with all that this implies: the inability to meditate discursively and the absence of affective prayer are other signs that the soul is becoming more and more possessed by the Holy Spirit. With loving and mysterious unction, the Spirit of God reveals fruits of peace and an ever more perfect conformity with the will of the Father. In an imperceptible way the person passes from the ascetical way to the mystical way to which this dark night belongs. Only in hindsight will the person know exactly what has transpired in the soul.

It must be repeated that the reason a person does not make it this far in the spiritual itinerary or does not advance from this point is owed to his lack of generosity and responding to divine inspirations, by not abandoning himself completely to the loving demands of God, giving into pusillanimity, cowardice, natural thinking, and "human" prudence. Other times it is owed to attachment to spiritually sensible attachments, such as consolations.

In these present mansions the Lord does not fail to recompense us with just measure, and even generously, for he always gives us much more than we deserve by granting us the special sweetness much greater than we can obtain from the pleasures and distractions of this life. But I did not think that he

---

[133] *Ibid.*, 1, 8-9.

gives many consolations, except when he occasionally invites us to see what is happening in the remaining mansions, so that we may be prepared to enter them.[134] Abbe Saudreau says:

> Now, as in the days of St. Teresa, there are many such in the world. Doubtless, as we shall soon show, they are far from being without defects, but they are nevertheless the life of the Church, the support of good works, the instruments that God often uses to bring back sinners and to strengthen the weak. Strongly attached to God's calls, these devout Christians feel a great aversion for the enemies of the Church. Their faith is much stronger and more enlightened than in the lower degrees. If, unfortunately, they fall, they are deeply conscious of the gravity of their faults, and the remorse is bitter. They understand God's love for them, and not by a reasonable affection only, but with the sentiments of filial tenderness, their hearts go out towards him.
>
> Who has not encountered numbers of Christians in these excellent dispositions? Dispositions which are so far from natural presuppose quite an extraordinary action of grace, not only upon the intellect, but also upon the heart...
>
> Those who have only just entered upon this life of piety cannot possess all virtues in a very high degree at the outset. The natural failings are more or less flattered by the sensible action of grace, but they are not really weakened and reduced (as will be the case later on) by a sustained practice of virtue and by trials borne in a right spirit...

---

[134] Ibid., 2, 9.

Some Christians spend their whole life in this state. They are too changeable, too weak in the fight against self…

But even for such as these, falls, although rare, are not unprecedented. A dangerous occasion which they were not willing to forgo, a disordered affection for a creature, numerous faults consented to, a failing such as pride, sensuality, or avarice not combated, a willful and persistent dissipation, for long neglect of devotional exercises – these are the causes which bring about the spiritual deterioration, and ultimately lead to the most tragic consequences.

Qui spernit modica paulatim decidet – He that neglects small things, shall fail little by little (Sir 19:1). Such a person, formerly devout, frequently gives way to sin in some slight matter; it makes light of its faults. In other words, it does not conceive sorrow for them. It does not seek to make reparation for them. It excuses itself, and strives to lessen them in his own eyes by poor excuses. So long as it recognized its faults humbly, and repented of them, its conscience remained sensitive, and the will, despite its weakness, continued to be sincerely attached to good. But later, having desired to reject the light, it has succeeded only too well in clothing itself with darkness. Then the understanding is less enlightened, and at the same time the will turns away from good, and attaches itself to what is to be condemned. Enlightened as to certain duties which this person continues to fulfill faithfully, he no longer understands the exigencies and delicacies of the virtues that he neglects. But if the evil extends, if the right actions become rarer, and falls multiply, then the good dispositions grow weak and the bad develop. Such is the story of all those who descend from the degrees of perfection to which they were raised. Their collapse is not due to frailty, but to culpable blindness of the spirit in the will's attachment to sin.

To arrive afresh at the degree of perfection from which one has fallen, the person must strive even more diligently than at the time of its first ascent. Let no one believe that he will recover what he has lost except with great penance. One must also understand that generous sacrifices are necessary to reorient the will and render it supple under the action of grace.[135]

Teresian Doctrine of Prayer for People in this Stage

Prayer of Simplicity: It is simply the prayer of acquired recollection, a simple love or gaze on some divine object, whether on God himself, his nature, the Holy Eucharist, some Christian truth or mystery. The former reasoning and affection have now been transformed into a simple loving attention on the divine. The prayer is the last grade of ascetical prayer, meaning that the person can attain to this prayer by its own effort with the help of ordinary grace. There is no particular method for this prayer. All it takes is a simple loving gaze and attention amidst a great deal of sacred space and quietude. However, it takes a certain intensity of God's grace or energy to do so, i.e., the intensity that builds up through the former three grades of prayer.

After the purification of the intellect and the will has been brought to a satisfactory degree in equal measure, such a degree

---

[135] Degrees of the Spiritual Life, pp. 92-94.

of prayer is possible. We all need this simple, sacred quietude regularly for sufficient nourishment, recollection, concentration and rest in the Lord. God is always willing and eager to grant us this prayer, as we read: *The Lord is my shepherd, there is nothing I lack. In green pastures he makes me lie down; to still waters he leads me; he restores my soul. He guides me along right paths for the sake of his name* (Ps 23:1-3). Hence, each time when we go to prayer, we should cooperate with the Lord and generously give ourselves sufficient time also for this prayer. This is when God's love, joy, peace, wisdom, discernment, rest, etc., would begin to slowly permeate and even overflow our soul. This is when we begin to experience the following more deeply: *Even though I walk through the valley of the shadow of death, I will fear no evil, for you are with me; your rod and your staff comfort me. You set a table before me in front of my enemies; You anoint my head with oil; my cup overflows. Indeed, goodness and mercy will pursue me all the days of my life* (Ps 23:4-6a).

One begins to long for more time in the Lord's presence. *I will dwell in the house of the Lord for endless days* (Ps 23:6b). Yet, in varying degrees, one finds oneself continuously hindered by various unknown forces. Prayer is indeed a daily battle. Various types of unholy and unwanted energies seem to disorient the mind and put up roadblocks to God's holy presence. However, the Lord is always the Good Shepherd who delights in blessing his beloved. He is the patient Guide. Fr. Aumann cautions us as follows:

During the practice of the prayer of simplicity, the soul should strive to preserve the loving attention that is fixed on God, but without forcing itself. It must avoid distractions and slothfulness, but if it exerts too much effort it will destroy the simplicity of the prayer. Psychologically it is difficult for us to remain attentive over a long period of time, and therefore we should not expect, especially in the beginning, to be able to practice the prayer of simplicity for long periods of time. As soon as the loving attention begins to waver, we should turn to the use of affective prayer or simple meditation. All must be done gently and without violence. Nor should the soul be upset if periods of dryness occur. The prayer of simplicity is not always a sweet and consoling type of prayer; it is also a transition from ascetical to mystical prayer, and therefore the soul may experience the aridity that normally accompanies transitional states.[136]

The Fervent

The second degree of piety belonging to the illuminative way is made up of "the fervent;" that is, those who practice the virtue in a way far superior to those who are simply pious.

The pious, as we have seen, not content with avoiding mortal sin and working toward their own salvation have a sincere will to apply themselves to the service of God in the practice of virtue. And alongside their excellent dispositions there is a lamentable void: they do not grasp sufficiently the need for mortification as preached by our Lord and, as such, they do not work to attain it. As a result, they remain bogged down by numerous defects.

The most marked difference between the pious and fervent is this understanding of Christian abnegation and mortification - the truly Christian penitential spirit and the will to achieve it. The fervent are firmly convinced that God did not put them in

---

[136] Spiritual Theology, p. 328.

the world for anything else except to be sanctified, and thus rendering unto God the greatest glory possible: *Gloria Dei est vivens homo* ("the glory of God is man truly alive").[137] The fervent use their every effort to achieve the supreme objective amid intense acts of love for God and the practice of abnegation according to Gospel norms (*cf.* Mt 16:24). Missing in them are the defects found in the inhabitants of the previous mansions: vanity, fullness of self, attachment to one's own judgment, the predominance of human prudence over divine prudence, pusillanimity, hypersensitivity, worries about self, attachment to spiritual conversations, concerns about what others think of them, desire for comfort – all of which one finds mixed in with true faith among other Christians.

It is true that the fervent have not yet arrived at perfection, but their faults are passing, stemming from simple human fragility and all the while sincerely deplored by them. They do not spring from habitually disordered dispositions or permanent character flaws; they do not excuse themselves or fight halfheartedly against them as can be witnessed among the pious. The fervent person knows himself very well and sets about to overcome whatever is un-Christ-like in himself.

These truly Christian and fervent people are capable of frequent and intense acts of love for God, far superior to those practiced by people who are simply pious. Since their faith is more alive, their minds more illumined, they more easily recognize the beauty of God's holiness, and content themselves with that alone. Further, since their abnegation is far more complete it costs them very little to overcome temptations to mortal sin, while the rejection of venial sins and even

---

[137] St. Irenaeus, *Adversus haereses*, IV, 20, 5-7.

imperfections comes with ease. Their desire to see God glorified in his creatures - the love of benevolence – is much more alive. As a result, their supernatural merit before God is far superior to the pious given the motive, extension, and the intensity of their acts of love.

In fact, the hearts of these Christians are lifted up to God habitually; it may be either in their acts of love directed towards him, the object of their love; or, again, in the actual works which they accomplish, the duties they fulfill, which are offered to God and performed with the loving submission to his will; the patience with which they endure trials here below, and the victories which they win whilst striving against temptations. All these are true acts of charity. The love of God is not a mere occurrence, but the very foundation of their lives, for they are animated by a continual desire to refer everything to God. 'Night and day,' Says blessed Henry Suzo, 'they strive with great solicitude to overcome their nature and conquer themselves.'[138]

Naturally, from this fervent love proceed other virtues that are not possessed in equal degree among the simply pious people. In the first place the fervent have a great confidence in God which is born of the sweet tenderness with which they love him, above all when they surrender themselves to him in prayer – something which is increasingly contemplative or mystical. They enjoy infused recollection of quiet, which St. Teresa beautifully describes in the fourth mansion of her *Interior Castle*:

So this gentle movement in this interior dilation causes the soul to be less constrained in matters relating to the service of God that was before and gives it much more freedom. It is not

---

[138] Degrees of the Spiritual Life, Vol 1, 4, 1., n. 305.

oppressed, for example, by the fear of hell, for, though it desires more than ever not to offend God (of whom, however, it has lost all servile fear), it has firm confidence that it is destined to have fruition of him.[139]

This absolute confidence in God serves as a platform for many other virtues. Such a fervent person believes himself capable of accomplishing very difficult tasks out of love for God and, indeed, the Lord asks it of them. St. Teresa, who was writing primarily for Carmelite nuns, that is, consecrated persons called to the practice of all sorts of austerities, points out the ardor in the soul brought about through penance. While in the preceding mansions the spirit was timorous and somewhat pusillanimous and did not dare mortify itself out of concern for health or a false sense of discretion, it has graduated to an attitude more in line with the Gospel:

A person who used to be afraid of doing penance lest he should ruin his health now believes that in God he can do everything and has more desire to do such things than he had previously. The fear of trials that he was want to have is now largely assuaged, because he has a more lively faith, and realizes that, if he endures these trials for God's sake, his Majesty will give them grace to bear them patiently, and sometimes even to desire them, because he also cherishes a great desire to do something for God.

The better he gets to know the greatness of God, the better he comes to realize the misery of his own condition; having now tasted of the consolations of God, he sees that earthly things are mere refuse; so, little by little, he withdraws from them and in this way becomes more and more his own master.

---

[139] Fourth Mansion, 3, 9.

In short, he finds himself strengthened in all the virtues and commits offenses against God – when that happens, everything is lost, however far a man may have climbed towards the crest of the mountain.[140]

The acts of faith, the submission to the will of God, its detachment, fraternal charity, etc. are generally much more rapidly forthcoming than in the pious. There is no longer an internal discourse or prolonged consideration about whether one will accept the trials and pains that the fulfillment of duty demands. One glance is enough, illumined by contemplative light, the person sees and understands what he must do. The human will has been generously placed in the will of God. It has weaned itself off the desire of natural affection and seeking of one's own gain that hamper the simply pious person and rob it of its liberty. With rectitude of conscience and purity of heart he can appreciate God's will and fulfills it.

Those who most promptly conceive these particularly praiseworthy desires are also those who are most favored with sensible graces. They tend towards a very sweet and intensely affective prayer and they wander into the first stages of contemplation, in which God bestows upon them many lights. God, who wants to bring them to perfection, helps them understand his project and the blessings resulting from it.

The impressions of grace are stronger and more copious in the people who live a recollected and penitential life. Nonetheless, even amongst them, this effect is not brought about by the first mystical experience. About this St. Teresa says:

---

[140] Ibid.

It must not be understood, however, that all these things take place because once or twice God has granted a soul this favor; it must continue receiving them, for it is from their continuance that all our good proceeds.[141]

Little by little they enter the light. This light will shine on the person's sinfulness and open his eyes to their horror. He will feel himself pierced by pain for having offended such a good God.

If, however, under the impression of this sentiment, the person shows himself to be evermore faithful to recollection and mortification these impressions of grace will multiply even amongst its daily tasks, inspiring it to such a living and ardent love for God that it will joyfully surrender itself to penance and the desire of total abnegation.

Sometimes our Lord achieves this and by granting the person the ability to contemplate the suffering and death of the holy Passion. If one is capable of contemplating this mystery with love and sorrow; if one knows how to distance himself from daily distractions and worries that might diminish this impression; if he seeks to identify himself and be configured with Jesus Christ crucified, offering love for love, sacrifice for sacrifice, soon he will feel himself embraced by the love of Jesus Christ crucified and its one longing will be to be immolated with him.

This latter way is the shortest and most effective; it is the quickest road to contemplation and fervor. Many reach the same results by way of other considerations; for the greatest number of cases not one consideration only, but the combined

141 *Ibid.*

result of all the lights received in prayer and moments of recollection, will enlighten them, little by little, upon the necessity of dying to themselves, and will inspire them with a sincere desire of living henceforth for God alone. Those who pray less will obviously receive less help from this whole exercise.[142]

To sum up, let us look at what constitutes "the fervent".

Mortal sin: Never. Maximum, an unforeseen and violent surprise on a very rare occasion. Even in these cases, whether it is mortal or not is doubtful, but it is always followed by profound repentance, immediate confession, and reparation.

Venial sin: There is a serious vigilance to avoid it. Rarely is it deliberate. This person submits himself to a serious particular exam in order to overcome it.

Imperfections: This person does not examine himself overly much to not oblige himself to combat it sufficiently. He loves abnegation in the renunciation of himself but only to a certain point and without great effort.

Practices of piety: Mass and daily Communion with fervent preparation and profound thanksgiving. Frequent and carefully prepared confession. Straightforward and deep spiritual direction focused on advancing in virtue. Tender devotion to Mary.

Prayer: Fidelity to it amid dryness and trials proper to the night of the senses. Enjoys the prayer of simplicity and casts loving gaze as the transition to contemplative prayer. In moments of particular intensity, this person may be graced with infused recollection and quiet.

After a period of purification that takes place in the first dark

---

[142] Degrees of the Spiritual Life, Vol 1, 4, 2, nn. 320-321.

night of the senses, there comes a time of relative peace and consolation.

There breaks into this person's life a new freedom in which he begins to experience a transformation. There is a closer intimacy with God and deeper awareness of resting in his love.

In this person's relationship with other people he becomes less judgmental and more compassionate, more realistic (through humble self-knowledge) about his own strengths and weaknesses. More respectful of God, less angry, more trusting, more accepting of other people's differences, not trying to control other people, willingness to carry the cross that comes his way. Life becomes simpler; all that matters is to try to live day by day for the love of God and neighbor.

Persons will not count the cost of taking care of those in physical or spiritual need. They will attempt very difficult acts of charity. The test will be the fruit of remaining in God's presence.

Teresian Doctrine of Prayer for People in this Stage

Infused Contemplation: As the intensity of God's presence, grace within the soul continues to increase through the first four grades of prayer, one may be granted the grace to advance to this first grade of mystical prayer, i.e., infused recollection or contemplation. From here on, God would become increasingly active while the person becomes ever more passive in prayer. Here, we are not implying anything that smacks of quietism, but rather a divine initiative. One cannot jump into this grade by one's own effort. This prayer is totally beyond human control. The recipient of such a grace can, at most, cooperate with God. As soon as this movement of the Holy Spirit is experienced that is the moment to instantly abandon all vocal

212

prayer, meditation, affective prayer and prayer of simplicity.

God gives to the soul a deep intellectual, experimental taste of His presence which cannot be depicted clearly and distinctively. Fr. Aumann lists twelve characteristics of Infused Contemplation for us as follows:[143]

It is an unmistakable experience of God's presence, experimentally and intellectually.

This is also an invasion of the soul by the supernatural as God inundates the soul with supernatural life.

The experience will not last a second longer than is desired by the Holy Spirit who causes it with the operation of His gifts.

The soul cannot contemplate whenever it wants, but only when God desires and in the measure and degree he so wishes.

The experimental knowledge of God enjoyed is not clear and distinct but obscure and baffled.

During this mystical prayer it is impossible for the soul to doubt about God's very presence and activity within, although the soul may doubt about it afterwards.

The soul also enjoys a certain moral certitude of being in the state of grace. Yet this certitude is far superior to that possessed by ordinary Christians in the ascetical state.

This mystical experience is indescribable as such, beyond the expression of human languages.

Although this mystical union with God may last for a long time, sometimes it is so brief as if it is nothing more than a divine touch. It also admits of variations and fluctuations in

---

[143] Spiritual Theology, cf. pp. 331-336.

intensity.

When mystical contemplation is very intense, the body may react visibly. The eyes become clouded and dull, the organism is weak and intermittent, with an occasional deep breathing as if trying to absorb the necessary quantity of air; the limbs are partly paralyzed; the heat of the body decreases, especially in the extremities.

This prayer may be so intense that it results in an ecstatic trance. Because of the absorption in God, it is often difficult and even impossible for a mystic to give attention to any other prayers or activities during this prayer.

A surest sign of true contemplation is that the soul often leaves this prayer with a great impulse toward a virtuous life. Sometimes the soul may be given a degree of progress in a certain virtue which has been impossible to attain despite great efforts. However, this prayer does not instantaneously bring us to perfection.

Father Aumann further counsels us:[144]

We should not cease discursive meditation until we clearly perceive the call to a higher grade of prayer. As St. Teresa warned us, when the soul is not sure, it should not try to remain passive and inactive. Such self-direction or pride would produce only empty aridity and restlessness which goes nowhere.

We should immediately terminate all discursive prayer as soon as we feel the impulse of grace toward infused contemplation. "Since this is God's activity, it would be most

---

[144] Cf. Ibid. 336-337.

imprudent for a spiritual director to command a particular soul to discontinue mystical prayer in order to return to ordinary prayer."[145]

People so graced should give themselves completely to the interior life and the practice of virtues. They should also break with all attachments that keep them in unholy or ungodly bondage. The so-called fervent, belonging to the last period of the illuminative stage enter into the prayer of quiet.

Prayer of Quiet: The prayer of quiet is a type of mystical prayer in which the intimate awareness of God's presence captivates the will and fills the soul and body with ineffable sweetness and delight. The fundamental difference between the prayer of quiet and that of infused recollection, apart from the greater intensity of contemplative light and more intense consolations, is that the prayer of quiet gives the soul an actual possession and joyful fruition of the sovereign Good.[146]

Infused contemplation principally affects the intellect, which is withdrawn from the other faculties, but the prayer of quiet especially affects the will. Although the intellect and the memory are now tranquil, they still remain free to realize what is occurring, but the will is completely captivated and absorbed in God. For that reason, the prayer of quiet, as its name indicates, tends to contemplative silence and repose. Since the other faculties remain free, however, they can be occupied with the work of the active life, and they may do so with great intensity. The will does not lose its sweet quietude, but the activities of Martha and Mary begin to merge in a beautiful

---

[145] *Ibid.* p .332.
[146] *Spiritual Theology,* p. 337.

manner, as St. Teresa points out. Yet the perfect blending of the active and contemplative life will not be achieved until the soul has reached the state of union with God.[147]

St. Teresa describes the prayer of quiet in the following way: 'From this recollection there sometimes proceeds an interior quiet and peace that are full of happiness because the soul is in such a state that it does not seem to lack anything, and even speaking [e.g., vocal prayer and meditation] wearies it; it wishes to do nothing but love. This state may last for some time and even for long periods of time.' The sanctifying effects produced in the soul by the prayer of quiet are enumerated by St. Teresa in the Fourth Mansions of her *Interior Castle*: (1) great liberty of spirit; (2) filial fear of God and great care not to offend him; (3) profound confidence of God; (4) love of mortification and suffering; (5) deep humility; (6) disdain for worldly pleasures; and (7) growth in all the virtues.[148]

Firmly grounded in St. Teresa, Fr. Aumann underlines the following norms of conduct for us:[149]

The general rule of conduct in any of the states of contemplative prayer is to cooperate with the working of grace and cultivate an increasingly profound humility. For the prayer of quiet in particular, the following rules should be carefully followed:
Never attempt to force oneself into this grade of prayer.
Cooperate with the divine movement as soon as it is experienced.

---

[147] *Ibid,* pp. 337-338.
[148] *Ibid.* p. 338.
[149] *Ibid.* p. 339.

Do not disturb the quiet of the will by attending to the activities of the lower faculties. (The memory and the imagination, since they are still free for their operations, could easily become a distraction in the prayer of quiet. St. Teresa advises this person not to pay any attention to these operations, but to ignore them until such time as God will bind them and captivate them.)

Scrupulously avoid any occasion of offending God.

Never abandon the practice of prayer in spite of any difficulty or obstacle.

Moreover, the experience does not last for a long time, although the person may return to this experience. Above all, we should not take this phenomenon as a sign that we are far advanced in the spiritual life, but should humble ourselves before God and never seek to practice prayer purely for obtaining consolations from God.

Challenges during this phase

Summing up St. Ignatius of Loyola's rules for those in the illuminative way we find the following points regarding spiritual consolations, and desires and projects for the future.

Rules concerning consolations[150]:The distinctive work of the good spirit and well-disposed person is true spiritual joy and peace. The evil spirit, on the contrary, labors to destroy this joy by means of sophistries, subtleties, and delusions. This rule is based on the fact that God is the author of peace, while the devil casts trouble upon the soul in order to discourage it.

---

[150] See *The Spiritual Life, Treatise on Ascetical and Mystical Theology*, Adolphe Tanquerey, Society of St. John the Evangelist, Desclee & Co, Tournai, Belgium. 1930. Nos. 1281-1288.

God alone can infuse true consolation without any antecedent natural cause, for he alone can penetrate into the inmost recesses of the soul and draw it to himself. We say that such consolation has no antecedent cause when nothing has intervened capable of producing it. For instance, a person is plunged into desolation, and suddenly, in an instant, he finds himself reassured, full of joy, strength and of goodwill. This was the case with St. Francis de Sales after violent scruples that assailed him.

When consolation has been preceded by some cause, it may come either from the good or the evil spirit. It proceeds from the former, if the said consolation enlightens and strengthens the soul to know and to do good. It proceeds from the latter, if it causes laxity, softness, love of pleasure or of honors, and presumption. In other words, the tree is judged by its fruits.

It is the part of the devil to transform himself into an angel of light to enter at the outset into the pious desires the person has, and end by suggesting his own designs. That is when he sees someone given to the practice of virtue, he first suggests sentiments in harmony with that person's good disposition; after that, relying on the person's self-love, he suggests sentiments of vain complacency or of presumption, excessive penances, so as to drive it to discouragement, or, on the contrary, less strictness of life, under pretexts of health or study. In this way he succeeds in making the person lower his standards little by little.

Rules concerning desires or projects for the future: We must submit such inspirations to a strict examination, considering it in their inception, in the course of their formation, and in the final unfolding, they tend towards good; for if any of these stages there should be anything of evil, anything to distract us from God, anything less good than what we had previously proposed; or again, if these desires disturb, trouble and weaken the soul, this is a proof that they proceed from the enemy of our spiritual progress and salvation. For an action to be good, there must not be in it anything contrary to the will of God or the spiritual welfare of the person. Hence, if any of these elements are present, there is the mark of the evil spirit.

Once the intervention of the evil spirit is discovered, the best course is to review the entire line of thought from the beginning and find out the way in which he entered to disturb the soul. This study will enable us to be on our guard against his maneuvers in the future.

There is another rule deduced from the difference in the mode of action of the two spirits. The good spirit comes with sweetness upon the person advancing in the way of perfection, like the morning dew penetrating the sponge; the evil spirit rushes in violently, noisily, like a heavy rain beating on a rock.

Even when consolations come from God, we must know how to distinguish between the moment itself of consolation and the time that follows. In the former, we act under the inspiration of grace; in the latter we form resolutions and projects which are not directly inspired by God, and which must therefore be scrutinized according to the preceding rules.

Further rules: To aspire to perfection inconsistent with our present duties, to practice showy virtues, to become singular, all this bears the mark of the bad spirit; for the good spirit inclines us indeed to the attainment of high perfection, but true perfection is compatible with the duties of our state and in keeping with a humble, hidden life.

Contempt for little things and the desire to be sanctified in a grandiose manner are not characteristic of the good Spirit, which urges us to perfect fidelity toward duties of state into every day virtues.

To reflect complacently upon self, to think one has done well, to desire to be held in esteem on account of one's piety and virtue, is also in opposition to the Christian spirit, whose first concern is to please God alone: *If I were still trying to please people, I would not be a slave of Christ* (Gal 1:10). Hence, false humility, which blames self that self maybe praised, and false meekness, which is in reality but the desire to please men, are contrary to the spirit of God.

To complain, to lose patience, to lose heart amid trials and aridity of soul is a sign of human spirit; the Spirit of God leads us, on the contrary, to the love of the Cross, to resignation, to a holy abandonment, and causes us to persevere in prayer amidst dryness and distraction.

Having left the purgative way behind, the person embarks upon wholly new terrain, incomparable to what he has experienced thus far.[151] This new phase is marked by a predominance of the spirit, is also called the way of the proficients, and includes illuminative prayer, a type of infused contemplation.[152]

Normally this phase lasts a long time – many years, in fact,[153] during which the person is prepared for the arduous and transforming dark night of the spirit, passing through the narrow lanes of divine love.[154]

The devil, who in his great malice is envious of all the good he sees in the soul, knowing of her prosperity, now employs all

---

[151] D 1, chpt. 10, 2.
[152] D 1, chpt. 14, 1.
[153] D 2, chpt. 1, 1.
[154] C 22, 3.

his ability and engages all his crafts to disturb this good, even if only a slight part of it. It is worth more to him to hinder a small fraction of this soul's rich and glorious delight than to make many others fall into numerous serious sins, for these others have little or nothing to lose; but this person has very much to lose because of all her precious gain. The loss of a little pure gold is much worse than the loss of many other base metals.[155]

What occurs during this phase is similar to what St. John of the Cross describes previous to spiritual marriage, which occurs during the unitive phase. As a result, it behooves us to accurately distinguish the influence of the evil spirit in his accidental aspect during this phase, such as the secondary mystical phenomena in contrast to those direct assaults against its epicenter and nucleus, which is contemplation.

Secondary Phenomena: These are made up of those supernatural communications which often, though not necessarily, accompany the early stages of the mystical life: *i.e.,* visions, locutions, the revelation of hidden mysteries, spiritual sentiments, etc.[156]

Many proficients enjoy a tide of visions, in the senses as well as in the spirit: nonetheless, these more often than not take place in the imagination than in the exterior senses.[157]

We shall now begin to treat of those other four apprehensions of the understanding, which are purely spiritual -- namely, visions, revelations, locutions and spiritual feelings. These we call purely spiritual, for they do not (as do those that are corporeal and imaginary) communicate themselves to the

---

[155] C 16, 2.
[156] A 2, chpt. 11,1.; A 2, chpt. 17, 4.
[157] D 2, chpt. 2, 3; A 2, chpt. 16, 3.

understanding by way of the corporeal senses; but, without the intervention of any inward or outward corporeal sense, they present themselves to the understanding, clearly and distinctly, by supernatural means, passively -- that is to say, without the performance of any act or operation on the part of the soul itself, at the least actively.

Speaking broadly and in general terms, all these four apprehensions may be called visions of the soul; for we term the understanding of the soul also its sight. And since all these apprehensions are intelligible to the understanding, they are described, in a spiritual sense, as 'visible.' And thus, the kinds of intelligence that are formed in the understanding may be called intellectual visions.[158] Throughout all of this Satan does not remain idle.

They receive an abundance of spiritual communications and apprehensions in the sensory and spiritual parts of their souls and frequently behold imaginative and spiritual visions. All of this as well as other delightful feelings are the lot of those who are in this state, and a person is often tricked through them by auto-suggestion as well as by the devil.

The devil entertains himself by such deceits, impressing upon people every sort of apprehension and feeling. Consequently, these proficients are easily charmed and beguiled if they are not careful to renounce such apprehensions and feelings and energetically defend themselves through faith.

This is the stage in which the devil induces many into believing vain visions and false prophecies. He strives to make them presume that God and the saints speak with them, and frequently they believe their fantasy. It is here that the devil

---

[158] A 2, ch[t. 23, 2.

customarily fills them with presumption and pride. Drawn by vanity and arrogance, they allow themselves to be seen in exterior acts of apparent holiness, such as raptures and other exhibitions. They become audacious with God and lose holy fear, which is the key to and guardian of all the virtues. Illusions and deceptions so multiply in some, and they become so inveterate in them, that it is very doubtful whether they will return to the pure road of virtue and authentic spirituality. They fall into these miseries by being too secure in their surrender to these apprehensions and spiritual feelings and do this just when they were beginning to make progress along the way.[159]

Given what St. John of the Cross says above, we understand why so few people pass from the illuminative stage to the unitive. The devil does not limit his influence to visions and corporeal apprehensions, but also employs spiritual communications to exercise his influence.[160]

If he perceives that God or a good angel is blessing the person with communications, he will attempt to spoil this interior feast. His tactic is to meet spiritual experience with spiritual experience,[161] enjoying a relative success as a result and sometimes finding his advances completely rebuffed.

In fact, so says the Mystical Doctor, the spiritually advanced person often vanquishes the foe in such a way that he causes the devil such distress that he flees in confusion – especially, if the proficient makes contemplation his hiding place, thus advancing spiritually and winning for himself still more grace which God is happy to grant him.

---

[159] D 2, chpt. 2, 3.
[160] D 2, chpt. 23, 8.
[161] Ibid.

Not only does the devil imitate this kind of corporeal vision, but he also simulates and interferes with spiritual communications coming from a good angel, since he can discern them, as we said; and as Job says, *omne sublime videt* - "he sees all sublime things" (Job 34:21), imitates and interferes with them. Yet he cannot imitate and form these spiritual communications as he can those granted under some appearance or figure, for these are without form and figure, and it is of the nature of the spirit to be formless and figureless. He represents his frightful spirit to the soul to attack it in the same way in which it receives the spiritual communication, and to assail and destroy the spiritual with the spiritual. In this case, when the good angel communicates spiritual contemplation, the soul cannot enter the hiding place of this contemplation quickly enough to go unnoticed by the devil. He then presents himself to it with some spiritual horror and disturbance, at times very painful. Sometimes the soul can withdraw speedily without giving this horror of the evil spirit an opportunity to make an impression on it, and it recollects itself by the efficacious favor the good angel then gives it.[162]

Inconstancy of vigilance opens a breach for the enemy:

At other times the devil prevails, and brings about disturbance and horror in the interior. This terror is a greater suffering than any other torment in life. Since this horrendous communication proceeds from spirit to spirit manifestly and somewhat incorporeally, it surpasses all sensory pain. This spiritual suffering does not last long, for if it did the soul would depart from the body on account of this

---

[162] Ibid.

violent communication. Afterward the soul can recall this diabolic communication; doing so is enough to cause great suffering.[163]

Contemplation: An essential element of the mystical life is the divine invasion - an inflowing and influence of grace that transforms the soul.[164] In its first purgative phase the presence of God is purgative and painful, working toward the passive night of the spirit. Continued growth on the way to union, the soul undergoes illumination of the intellect[165] and a loving inflammation of the spirit,[166] making the soul catch fire bringing it to become fire itself, just as a cold, damp log submitted to flame over time becomes one with the fire. This is the transformation our Lord seeks for us: to be divinized.[167]

The spiritual person in this phase no longer exercises his imagination and discursive meditation in prayer. Rather, he progresses along the ways of divine love with broader steps, greater satisfaction, and increased generosity,[168] nourished and renewed by the Lord without exerting nearly as much personal effort as before.[169]

Witnessing this progress, the Evil One experiences tremendous envy and pain.[170] Recognizing the signs of spiritual peace, prosperity, interior recollection with which the Holy Spirit delicately blesses this person, the devil flies into a rage of

---

[163] C 20-21, 9
[164] D 1, chpt. 1, 12.
[165] D 2, chpt. 5, 1.
[166] D 2, chpt. 11, 1.
[167] D 2, chpt. 10, 1.
[168] D 2, chpt. 1, 1.
[169] D 1, chpt. 14, 1.
[170] C 20-21,9.

disgust.[171] Witnessing the fruits of the blessings – the devil is blind to the economy of grace, therefore, he can only see its effects – he is reminded of those things he has freely refused. The good things of God he has rejected he wants to hinder in those who cooperate with grace. The spiritual growth of the proficient is a torture for the devil.[172] About this Thomas tells us:

> Now the envious man repines over the good possessed by another, inasmuch as he deems his neighbor's good to be a hindrance to his own. But another's good could not be deemed a hindrance to the good coveted by the wicked angel, except inasmuch as he coveted a singular excellence, which would cease to be singular because of the excellence of some other. So, after the sin of pride, there followed the evil of envy in the sinning angel, whereby he grieved over man's good, and also over the Divine excellence, according as against the devil's will God makes use of man for the Divine glory.[173]

Demons are so twisted, says St. John of the Cross, that "There is no devil who is not willing to suffer something for his own sense of honor."[174] From what we have seen thus far, it is clear that the devil has an exaggerated sense of himself. People who take themselves too seriously are rarely happy. The devil is never happy. And all the demonic assaults we have thus far considered have been peripheral circumventions, so to say,

---

[171] C 3, 63.
[172] C 16, 2.
[173] *S. Th.* I, q. 63, a. 2, c.
[174] *Censure and Opinion.*

inasmuch as they were indirectly and therefore, more or less successfully, aimed at the stronghold of contemplation. Contemplation constitutes the last bulwark of the spiritual edifice, which will determine the demon's twisted honor or confusion in spiritual combat.

Considering what St. John of the Cross has to say about how the devil attempts to hinder contemplation we find it laid out succinctly in *The Dark Night of the Soul* (book 2, chapter 23), *Spiritual Canticle* (chapters 16 and 18), and *The Living Flame of Love* (chapter 3). Reading these texts next to each other we discover a beautiful complementarity in which the spiritual doctrine of one text illumines the content of the others.

From the contents of these chapters we will limit ourselves to consider the following notions: objective, tactics, attacks of the devil.

Objectives: The proximate objective of the devil consists of defending the wall of contemplation so that the soul may not enter,[175] because within lies the hiding place of recollection where the soul is alone with its divine Spouse.[176] The devil knows that once the soul enters this place he will find it nearly impossible to harm it.[177] Satan commands his demons to do everything possible to block the passage to contemplation [178] and impede advances.[179]

Tactics: The devil attacks the sensed part of the soul to impede secret spiritual communications. He knows well that the encounter of these two lovers, the soul and its Spouse – the only

---

[175] C 10, 3.
[176] C 40, 4.
[177] C 16, 6.
[178] C 3, 63.
[179] D 2, chpt. 15, 1.

begotten Word of God – requires solitude and detachment from everything.[180] As a result, all of the senses and their interior and exterior powers must come to rest, be emptied, and in a state of quiet.[181] In order to impede the soul's entrance into the fortress of contemplation, the devil will attempt to disquiet and disturb the person[182] in the different faculties. In this way the devil's attacks are peripheral – not attacking contemplation itself, but those things it requires for success.

In other words, since the devil cannot reach the depths of one's soul,[183] he settles for more superficial attacks on the senses where he can have more success: creating diversions and sowing confusion in hopes of disturbing contemplation and its contingent graces:

It is quite true that even though the devil is ignorant of the nature of these very interior and secret spiritual communications, he frequently perceives that one is receiving them because of the great quietude and silence some of them cause in the sensory part. And since he is aware that he cannot impede them in the depths of the soul, he does everything possible to excite and disturb the sensory part, which he can affect with sufferings, horrors, and fears. He intends by this agitation to disquiet the superior and spiritual part of the soul in its reception and enjoyment of that good.

Yet when the communication of such contemplation shines in the spirit alone and produces strength in it, the devil's diligence in disturbing the soul is often of no avail. It receives instead new benefits and a deeper, more secure peace. For what a wonderful

---

[180] C 14-15, 2.
[181] C 16, 10.
[182] D 1, chpt. 4, 3.
[183] C 20-21,9

thing it is! In experiencing the troublesome presence of the enemy, the soul enters more deeply into its inner depths without knowing how and without any efforts of its own, and it is sharply aware of being placed in a certain refuge where it is more hidden and withdrawn from the enemy. There the peace and joy that the devil planned to undo increase. All that fear remains outside; and the soul exults in a very clear consciousness of secure joy, in the quiet peace and delight of the hidden Spouse that neither the world nor the devil can either give or take away. The soul experiences the truth of the bride's exclamation in the Song of Songs: Behold, sixty men surround the bed of Solomon, etc., because of the fears of the night [Song 3:7-8]. She is aware of this strength and peace even though she frequently feels that her flesh and bones outside are being tormented.[184]

Attacks: These are many and take varied forms, albeit they are identical inasmuch as they always attack the sensitive part of the intellect.

The practical results of these depends less on the expertise of the aggressor or degree of violence with which he attacks the proficient, but rather on the degree of foresight of the person under attack and the degree of contemplation achieved.

A first type of spiritual communication is that which is inexplicable without part of the senses. In other words, this is contemplation that is not wholly pure, but still dependent upon the senses and still wrapped up in those activities in the lower parts of the soul:

At other times, when the spiritual communication is not bestowed exclusively on the spirit but on the senses too, the

---

[184] D 2, chpt. 23, 4.

devil more easily disturbs and agitates the spirit with these horrors by means of the senses. The torment and pain he then causes is immense, and sometimes it is ineffable. For since it proceeds nakedly from spirit to spirit, the horror the evil spirit causes within the good spirit (in that of the soul), if he reaches the spiritual part, is unbearable. The bride of the Song of Songs also speaks of this disturbance in telling of her desire to descend to interior recollection and enjoy these goods: I went down into the garden of nuts to see the apples of the valleys and if the vineyard was in flower; I knew not; my soul was troubled by the chariots (by the carts and roaring) of Aminadab (the devil) (Song 6:11-12).[185]

Juxtaposed to the success the devil has on beginners, his assaults on the senses of the proficient are usually negligible. The proficient have, in most cases, sufficiently mortified their senses to such an extent that whatever demons attempt, it usually comes to nothing or very little.

The devil at this point takes advantage of the sensory appetites, although most of the time he can do very little or nothing, since these appetites are already deadened in persons who have reached this state. When he is unable to stir these appetites, he produces a great variety of images in the imagination. He is sometimes the cause of many movements of the sensory part of the soul and of many other disturbances, spiritual as well as sensory. It is not in a person's power to be free of these until the Lord sends his angel, as is said in the psalm, round about them that fear him and delivers them [Ps. 34:7], and until he brings peace and tranquility in both the sensory and spiritual parts of the soul.[186]

---

[185] D 2, chpt. 23, 5.

In the face of such a route, the devil does not give up, but changes his approach, attacking the fantasy and the imagination, thus causing many distractions.[187] The least attachment to the created provides an entry for the Evil One.

When the soul is in the loftiest solitudes, receiving the infusion of the delicate unction of the Holy Spirit insofar as it is alone, despoiled, and withdrawn from every creature and trace of a creature, the devil, with great sadness and envy, seeing that the soul is not only enriched but flying along at such a pace that he cannot catch it in anything, strives to intrude in this withdrawal with some clouds of knowledge and sensible satisfaction. This knowledge and satisfaction he gives is sometimes good, so he may feed the soul more and make it revert to particular things and the work of the senses, and make it turn thus to this good knowledge and satisfaction, embrace it, and slow the journey to God by leaning upon it.

With this new-found dependence, he distracts the soul very easily and draws it out of that solitude and recollection in which, as we said, the Holy Spirit is bringing about those secret marvels. Since humans of themselves are inclined toward feeling and tasting, especially if they are seeking something and do not understand the road they are traveling, they easily grow attached to the knowledge and satisfaction provided by the devil and lose the solitude God was providing. Since the soul was doing nothing in that solitude and quiet of the faculties, it thinks that this way is better because it is now doing something.

It is a great pity that, in not understanding itself and for the sake of eating a morsel of particular knowledge and satisfaction,

---

186 C 16, 2.
187 C 20-21,9.

the soul impedes God from feeding on it entirely, which God does in that solitude where he places it, since he absorbs it in himself by means of those solitary spiritual anointings.[188]

Awakening these thoughts, the devil manages to dissipate the contemplative soul and succeeds in undoing the effects of divine communications.[189] As the weakness of the one in the purgative way resides in the lower senses, the proficient's Achilles' heal is in activity – especially in the area of thoughts. If the devil can manage to distract the proficient from his solitary recollection, he scores a great victory.

Those who remain steadfast in their recollection are described as follows:

> Yet when the communication of such contemplation shines in the spirit alone and produces strength in it, the devil's diligence in disturbing the soul is often of no avail. It receives instead new benefits and a deeper, more secure peace. For what a wonderful thing it is! In experiencing the troublesome presence of the enemy, the soul enters more deeply into its inner depths without knowing how and without any efforts of its own, and it is sharply aware of being placed in a certain refuge where it is more hidden and withdrawn from the enemy. There the peace and joy that the devil planned to undo increase. All that fear remains outside; and the soul exults in a very clear consciousness of secure joy, in the quiet peace and delight of the hidden Spouse that neither the world nor the devil can either give or take away. The soul experiences the truth of the bride's exclamation in the Song of

---

[188] *Living Flame of Love*, 3, 63 (henceforth cited as L).
[189] L 3, 64.

Songs: Behold, sixty men surround the bed of Solomon, etc., because of the fears of the night (Song 3:7-8). She is aware of this strength and peace even though she frequently feels that her flesh and bones outside are being tormented.[190]

On the other hand, if the devil finds the proficient on guard and not exercising the intellect too much or focused on one thing in particular, his attack becomes even more crass:

> At other times, when the spiritual communication is not bestowed exclusively on the spirit but on the senses too, the devil more easily disturbs and agitates the spirit with these horrors by means of the senses. The torment and pain he then causes is immense, and sometimes it is ineffable. For since it proceeds nakedly from spirit to spirit, the horror the evil spirit causes within the good spirit (in that of the soul), if he reaches the spiritual part, is unbearable.[191]

If that produces no desired effect, sometimes God grants the devil still more license:

> If permission is given them they can do this very easily, for since the soul at this time enters into great nakedness of spirit for the sake of this spiritual exercise, the devil can easily show himself to her, because he is also spirit.[192]

Other attacks are: "on the rational intellect with "spiritual

---

[190] D, 2 chpt. 23, 4.
[191] Loc. Cit. 5.
[192] Ibid.

horrors,"[193] with fear and disturbances,"[194] "spiritual threats,"[195] or "disturbing him in times of devotion."[196]

St. John of the Cross describes these horrors as "intolerable"; the fear is "tremendous;" the torments and pain are "intense;" and says that these things cannot compare with other crosses life has to offer.[197]

The proficient will not be free of these sensitive and spiritual afflictions until the Lord – according to Sacred Scripture[198] - send his angels to those that fear him, thus instilling peace and tranquility in the senses and the spirit.[199]

A second form of spiritual communication is that which is granted to the higher regions of the soul. This contemplation is infused without images, forms, or figures and is expressed without interference of or the imperfections pertaining to the lower parts of the soul. John describes this communication as "confused, dark, and general,"[200] yet at the same time "loving, peaceful, and calm."[201]

When this loving communication is granted with purity and strength, the devil will celebrate no victory in his attempts to disturb the soul absorbed in God.[202] Nonetheless, he does not cease his attacks: the only thing left for him to do is attack the proficient exteriorly: physical assaults, strange noises, and other

---

[193] Ibid.
[194] C 25, 2.
[195] C 25-21,9.
[196] C 25, 2.
[197] D 2, chpt. 23, 9.
[198] Ps 34:7
[199] C 16, 2.
[200] A 2, chpt. 9, 2.
[201] Ibid. chpt. 12, 2.
[202] D 2, chpt. 25, 4.

frightening things.[203]

All these things Satan does when he sees that the soul is preparing to enter the garden enclosed where the divine Spouse awaits. At all costs he wants to hinder the divine communications that await the contemplative person.[204] St. John of the Cross, for sure speaking autobiographically, says that as soon as the soul perceives the approach of the demon, almost instinctively and without giving it any thought, it takes refuge in the hiding place of contemplation where it is safe and experiences profound joy.[205]

St. John paints a pathetic image of the devil screaming and pounding on the gate without, furious at the divine communications that are most certainly taking place. Sometimes he remains there for great lengths of time. Finally, upon seeing that he lost that fight, he leaves the soul in complete peace.[206]

This person, sure in his contemplation, remains at peace with his Spouse. Whatever fears there may have been, they are outside and far away their effect now brings about a new-found joy which St. John describes as "indescribable."[207]

His peace is more constant and the spiritual benefit greater.[208] This new-found situation is something akin to a person in a warm castle, safe and secure, watching a storm outside. The tests are now on the surface: attacks on the body, for sure, but the soul is serene.[209]

---

[203] L 3, 64.
[204] C 16, 6.
[205] Ibid.
[206] L 3, 64.
[207] C 16, 6.
[208] D 2, chpt. 23, 4.
[209] Ibid.

When these favors are bestowed in concealment (only in the spirit, as we said), a person is usually aware, without knowing how, that the superior and spiritual part of the soul is withdrawn and alienated from the lower and sensory part. This withdrawal makes one conscious of two parts so distinct that one seemingly has no relation to the other and is far removed from it. And, indeed, this is in a way true, for in the activity that is then entirely spiritual there is no communication with the sensory part.

A person in this way becomes wholly spiritual, and in these hiding places of unitive contemplation, and by their means, the passions and spiritual appetites are to a great degree eliminated. Referring thus to the superior part of the soul, he says in this last verse: my house being now all stilled.[210]

St. Ignatius' Rules for Discernment (proper to the Second Week, i.e., the illuminative stage)

First Rule: It is proper to God and to His Angels in their movements to give true spiritual gladness and joy, taking away all sadness and disturbance which the enemy brings on. Of this latter it is proper to fight against the spiritual gladness and consolation, bringing apparent reasons, subtleties and continual fallacies.

Second Rule: It belongs to God our Lord to give consolation to the soul without preceding cause, for it is the property of the Creator to enter, go out and cause movements in the soul, bringing it all into love of His Divine Majesty. I say without cause: without any previous sense or knowledge of any object through which such consolation would come, through one's acts

---

[210] D 2, chpt. 23, 14.

of understanding and will.

Third Rule: With cause, as well the good Angel as the bad can console the soul, for contrary ends: the good Angel for the profit of the soul, that it may grow and rise from good to better, and the evil Angel, for the contrary, and later on to draw it to his damnable intention and wickedness.

Fourth Rule: It is proper to the evil Angel, who forms himself under the appearance of an angel of light, to enter with the devout soul and go out with himself: that is to say, to bring good and holy thoughts, conformable to such just soul, and then little by little he aims at coming out drawing the soul to his covert deceits and perverse intentions.

Fifth Rule: We ought to note well the course of the thoughts, and if the beginning, middle and end is all good, inclined to all good, it is a sign of the good Angel; but if in the course of the thoughts which he brings it ends in something bad, of a distracting tendency, or less good than what the soul had previously proposed to do, or if it weakens it or disquiets or disturbs the soul, taking away its peace, tranquility and quiet, which it had before, it is a clear sign that it proceeds from the evil spirit, enemy of our profit and eternal salvation.

Sixth Rule: When the enemy of human nature has been perceived and known by his serpent's tail and the bad end to which he leads on, it helps the person who was tempted by him, to look immediately at the course of the good thoughts which he brought him at their beginning, and how little by little he aimed at making him descend from the spiritual sweetness and joy in which he was, so far as to bring him to his depraved intention; in order that with this experience, known and noted, the person may be able to guard for the future against his usual deceits.

Seventh Rule: In those who go on from good to better, the good Angel touches such soul sweetly, lightly and gently, like a drop of water which enters a sponge; and the evil touches it sharply and with noise and disquiet, as when the drop of water falls on the stone.

And the above-said spirits touch in a contrary way those who go on from bad to worse. The reason of this is that the disposition of the soul is contrary or like to the said Angels. Because, when it is contrary, they enter perceptibly with clatter and noise; and when it is like, they enter with silence as into their own home, through the open door.

Eighth Rule: When the consolation is without cause, although there be no deceit in it, as being of God our Lord alone, as was said; still the spiritual person to whom God gives such consolation, ought, with much vigilance and attention, to look at and distinguish the time itself of such actual consolation from the following, in which the soul remains warm and favored with the favor and remnants of the consolation past; for often in this second time, through one's own course of habits and the consequences of the concepts and judgments, or through the good spirit or through the bad, he forms various resolutions and opinions which are not given immediately by God our Lord, and therefore they have need to be very well examined before entire credit is given them, or they are put into effect.

-4-

The Unitive Way

This vocation to perfect love is not restricted to a small group of individuals. The invitation, "go, sell your possessions and give the money to the poor", and the promise "you will have treasure in heaven", are meant for everyone, because they bring out the full meaning of the commandment of love for neighbour, just as the invitation which follows, "Come, follow me", is the new, specific form of the commandment of love of God. Both the commandments and Jesus' invitation to the rich young man stand at the service of a single and indivisible charity, which spontaneously tends towards that perfection whose measure is God alone: "You, therefore, must be perfect, as your heavenly Father is perfect" (Mt 5:48).[211]

When recollection constitutes a habitual state and when the soul breathes the air of permanent prayer amid its daily occupations and duties proper to one's state in life – all of which are fulfilled with exacting fidelity; when intimate union with God in the arrival at the heights of Christian perfection

---

[211] Veritatis Splendor, 18.

constitute one's supreme and singular illusion for life, the person has entered into the unitive way.

St. Thomas speaks of it in these terms:

The spiritual increase of charity may be considered in respect of a certain likeness to the growth of the human body. For although this latter growth may be divided into many parts, yet it has certain fixed divisions according to those particular actions or pursuits to which man is brought by this same growth.

First we speak of a man being an infant until he has the use of reason, after which we distinguish another state of man wherein he begins to speak and uses reason, while there is again a third state, that of puberty when he begins to acquire the power of generation, and so on until he arrives at perfection.

In like manner the diverse degrees of charity are distinguished according to the pursuits to which man is brought by the increasing charity. For the first it is incumbent on man to occupy himself chiefly with avoiding sin and resisting his concupiscences, which move him in opposition to charity: this concerns beginners, in whom charity has to be fed or fostered lest it be destroyed: in the second place man's chief pursuit is to aim at progress in good, and this is the pursuit of the proficient, whose chief aim is to strengthen their charity by adding to it: while man's third pursuit is to aim chiefly at union with and enjoyment of God: this belongs to the perfect who *desire to be dissolved and to be with Christ.*

In like manner we observe in local motion that at first there is withdrawal from one term, then approach to the other term, and thirdly, rest in this term.[212]

Within this stage of the spiritual life we find three fundamental degrees: the Nearly Perfect, Heroic Sanctity and the Greatest of Saints.

The Nearly Perfect

It is a worthy endeavor to arrive to the degree of holiness of the fervent who are progressing to the 5th Mansion – that of the union. Nonetheless, there are still many weaknesses to overcome. It may be that for many years in this stage there is found a mixture of fervent sentiments, an attitude of prompt and generous abnegation, a multitude of crosses and trials to bear. These people also have their sights set on perfection – even with a tendency to perfect abnegation and self-emptying, but without fully achieving this. How does such a person arrive at the state of complete nudity and spiritual dispossession of everything that is not God? This is what we will examine now: *This perfect and the ritual conformity of the human will with the divine will – this constitutes relative perfection,* the first degree of the unitive way.

To aptly discern whether one has truly broken with all his attachments for created goods and has arrived at perfection is not always easy, for something similar is found amongst the fervent in whom such attachments are notably weakened and not readily apparent. It is easy to be mistaken in this material, above all when the sensible graces that are infused in the soul

---

[212] *S Th* II-II, 24,9.

impede the rebellion of passions and preserve the person from all sorts of spiritual dangers and occasions of sin.

One of the hallmarks of having achieved this first degree of the unitive way is to find oneself habitually in a state of contemplative prayer. Prior to this degree the person has journeyed in a sort of intermediate state, favored by the gift of contemplation and, nonetheless, finding it necessary to have recourse to the methods of meditation that are proper to the inferior states (discursive meditation, affective prayer, etc.). But when contemplation comes with great facility and it is almost habitual the person has arrived to a degree of supernatural life that can be called relative perfection. We consider now what St. John of the Cross, the Mystical Doctor says about this:

> For it must be known that the end of reasoning and meditation on the things of God is the gaining of some knowledge and love of God, and each time that the soul gains this through meditation, it is an act; and just as many acts, of whatever kind, end by forming a habit in the soul, just so, many of these acts bring knowledge which the soul has been making one after another from time to time come through repetition to be so continuous in that they become habitual.

This end of God is wont also to effect in many souls without the intervention of these acts (or at least without many such acts having preceded it), by setting them at once in contemplation. And gradually through its labour of meditation upon particular facts has now through practice, as we have been saying, become converted and changed into a habit and substance of loving knowledge, of a general kind, and not distinct or particular as before.

Wherefore when it gives itself to prayer, the soul is now like one to whom water has been brought, so that he drinks peacefully, without labour, and is no longer forced to draw the water through aqueducts of past meditations and forms and figures. So that as soon as the soul comes before God, it makes an act of knowledge, confused, loving, passive, and tranquil, wherein it drinks of wisdom and love and delight.[213]

Moreover, it often happens that this contemplative union which fills the soul with sweetness and love perseveres amidst many different occupations without the soul having to force itself to sustain this contemplation.

Teresian Doctrine: Prayer of Union (The Fifth Mansion)

The prayer of union is that grade of mystical prayer in which all the internal faculties are gradually captivated and occupied with God. In the prayer of quiet only the will was captivated; in the sleep of faculties the intellect was also captivated, although the memory and the imagination remained free. In the prayer of union all the interior faculties, including the memory and the imagination, are captivated. Only the external bodily senses are now free.[214] Indeed,

the intensity of the mystical experience caused by the prayer of union is indescribable. It is superior beyond compare to that of the preceding grade, to the point that the body itself is affected by the working of God in the soul. Without being entirely captivated, the external senses become almost helpless and inoperative. The person experiences divine

---

[213] A, 2, 14, 2.
[214] Spiritual Theology, p. 340.

reality with such intensity that it could easily fall into ecstasy. At the beginning, this sublime absorption of the faculties in God lasts but a short time (a half hour at most), but as the intensity increases, it may be prolonged for several hours.[215]

Accordingly, the essential characteristics of the prayer of union and the signs by which it can be recognized and distinguished from previous grades of prayer are: *absence of distractions* which are psychologically impossible; *certitude of being intimately united with God* in which the person cannot doubt that it experiences God during this prayer; *absence of weariness and tedium* in which the person in absorbed in God and never wearies of its union with the Beloved, however long it may last.

Moreover, the people enjoying such an intimate union with God seem to look at the world very differently. In the words of Fr. Aumann,

St. Teresa lists the principal effects of the prayer of union in the Fifth Mansions of her *Interior Castle*. The soul is so anxious to praise God that it would gladly die a thousand deaths for his sake. It has an intense longing to suffer great trials, and experience vehement desires for penance and solitude. It wishes that all souls would know God, and it is greatly saddened when it sees God is offended.

The soul is dissatisfied with everything that it sees on earth, since God has given it wings so that it can fly to him. And whatever it does for God seems very little by comparison

---

[215] Ibid. pp. 340-341.

with what it desires to do. Its weakness has been turned into strength, and it is no longer bound by any ties of relationship or friendship or worldly possessions.

The soul is grieved at having to be concerned with the things of earth, lest these things should cause it to sin against God. Everything wearies it because it can find no true rest in any created thing.[216]

Nonetheless, the phenomenon of mystical union is far from being confirmed, above all in its initial stages in which, as saint John of the Cross warns us, "Here it must be made clear that this general knowledge whereof we are speaking is at times so subtle and delicate, particularly when it is most pure and simple and perfect, most spiritual and most interior, that, although the soul be occupied therein, it can neither realize it nor perceive it."[217] Only when contemplation supersedes the so-called quietude, thus becoming true union is it possible that the soul is allowed to perceive this phenomenon, Since the joy of this sweetness is so intense the soul, so says St. Teresa of Avila,

(One) cannot possibly doubt that God has been in it and it has been in God; so firmly does this truth remain with in it that, although for years God may never grant that favor again, it can neither forget it nor doubt that it has received it (and this quite apart from the effects would remain within it).[218]

---

[216] *Ibid.* p. 342.
[217] *Ibid.*, n. 8.
[218] Fifth Mansion, c. 1, n.9.

Aside from this hallmark another great sign that the soul has arrived to the degree of relative perfection – this is habitual contemplative prayer – is recognizable in certain habitual dispositions which we will discuss presently.

Lights granted by God to souls in union: Up to this point it has been apparent that the lights of grace increase in the soul in the measure to which it progresses: the pious receive more and more pronounced lights than the simply good souls. The fervent receive more than those who are merely pious.

This illumination is resplendent among those who have attained union, that is, those who are relatively perfect. The gifts of the Holy Spirit are at work in them in an almost habitual way and with greater energy. Having at their disposition lights and the gifts of understanding and wisdom, they are nursed by the memory of the greatness and the benefits of God.

Much more than the imperfect, the perfect truly understand what it means to be loved. Thanks to the increase of the gift of knowledge they understand more clearly the relative and, therefore, passing value of created goods, the emptiness and vanity of transitory things.

Take for example, the Carthusian motto, *Stat Crux dum volvitur orbis* (the Cross is steady as the world turns). These very same words are heard by sinners, the imperfect, the fervent, and those in union; yet each one understands these words differently. Sinners who are passionate about passing joys will not understand very much of these words; the imperfect, who are sensitive to all sorts of privations, disappointments, human judgment, fear of being offended or not appreciated, will understand these words to a lesser degree than those who are united to God. Thanks to the gift of knowledge, people in union will understand much better the meaning of these words because they describe their habitual attitude.

Intense love for God: Those who have arrived at this state of relative perfection have but one sole desire: to be united with God, to possess God, to enjoy God. They do not see death as loss but as a necessary door opening them up to the eternal joy of God. As St. Teresa of Avila famously said, "I die because I do not die." They look forward to death as an intense act of love for God. In fact, the most frequent object of their thought and longing is the love of God which is the foundation of their mystical contemplation. For the most part, in its impetus of love, the contemplative forgets himself and has a mind and heart for God alone. Sometimes the only words they can say are, "My God," and more often they prefer to say nothing, rejoicing in God's perfections and experiencing a loving desire for God and satisfaction in only that which pertains to him. These acts of pure love – springing from the gift of wisdom in full force – are free and meritorious and are increased much more than discursive acts of reason or meditative prayer.

Thus, for example, a contemplative, upon embracing a crucifix would immediately make more meritorious and intense acts of love for God than a pious person would in a prolonged prayer. Further, this soul arrives at contemplation with such frequency that even amidst its daily occupations it can prolong an intimate sense of the presence of God without ever being disturbed.

This sentiment brings with it profound movements in its heart. Even when it does not feel this impression in times of dryness, a latent tendency towards God remains in the perfect. The most insignificant occasion – for example glancing at an image of Jesus or a simple thought about him – is enough to provoke secret but ardent sentiments of love for Christ.

The sincerity of these affections is proven and made manifest in the conduct of radical detachment from one's self and the sense of perfect abnegation. Amongst the imperfect affective sentiments are frequent, simple desires more than acts of true will. They indicate the tendencies of a heart that would like to love God more than anything else, but they are still not yet fully resolved to sacrifice everything for him. The loving sentiments of the perfect, presupposes total abnegation and is, therefore, truer and more meritorious.

As a result, it is logical that the space of just one day in the life of the perfect is so filled with meritorious acts that it illustrates what St. Francis de Sales famously said: "Just one ardent soul gives more glory to God than a thousand mediocre Christians." St. John of the Cross agrees: "For a little of this pure love is more precious to God and the soul and more beneficial to the Church, even though it seems one is doing nothing, than all these other works put together."[219]

Love for solitude: One who has arrived at this degree of perfection would rather spend all his time alone with God, enjoying his sweetness. Even in times of dryness, when the faculties experience emptiness and aridity, the soul is constantly attracted to God.

This person counts himself blessed when deprived of human company so that it can be alone with its divine Beloved. Even amid liturgical services, the contemplative spends no effort in recollecting itself, finding itself in the Heart of God. In fact, the previous methods, formerly so helpful when used in meditation, are experienced as cumbersome and obtuse: "It sets no store by the things it did when it was a worm – that is, by its

---

[219] C, 29, 2.

248

gradual weaving of the cocoon. It has wings now: how can it be content to crawl along slowly when is able to fly?"[220]

Spirit of detachment: Those who have arrived at this degree of perfection manifest perfect detachment. The person in union has God as his only treasure. Natural desires to possess, worries and concerns that previously caused suffering for the fervent mean nothing now. Things which would be of great concern and worry for many people – for no one, regardless of his degree of holiness, is exempt from them – merely ruffle the heart of the perfect, without going any deeper. What truly concerns a person in this stage are God's interests:

> But it must not be supposed that perfect souls are less distracted by natural inclinations and preoccupations because they are no longer a subject of temptations to them. When St. Paul made such lamentation with regard to the buffets of Satan he was in a much higher state of perfection than the souls of which we now speak. If there are many temptations that no longer avail these perfect souls, others still persist. Devils, even more malignant and powerful than those that assail the common run of Christians, at times succeed in arousing their slumbering passions. Our Lord who permits these conflicts to his faithful servants for the ultimate glory, knowing them to be capable of resisting and overcoming allows these accursed angels fuller liberty... Perfect souls are more indifferent regarding the things of the world, and their only weapons with which to combat wrong desires are acts of love.

A perfect soul does not ignore the distinction between good

---

[220] *Fifth Mansions*, 2, 8.

and evil, pleasure and pain. If God sends temporal blessings, health, talent, or wealth, it offers him gratitude, and these good gifts of God become for it occasions for rendering him a more perfect service. If at times it desires them, it is in order to use them for the Master's glory, and its entire reliance upon providence causes this desire, when it occurs, to be always moderate and quiet."[221]

Desires of heaven, love's longings: "The very discontent," so says St. Teresa, "caused by the things of the world arouses a desire to leave it, so grievous that any alleviation it finds can only be in the thought that it's life in this exile is God's will."[222] On the one hand, one feels no great satisfactions in this world: diversions, passing joys have lost their enchantment and make the person feel himself to be a stranger and sojourner in this world. On the other hand, this person must endure much suffering; attracted to the love of God alone, he recognizes with all the more pain his own weakness; as a result, he feels the temptations that make it feel distant from God to such a point that he considers himself hateful in God's sight: *Miserable one that I am! Who will deliver me from this mortal body?* (Rom 7:24).

The yearning for heaven which these souls experience is thereby accentuated. In heaven alone can they love God freely; there nothing will hinder the full flow of their love. Their thirst will be quenched. Their every aspiration satisfied. They can praise him, exalt him, unite themselves to him, and rejoice in him to their heart's content. So says St. Thomas, 'While man's third pursuit is to aim chiefly at union with and enjoyment of

---

[221] *Degrees of the Spiritual Life,* vol. 2, bk. 5, part 2, ch. 3, nn. 108-109.
[222] Fifth Mansions, 2.

250

God: this belongs to the perfect who *desire to be dissolved and be with Christ.*[223]

Zeal and love for the cross: From this pure love is born, naturally, ardent zeal. This person "has the most vehement desires for penance, for solitude, and for all to know God. And hence, when it sees God being offended, it becomes greatly distressed."[224] It experiences profound desires to glorify God and obtain the salvation and sanctification of others even at the cost of great sacrifice, completely forgetting his own interests.

Realizing that in accordance with the example of Jesus Christ he cannot promote the glory of God without suffering, the perfect soul feels a sincere desire to bear heavy crosses for his sake... Further, all that it manages to accomplish for God seems nothing in comparison with what it desires to do. This is what keeps it humble and enables it to face without difficulty the trials which God will permit to the proving of its love.[225]

Hunger for Communion: Thirsting for God, longing more than the deer longs for streams of living water (*cf.* Ps 41:2), the perfect experience a burning hunger for Holy Communion. If they were to miss communion it would be the cause of great suffering, finding conformity to the divine will their only solace. Yet if they are deprived of Holy Communion over a prolonged period of time, they experience the deepest of sorrow and pain that is a grace and a work of the Holy Spirit.

Peace of soul: In all their endeavors, in the works – always inspired by their ardent zeal - there is no longer found the disquiet that previously moved them to act, something proper

---

[223] Saudreau, op. cit. nn. 110 and 112.
[224] Ibid.
[225] *Degrees of the Spiritual Life,* Vol. 2, bk. 5, part 2, ch. 3, n. 114.

to the less perfect. Nor are they disheartened or discouraged by humiliations and defeats, since God's grace is their true treasure and human means become of little regard.

Perfect purity of intention: Blessed with tranquil fortitude, freed of frenetic agitations of the imagination or sensitivity, and adhering to the will of God, the perfect tend to live with great rectitude and purity of intention.

God, the infinitely simple Being, communicates to these faithful people something of his own sublime simplicity. All the operations that God works in the soul for that sanctification may be reduced to one – its conformity with divine simplicity. The love of God present in the soul, now more perfect and more simple, becomes the sole motivation behind its actions: "I no longer tend the herd, nor have I any other work now that my every act is love."[226]

Great is their merit; this familiarity with God, this inward peace, this profound tranquility, this liberty of spirit, this vigor in action, this wisdom in all their works, are blessings greatly to be desired.

The sixth mansion,' says St. Teresa, 'only differs from the fifth in the magnitude of its results; but this difference is a very great one'…. But however immeasurably short of the lives of the saints the lives of the perfect souls my fall, they are nonetheless extremely beautiful.[227]

We should avoid the error of thinking that there is little difference between the perfect and those who have ascended to the heights of holiness. The dispositions of these latter are much more perfect by degree.

---

[226] C, 28.

[227] *Degrees of the Spiritual Life,* vol. 2, bk. 5, part 2, ch 6. N.134.

Heroic sanctity

The second degree within the unitive way (and sixth starting from base sinners) is made up of those deemed heroic, that is, those who habitually practice all the Christian virtues to a heroic degree. When proof of this habitual heroism can be demonstrated the Church has sufficient motive to officially recognize the process of beatification and subsequent canonization.

We class in the sixth degree souls who practice virtue after heroic fashion. Before virtue can be called heroic it is necessary, says Benedict XIV (*de canonizatione sanctorum* 1) that the matter should be arduous, and that the practice of virtue in those special circumstances should argue an energy above the ordinary power of humanity; that the acts of virtue should be accomplished promptly and unhesitatingly; that they should be performed joyfully and enthusiastically; and this not on one occasion alone, but habitually and whatever the location offers.[228]

This quickness and enthusiasm in the performance of arduous undertakings are properly attributed by the learned Pontiff to the influence of the gifts of the Holy Spirit. Thus, he attributes heroic faith to the gift of understanding, heroic hope to the gift of fear of the Lord, heroic charity to the gift of wisdom, heroic prudence to the gift of counsel, etc.

We who yet do not partake so abundantly of the gifts of the Holy Spirit must labor and toil in the practice of virtue. We are like those who make way by dint of rolling against wind and tides; a day will come, if it please God, when, having received the gifts of the Holy Spirit, we shall speed full sail before the

---

[228] *Ibid.*, ch. 1, n. 173.

wind; for it is the Holy Spirit who by his gifts disposes of the soul to yield itself easily to his divine inspiration. With the assistance of the gifts of the Holy Spirit, saints reach such a height of perfection, as to accomplish without labor things of which we should not venture so much as to think; the Holy Spirit's moving away all their difficulties and enabling them to surmount every obstacle.[229]

Heroic virtues are practiced in a virtual way by the people who have arrived at the sixth mansions of St. Teresa of Avila.

Teresian Doctrine: The Prayer of Conforming Union (The Sixth Mansion)

It would be impossible to summarize here St. Theresa's inspired doctrine in which she masterfully describes (in 11 long chapters) the sixth mansion.

There she describes in her own inimitable way the so-called ecstatic union, in which the soul, deeply wounded by divine love, goes so far as to lose the use of it senses upon experiencing the most intense delights which supersede all its physical capabilities. Ecstasy, in as much as an exterior and visible phenomenon, seems to be something of a fainting spell, the sort of failing of all the physical senses, incapable of resisting the immense weight of glory which the soul experiences, bathed in the most intense divine delights of heaven.

In this sixth mansion the saint describes the different lights and divine communications that the soul receives. She speaks of a mystical nuptial and the great and terrible tests that precede and follow it – all part of the most frightening night of the spirit.

Through this process of the dark night of the spirit, the soul is

---

[229] Louis Lallemant, *Spiritual Doctrine,* principle IV, ch. 3, art. 2, section 5.

stripped naked, renewed, and transformed. These steps form the last preparations in order to enter into the seventh and last of the mansions where divinization of the soul occurs, and it is in which the soul is joined in matrimonial union with God through love.

Amongst the favors the soul receives in the sixth mansions St. Teresa describes the: "mysterious substantial touches" – impossible to imagine by those who have never experienced them, wounds of love, immense impulses which drive the soul outside of itself; raptures and flights of spirit joined to visions and locutions, all accompanied by profound consolation.

The tests that the person must endure take the form of persecutions by good people, made much more painful than if they were done by evil people; even spiritual directors and confessors become agents of these trials leaving the person in mortal anguish and deprivation.

To this is added a sense of the absence of God, which makes one feel completely abandoned regardless of how much it longs to be united with God and desires to be faithful. This person is made to undergo unbearable weights of divine justice to such an extent that it feels condemned, rejected by God, bringing about a mortal torture (seemingly endless) regardless of the degree of faith and ardent love for God present in the soul.

The fruits of these divine communications and these terrible trials are admirable and desirable. What follows is a selection of texts regarding this state.

It is conscious of having been most delectably wounded but cannot say how or by whom; but it is certain that this is a precious experience and it would be glad if it were never to be healed of that wound.

The soul complains to its spouse with words of love, and

even cries aloud, being unable to help itself, for it realizes that he is present but will not manifest himself in such a way as to allow it to enjoy him, and this is a great grief, though a sweet and delectable one; even if it should desire not to suffer it, it would have no choice – but in any case it never would so desire. It is much more satisfying to a soul than is the delectable absorption, devoid of distress, which occurs in the prayer of quiet.[230]

But, although relief comes, the ecstasy has the effect of leaving the will so completely absorbed and the understanding so completely transported – for as long as a day, or perhaps for several days – that the soul seems incapable of grasping anything that does not awaken the will to love; to this it is fully awake, while asleep as regards all that concerns attachment to any creature.[231]

Oh, what confusion the soul feels when it comes to itself again and what ardent desire it must be with God in any and every way in which he may be pleased to employ it! It has tremendous desires to do penance; and whatever penance it does it counts as very little, for its love is so strong that it feels everything it does to be a very small account and realizes clearly that it was not such a great matter for the martyrs to suffer all their tortures, for with the aid of our Lord such a thing becomes easy. And thus, the souls may complain to our Lord when he offers them no means of suffering."[232]

Having won such great favors, the soul is so anxious to have complete fruition of their Giver that its life becomes sheer,

---

[230] Second Mansion, *n.1.*
[231] *Fourth Mansion4, n.* 14.
[232] *Ibid,* 4, n. 15.

though delectable, torture. It has the keenest longings for death, and so infrequently and tearfully begs God to take it out of this exile. Everything in this life that it sees wearies it; when it finds itself alone it experiences great relief, but immediately this distress returns hardly knows itself when it is without it.[233]

It is fitting to read these texts of the great saint of Avila as she describes the marvels that God works in souls who arrive to the sixth mansion. These divine treasures are, as such, open to all generous people who are decided to not deny God anything. In other words, all of us can arrive to these heights if we were so disposed. St. Teresa affirms just this:

Forgive me, sisters; and believe me, now that I have come to these great things of God, I cannot help feeling the pity of it when I see how much we are losing, and all through our own fault. For, true though it is that these are things which the Lord gives to whom he will, he would give them to us all if we loved him as he loves us. For he desires nothing else but to have those to whom he may give them, and his riches are not diminished by his readiness to give.[234]

While St. Teresa calls this degree of prayerful union with God *the spiritual betrothal or espousal*; others call it the prayer of ecstatic union, taking the name from the primary external phenomenon of this grade. However, Father Aumann prefers to use *conforming union* and *transforming union* for the last two degrees of mystical prayer. Accordingly,

in the prayer of simple union all the interior faculties of the soul are centered on God alone; only the external senses are

---

[233] *Sixth Mansion*, n. 1.
[234] *Ibid*, n. 12.

still free. But in the prayer of conforming union God captivates even the external senses, with the result that the soul is totally divinized, so to speak, and prepared by God to move to the full and final commitment of the transforming union.[235]

Fr. Aumann continues,

In the prayer of conforming union, therefore, the soul loses the use of its external senses, either partially or totally, because all the interior faculties are absorbed in God and the senses are alienated from their proper natural functioning.

It is with difficulty that the soul turns its attention to external activity, though it knows that sometimes it must 'leave God for God' in performing its duties or services of charity for others. But the predominant sentiment of these souls is the longing for full and perfect union with God, accompanied by a longing for death. The soul now echoes the yearning of St. Paul to be dissolved and to be with Christ (Phi. 1:23) and the statement of St. Teresa as a child: 'I want to see God, but to see God we must die.'[236]

In the ecstatic experience of the conforming union, the soul not only has contact with God in the very center of its soul, but also it seems to peer into the very essence of God and discover divine secrets... The soul experiences that it is in God and God in the soul, and the concentration is so complete that all the

---

[235] *Spiritual Theology,* p. 344.
[236] *Ibid.* p. 345.

faculties are absorbed in this union.

Mystical ecstasy is therefore a concomitant or normal phenomenon of the prayer of conforming union. Unlike prophetic ecstasy, mystical ecstasy is both sanctifying and meritorious. The essential element in this prayer, however, is the absorption of the soul in God; the ecstasy is a secondary but concomitant element. Both elements are necessary for the true mystical ecstasy. Without the union with God in infused contemplative prayer, the ecstasy would be a natural ecstasy or trance, a falsification of mystical ecstasy caused by an evil spirit, or the *gratia gratis data* of prophetic ecstasy.[237]

We are also told that the principal forms of ecstasy that occur here can be gentle and delightful, as well as violent and painful (*cf. ibid.* p.347). Except perhaps for their apparent difference between delight and pain, even St. Teresa found it difficult to distinguish clearly the essential difference between them, as we read: "I should like, with the help of God, to be able to describe the difference between union and rapture, or elevation, or what they call flight of the spirit, or transport --- it is all one. I mean that these different names all refer to the same thing, which is also called ecstasy. It is much more beneficial than union: the effects it produces are far more important, and it has a great many more operations, for union gives the impression of being just the same at the beginning, in the middle, and at the end, and it happens interiorly. But the ends of these raptures are both interior and exterior."[238]

Great saints

---

[237] *Ibid.* p. 346.
[238] *Ibid.* p. 347.

Within the limits of this small work we shall now embark upon the immeasurable heights to which, with divine assistance, the greatest of saints ascend.

It is not an exaggeration to say that, for as far from our own spiritual misery these great saints have journeyed, few things are more provocative and stimulating and encouraging for us than the consideration of the infinite riches which we too may encounter even in this life.

To attain to these heights, we must decide to surrender ourselves totally to God with all of those consequences and the progressive influence of grace – resulting in its fullest expansion and development under the action and direction of the Holy Spirit, by the means of his gifts and charismatic graces.

How could one renounce such an infinite treasure – infinitely above all the treasures of this world – and yet it is within our grasp, if only we would surrender ourselves completely to the action of grace exercising the most careful and delicate fidelity to the inspirations of its demands? St. John of the Cross says that upon the heights of these mountains is found only the honor and glory of God. What occurs on those sublime heights only the saints know. As such, we will allow the saints to describe what they found there on the heights.

Teresian Doctrine: Prayer of Transforming Union (The Seventh Mansion)

The last grade of prayer is the transforming union, identified by many mystics as the spiritual marriage. It constitutes the seventh mansions of *The Interior Castle* of St. Teresa and is the highest degree of perfection that one can attain in this life. It is, therefore, a prelude to the beatific life of glory... In this grade of prayer there is a total transformation of the soul into the

Beloved.

The soul has entered its very center, so to speak, which is the throne room of the interior castle where the Trinity dwells through grace. There God and the soul give themselves to each other in the consummation of divine love, so far as is possible in the present life. There is no more ecstasy, for the soul has now been strengthened to receive the full power of love, but in the brightness of an intellectual vision the soul experiences the Trinity with vivid awareness"[239] Fr. Aumann continues:

> We can distinguish three elements in this loftiest degree of the prayer of union: transformation in God, mutual surrender, and the permanent union of love... Concomitant with the permanent union of love is the soul's *confirmation in grace*. St. John of the Cross maintains that the transformation union never falters and the soul is confirmed in grace, but St. Teresa warns that as long as we are in this world we must walk with caution, lest we offend God.

> However, the apparent contradiction is readily resolved when we say that confirmation in grace does not mean intrinsic impeccability, for the Church teaches that it is an impossibility in this life. Nor is it a question of avoiding all venial sins in this life, for that would require a special privilege of grace as was bestowed on the Virgin Mary. Consequently, confirmation in grace must be understood as the special grace and assistance from God to avoid all mortal sins and thus have moral certitude of salvation.[240]

---

[239] Spiritual Theology, pp. 350-351.
[240] *Ibid.* p. 352.

Finally, Fr. Aumann sums up this ideal of Christian perfection as follows:

Such is the bittersweet path that leads to the heights of contemplative prayer and the transforming union. It is the sublime ideal of Christian perfection, and it is offered to all souls in grace.

When Jesus pronounced the precept: 'You must be made perfect as your heavenly father is perfect' (Matt. 5:48), he was speaking to all souls without exception. The Christian life, if it is developed according to the supernatural powers that are inherent in it, will lead to the transforming union of charity, which is in turn the prelude to the beatific vision."[241]

St. Teresa was about 40 years old when the long and terrible anguish of the night of the spirit came to an end. During that period, she exercised the virtues to a heroic degree and with exquisite fidelity to grace, exercising a firm constancy despite many difficulties. The years that followed served to increase her merits before God.

At the age of 40, St. Teresa experienced the wound in her heart at the hands of an angel who pierced her with a burning arrow, symbolic of her ardent charity. At the age of 45 she made the vow to work for that which was most perfect; that is when she took to the path of the reform of Carmel and succeeded in founding numerous convents of the Reform. At this time she was already an extraordinary saint and, nonetheless, until she

---

[241] *Ibid.* p. 354.

was around 55 years of age, she had not yet been elevated to the supreme grade of the mystical life – the transforming union or, spiritual matrimony – which she masterfully describes in the seventh mansion of her *Interior Castle*.

St. Theresa begins the exposition of the seventh mansion with the following words: "You will think, sisters, that so much has been said about the spiritual road that there cannot possibly be any more to say. It would be a great mistake to think that; 'just as the greatness of God is without limit, not so his works.'[242] In fact, she goes on to say:

> For you who understand that there is the greatest difference between all the other visions we have mentioned in those belonging to this mansion, and there is the same difference between the spiritual betrothal and the spiritual marriage as there is between two betrothed persons and two are united so that they cannot be separated anymore.[243]

This instantaneous communication of God to the soul is so great a secret and so sublime a favor, and such delight is felt by the soul, that I do not know with what to compare it, beyond saying that the Lord is pleased to manifest to the soul at that moment the glory that is in heaven, in a more sublime manner than is possible through any vision or spiritual consolation.

It is impossible to say more than that, as far as one can understand, the soul is made one with God, who, being likewise a spirit, has been pleased to reveal the love that he has for us by showing to certain persons the extent of that love, so that we

---

[242] 1, n.1.
[243] 2, n.2.

may praise his greatness. For he has been pleased to unite himself with his creature in such a way that they have become like two who cannot be separated from one another: even so he will not separate himself from her.[244]

The spiritual betrothal is different: here the two persons are frequently separated, as is the case with union, for, although by union is meant the joining of two things in one, each of the two, as is a matter of common observation, can be separated and remain the things by itself. This favor of the Lord passes quickly and afterwards the soul is the product of the companionship – I mean so far as it can understand. In this other favor of the Lord it is not so: the soul remains all the time in that center with its God.[245]

You might say that union is as if the ends of two wax candles were joined so that the light they give it is one: the wicks and the wax and the light are all one, yet afterwards the one candle can be perfectly well separated from the other and the candles become too again, or the wick may be withdrawn from the wax. But here it is like rain falling from the heavens into a river or a spring; there is nothing but water there and it is impossible to divide or separate the water belonging to the river from that which fell from the heavens. Or it is as if a tiny streamlet enters the sea, from which you will find no way of separating itself, or as if in a room there were two large windows through which the light streams in: it enters in different places, but it all becomes one.

Perhaps when St. Paul says: *He who is joined to God becomes one spirit with him,* (1 Cor 6:17) he is referring to his sovereign

---

244 2, n.4
245 2, n.5.

marriage, which presupposes the entrance of his majesty into the soul by union. And he also says: *For to me to live is Christ, to die is gain* (Phil 1:21). This, I think, the soul may say here, for it is here that the little butterfly to which we have referred to dies, and with the greatest joy, because Christ is now its life.[246]

A little before this passage, St. Teresa explains in what way this transformed soul feels the divine persons permanently inhabiting it. It is brought into this mansion by means of an intellectual vision, in which, by representation of the truth in a particular way, the most Holy Trinity reveals itself, in all three Persons.

First, the spirit becomes enkindled and is illumined, as it were, by a cloud of the greatest brightness. The soul sees these three Persons, individually, and yet by a wonderful kind of knowledge which is given to it, it realizes that most certainly and truly all these three Persons are one substance and one power and one knowledge in one God alone. In this way, that what we hold by faith the soul may be said here to grasp by sight, although nothing is seen by the eyes, either of the body of the soul, for it is no imaginary vision.

Here all three Persons communicate themselves to the soul and speak to the soul and explain to it those words which the Gospel attributes to the Lord – namely, that he and the Father and the Holy Spirit will come to dwell with the soul which loves them and keeps his commandments.

Oh, God help me! What a difference there is between hearing and believing these words and in being led in this way to realize how true they are. Each day this soul wonders more,

---

[246] 2, n.6.

for she feels that they have never left her, and perceives quite clearly, and the way I described, that they are in the interior of her heart – in the most interior place of all and its greatest depths. So although, not being a learned person, she cannot say how this is, she feels within herself this divine companionship.[247]

This sublime transformation in God – which, nonetheless, should not be understood in a pantheistic sense, as a fusion of substances, but rather as a sublime fusion of love and exchange of hearts – produces in the soul some admirable effects of sanctification, that the great saint of Avila describes in the third chapter of the seventh mansions. Although one ought to read the entire chapter, here we will limit ourselves to underline its most salient notions.

First, there is a self-forgetfulness so complete that it really seems as though the soul no longer existed, because it is such that she has neither knowledge nor remembrance that there is either heaven or life or honor for her, so entirely is she employed in seeking the honor of God.

The second effect produced is a great desire to suffer, but this is not of such a kind as to disturb the soul, as it did previously. So extreme is her longing for the will of God to be done in her that whatever his Majesty does she considers to be for the best: if he wills that she should suffer, well and good; if not, she does not wear herself to death as she did before.

When these people are persecuted again, they have a great interior joy, and much more peace than in the state described above. They bear no enmity to those who mistreat them, or desire to do so. Indeed they conceive a special love for them, so

---

[247] 1, nn. 7-8.

that, if they see them in some trouble, they are deeply grieved and would do anything possible to relieve them; they love to commend them to God, and they would rejoice at not being given some of the honors which his Majesty bestows upon them if their enemies might have them instead and thus be prevented from offending our Lord.

You have already seen what trials and afflictions these people have suffered because of their desire to die and thus to enjoy our Lord. They have now an equally strong desire to serve him, and to sing his praise, and to help some soul if they can.

What they desire now is not merely not to die but to live for a great many years and to suffer the severest trials, if by doing so they can become the means whereby the Lord is praised, even in the smallest thing. If they knew for certain that, on leaving the body, they would have fruition of God, their attitude would not be affected, nor is it altered when they think of the glory belonging to the saints, for they do not desire as yet to attain this. Their conception of glory is of being able in some way to help the Crucified, especially when they see how often people offend him and how few there are who really care about his honor and are detached from everything else.

True, they sometimes forgot this, turn with tender longing to the thoughts of enjoying God and desire to escape from this exile, especially when they see how little they are doing to serve him. But then they turn back and look within themselves and remember that they have him with them continually; and they are content with this and offer his majesty their will to live as the costliest oblation they can give him. They are no more afraid of death then they would be of gentle rapture.

These people have a marked detachment from everything and the desire to be always either alone or busy with something that is to some soul's advantage. They have no aridities or interior trials but a remembrance of our Lord and a tender love for him, so that they would like never to be doing anything but giving him praise.

There are hardly any of the periods of aridity or interior disturbance in it like those that, at one time or another, have occurred in all the rest, but the soul is almost always in tranquility. It is not afraid that the sublime favor may be counterfeited by the devil but retains the unwavering certainty that comes from God.

As has been said, the senses and faculties have no part in this: His Majesty has revealed himself to the soul and taking it with him into a place where, as I believe, the devil will not enter, because the Lord will not allow him to do so; and all the favors which the Lord grants the soul here, as I have said, come quite independently of the acts of the soul itself, apart from that of its having committed itself wholly to God.

These are a summary of the dispositions of the greatest of saints, those generous people who have ascended to the heights of mystical union with God atop Mount Carmel. Of it, St. John of the Cross Says, "Here on this mountain only God's honor and glory reside."

St. John of the Cross' Doctrine

In complete conformity with Teresian thought, St. John of the Cross describes the characteristics of this transforming union or, as he calls it, spiritual matrimony, in the following way.

This spiritual marriage is incomparably greater than the spiritual betrothal, for it is a total transformation in the beloved, in which each surrenders the entire possession of self to the other with a certain consummation of the union of love. The soul thereby becomes divine, God through participation, in so far as is possible in this life. And thus, I think that the state never occurs without the soul's being confirmed in grace, for the faith of both is confirmed when God's faith in the soul is here confirmed. It is accordingly the highest state attainable in this life.

Just as in the consummation of carnal marriage they are two in one flesh, as Sacred Scripture points out (*cf.* Gen 2:24), so also when the spiritual marriage between God and the soul is consummated, there are two natures in one spirit and love, as St. Paul says in making the same comparison: *Whoever is joined to the Lord becomes one spirit with him* (1 Cor 6:17).
This union resembles the union of the light of a star or candle with the light of the sun, for what then sheds light is not the star or candle, but the sun, which has absorbed the other lights into its own.[248]

Describing the divine activity of the soul who is arrived at the sublime heights, the mystical doctor writes these awe–inducing words:

By his divine breath-like spiration, the Holy Spirit elevates the soul sublimely and informs her and makes her capable of breathing in God the same spiration of love that the Father breathes in the Son and the Son in the Father.

---

[248] Spiritual Canticle, 22, 3.

There would not be a true and total transformation if the soul were not transformed in the three Persons of the Most Holy Trinity in an open and manifest degree…

One should not think it impossible that the soul be capable of so sublime an activity as this breathing in God through participation as God breathes in her. For, granted that God favors her by union with the Most Blessed Trinity, in which she becomes deiform in God through participation, how could it be incredible that she also understands, knows, and loves – or better that this be done in her – in the Trinity, together with that, as does the Trinity itself!

Yet God accomplishes this in the soul through communication and participation. This is transformation in the three persons in power and wisdom and love, and thus the soul is like God through this transformation. He created her in his image and likeness that she might obtain such resemblance."[249]

To not confuse this sublime transformation with the absurd notion of pantheist fusion – which, in effect, would be a negation of union, since the soul would disappear, being absorbed by the divinity – The Mystical Doctor clarifies:

In thus allowing God to work in it, the soul (having rid itself of every mist and stain of creatures, which consists of having its will perfectly united with that of God, for to love is to labor to detach and strip itself for God's sake of all that is not

---

[249] *Ibid.*, 39, n. 3-4.

God) is that once illumined and transformed in God, and God communicates to it his supernatural Being, in such a way that it appears to be God himself, and has all that God himself has.

This union comes to pass when God grants the soul the supernatural favor, that all the things of God and the soul are one and participant transformation; and the soul seems to be God rather than a soul, and is indeed God by participation; although it is true that its natural being, though thus transformed, is as distinct from the being of God as it was before, even as the window has likewise a nature distinct from that of the ray, though the ray gives it brightness.[250]

According to Saint John of the Cross, all people in grace are called to these unimaginable heights and all would arrive if they were perfectly faithful to the sanctifying action of the Holy Spirit within them and never voluntarily placed obstacles to this divine action. In fact, immediately after describing transforming union He makes this claim:

Oh souls, created for these grandeurs and call to them! What are you doing? How are you spending your time? Your aims are base and your possessions miseries! Oh wretched blindness of your eyes! You are blind to so brilliant a light and deaf to such loud voices because you failed to discern that insofar as you seek eminence and glory to remain miserable, base, ignorant, and unworthy of so many blessings![251]

---

[250] Ascent of Mount Carmel, II, 5, 7.

Challenges during this phase

Contemplatives tending towards this phase ought to keep in mind two extremes to be avoided: Spurring oneself on indiscriminately towards contemplation – thinking it can be gained by much effort; and complacency – believing oneself completely converted when that is not the case.

In order to avoid the first mistake one ought to remember that one does not usually receive the gift of contemplation except after one has for a long time exercised himself in prayer and in the practice of the Christian virtues, purity of heart, detachment from self and from creatures, humility, obedience, conformity to the will of God, spirit of faith, trust, and of love. The "Last of the Fathers", St. Bernard, says:

> If among the monks there are any contemplatives, they are not the novices in virtue, who but erstwhile dead to sin, labor in tears and in the dread of judgment to heal their yet fresh wounds. They are rather those who after a long cooperation with grace have made solid progress in virtue, need no longer consider again and again in their minds the sorrowful picture of their sins, but, on the contrary, find their delight in meditating day and night and in keeping the law of God.[252]

The danger here is that this desire for contemplation is presumptuous. It is helpful to recall that no one may force his way into contemplation, and that moreover the joys of prayer generally come only after bitter trials.

---

[251] Spiritual Canticle, 39, 8.
[252] *In cantica*, Sermo LVII, n. 11.

To avoid the second error – that of complacency - one ought to remember that God, ever prodigious with his gifts, gives himself generously to the docile and, above all, to the humble in the degree and when he pleases.

After the person has passed through the bitterness of mortification and the struggles contingent of meditation,[253] after the Lord has brought this person through the periods of anguish, doubts, fear, diabolical visitation and communications,[254] and having been purified at the root[255] by the dark ray,[256] God may call the soul to divinization in which two natures become one in spirit and love,[257] as has been just described.

Because of this new situation for the soul immersed in God and transformed, its relationship with other creatures is, in turn, transformed:

The reason for this security has been clearly explained. Usually a person never strays except through its appetites, its gratifications, or its discursive meditation, or through its knowledge or affections. By these, people usually fail through excess or defect, or they change because of them or go astray, or experience inordinate inclinations. Once all these operations and movements are impeded, individuals are obviously freed from error in them, because they are not only liberated from themselves but also from their other enemies, the world and the devil. The world and the devil have no other means of warring against the soul when its affections and operations are deadened.[258]

---

[253] C 22, 4.
[254] D 2, chpt. 15, 1.
[255] D 2, cpt. 2, 1.
[256] C 14-15, 16.
[257] C 22, 3.

Until now the soul has been purged, illumined, and has entered spiritual betrothal. Consequently, it was subject to a myriad of attacks, irritations, and vexations – all taking place in the lower regions; yet in a state of spiritual marriage, all of this comes to a halt.[259] Strong in its heroic virtue it no longer engages in spiritual combat, neither against the world, nor the flesh, nor even the devil "who fears to attack her."[260] What interests us now is the person's reaction to all of this.

But before the soul reaches this full flourishing of spiritual matrimony, it must pass through to the last mansion. In other words, even within the unitive phase, there are trials to undergo:

> For Our Lord continues to prove the soul and to raise it ever higher, so that He first gives it things that are very unpretentious and exterior and in the order of sense, in conformity with the smallness of its capacity; to the end that, when it behaves as it should, and receives these first morsels with moderation for its strength and sustenance, he may grant it further and better food.

> If, then, the soul conquer the devil upon the first step, it will pass to the second; and if upon the second likewise, it will pass to the third; and so onward, through all seven mansions, which are the seven steps of love, until the Spouse shall bring it to the cellar of wine of His perfect charity.[261]

---

[258] D 2, chpt. 16, 2.
[259] C 14-15, 30.
[260] C 2, 4-5.
[261] A 2, chpt. 11, 9.

How one reacts to these trials will, as always, determine it progress or halt. Undoubtedly, if it strives faithfully against each of these heads, and gains the victory, it will deserve to pass from one step to another, and from one mansion to another, even unto the last, leaving the beast vanquished after destroying its seven heads, wherewith it made so furious a war upon it.[262]

These demonic attacks along the way to transforming union have the undesired effect, in many cases, of helping the soul along in its purification and sanctification. The devil loses twice: his efforts not only fail to impede progress, they help it along.

Self-Defense: "All we have mentioned here takes place passively without one's doing or undoing anything."[263] In other words, the soul has been provoked, obliged to undergo the horrors and assaults of the Evil One to varying degrees. The person has not sought this.

To think that St. John of the Cross means by "reaction," that a soul, now in a state of transforming union, becomes the aggressor would be to misunderstand him. Engagement in spiritual combat and vanquishing the last of the seven heads has nothing to do with revenge against the devil or self-vindication. Spiritual combat, "reacting", according to sanjuanistic doctrine will always take the form of simple self-defense.

It makes sense to understand what is to be done to best defend oneself in this phase, according to the teaching of the Mystical Doctor. We will consider two dominant themes:

---

[262] Loc. Cit. 10.
[263] D 2, chpt. 23, 10.

behavior and final success because of this behavior.

Behavior: The joy-filled state of transforming union ought not to be understood in terms of a "means" to something yet beyond it. Nonetheless, there are means to be used to protect this state.

The means that the Mystical Doctor offers us include an attitude to be adopted consisting of an absolute trust in our Lord's victory, yet it implies a marked defensiveness. To avoid the ambushes, set by the enemy, the soul must take to the narrow road, when leaving its house following these sanjuanistic indications: it should travel by night,[264] be well camouflaged or "disguised",[265] and be well accompanied.[266]

Certainly, the limits of this small book do not permit me to elaborate on these aspects with the depth they merit. I will have to settle for a glance at these elements, inspired by St. John's teaching.

Travelling by Night: Darkness, rather than a thing in itself, is a privation of light. This is the term our author uses for self-denial, a privation of likes and tastes in everything:

We here describe as night the privation of every kind of pleasure which belongs to the desire; for, even as night is naught but the privation of light, and, consequently, of all objects that can be seen by means of light, whereby the visual faculty remains unoccupied[83] and in darkness, even so likewise the mortification of desire may be called night to the soul. For, when the soul is deprived of the pleasure of its

---

[264] First line of *The Dark Night.*
[265] Loc. Cit. second stanza.
[266] A prologue, 3.

desire in all things, it remains, as it were, unoccupied and in darkness. For even as the visual faculty, by means of light, is nourished and fed by objects which can be seen, and which, when the light is quenched, are not seen, even so, by means of the desire, the soul is nourished and fed by all things wherein it can take pleasure according to its faculties; and, when this also is quenched, or rather, mortified, the soul ceases to feed upon the pleasure of all things, and thus, with respect to its desire, it remains unoccupied and in darkness.[267]

Deprivation of tastes and appetites, renunciation is night: "in the dark and with nothing."[268] Thomas says something similar: "The creature is darkness in comparison with the excellence of the Divine light; and therefore the creature's knowledge in its own nature is called "evening" knowledge.[269]

Active mortification must be exercised to develop true detachment of heart from created things. In this way, we manage to "banish the devil" for a time.[270] The devil has a certain power and ability to attack the soul – not only in itself, but also in the things it uses or those things around it.[271] He will especially pay attention to the affections, desires, and likes where Satan will torment the person, obscure his vision, in hopes of sullying and weakening the soul.[272]

With that in mind, detaching oneself from one's likes and purifying one's affections, the devil is disarmed in that regard.

---

[267] A 1, chpt 3, 1.
[268] Loc. Cit.
[269] S. Th. I, q. 64, a. 1, ad 3.
[270] A 1, chpt. 2, 1.
[271] Ibid. Also, St. Thomas says this in 4 Sent. D. 6, q. 1, a. 4, c.
[272] A 1, chpt. 6, 1.

To travel by night means to mortify oneself and, in that way, the contemplative defends himself from certain wiles and deceits of the Evil One.

Camouflage or disguise: The disguise St. John of Cross suggests is a three-piece habit which covers the soul, hiding it from the intrusive eyes of the enemy. Dressing up the soul in this way reorients it towards the divine Beloved and makes it pleasing to him. It also serves as a protection, allowing the soul to carry out its tasks unhindered.[273]

The soul progressing in grace must continuously face its three enemies: the world, the flesh, and the devil. To go about unseen by these enemies it must put on the three-colored uniform of faith (white), hope (green), and love (red).[274] Dressed in this fashion, the soul finds "total security against the wiles of the devil."[275]

"More than all the other virtues,"[276] it is faith that most directly and efficiently preserves the soul in its contemplative activity, protecting it from insidious attacks. In similar terms, St. Peter counsels faith against the attacks of the devil: *Stand up to him strong in the faith.*[277]

Faith is an inner tunic of such pure whiteness that it blinds the sight of every intellect. When the soul is clothed in faith the devil is ignorant of how to hinder her, neither is he successful in his efforts, for faith gives her strong protection - more than do all the other virtues - against the devil, who is the mightiest and most astute enemy.[278]

---

[273] D 2, chpt. 21, 2.
[274] Loc. Cit. 3.
[275] A 2, chpt. 6, 7.
[276] D 2, chpt. 21, 3.
[277] I Pet. 5:9.

St. John of the Cross calls faith a "dark ray,"[279] and in relation to the devil, the light of faith is darker than dark.[280] And thus the soul that journeys through this night, we may say, journeys in concealment and in hiding from the devil, as will be more clearly seen hereafter. Wherefore the soul says that it went forth 'in darkness and secure'; for one that has such happiness as to be able to journey through the darkness of faith, taking faith for his guide, like to one that is blind, and leaving behind all natural imaginings and spiritual reasonings, journeys very securely.[281]

The simple knowing through faith supersedes all forms, figures, imaginings, and ridding itself of all these natural phantasms and reasoning,[282] thus disarming the devil of his ability to suggest communications: his principal weapon. Therefore, "the less the soul works through its own powers, the more securely it advances, because it walks by faith."[283]

It is not enough to go out by night. One must immerse oneself in the darkness, travelling in the dense obscurity of faith.[284] Beyond the senses, the soul must blind its rational part to allow itself to be guided. One must abandon the familiar avenues of reason and sense (always woefully limited) and be led like a blind man: courageously taking to the incomprehensible path of God:

Wherefore, upon this road, to enter upon the road is to leave

---

[278] D 2, chpt. 21, 4.
[279] A 1, chpt. 1, 1.
[280] Loc. Cit. 3.
[281] A 2, chpt. 1, 2.
[282] Ibid.
[283] Loc. Cit. 3
[284] Ibid.

the road; or, to express it better, it is to pass on to the goal and to leave one's own way, and to enter upon that which has no way, which is God. For the soul that attains to this state has no longer any ways or methods, still less is it attached to ways and methods, or is capable of being attached to them. I mean ways of understanding, or of perception, or of feeling.... It enters within the limits of the supernatural, which has no way, yet in substance has all ways.[285]

St. John of the Cross states clearly that his purpose is not to lay out rules for discerning which supernatural phenomena are of God and which are demonic falsifications. Nonetheless, guiding principles are to be found in his doctrine.

I say, then, that with regard to all these imaginary visions and apprehensions and to all other forms and species whatsoever, which present themselves beneath some particular kind of knowledge or image or form, whether they be false and come from the devil or are recognized as true and coming from God, the understanding must not be embarrassed by them or feed upon them, neither must the soul desire to receive them or to have them, lest it should no longer be detached, free, pure and simple, without any mode or manner, as is required for union.[286]

The Mystical Doctor invites the contemplative to distinguish between essentials and accidentals, giving faith primacy above all other communications, considerations, and images – even those that have a divine source.

Does St. John mean willful rejection of divinely inspired communications? It is always well, then, that the soul should

---

[285] A 2, chpt. 4, 5.
[286] A 2, chpt. 16, 6.

reject these things, and close its eyes to them, whenever they come. For, unless it does so, it will prepare the way for those things that come from the devil, and will give him such influence that, not only will his visions come in place of God's, but his visions will begin to increase, and those of God to cease, in such manner that the devil will have all the power and God will have none.

So it has happened to many incautious and ignorant souls, who rely on these things to such an extent that many of them have found it hard to return to God in purity of faith; and many have been unable to return, so securely has the devil rooted himself in them; for which reason it is well to resist and reject them all.

For, by the rejection of evil visions, the errors of the devil are avoided, and by the rejection of good visions no hindrance is offered to faith and the spirit harvests the fruit of them.

Further, just when the soul allows them entrance, God begins to withhold them because the soul is becoming attached to them and is not profiting by them as it should, while the devil insinuates and increases his own visions, where he finds occasion and cause for them; just so, when the soul is resigned, or even averse to them, the devil begins to desist, since he sees that his efforts to harm the soul are fruitless; and contrariwise God begins to increase and magnify His favors in a soul that is so humble and detached, making it ruler over many things, even as He made the servant who was faithful in small things.[287]

The Mystical Doctor, while not having a negative view of possible divine communications, certainly counsels a negative reaction to them. Such an attitude will not offend God in the

---

[287] A 2, chpt. 11, 8.

slightest, since he knows that the prudent person does this out of love and a sense of protection of one's own spiritual life.

St. John's reaction to corporeal visions is practical:

...(H)ence it follows that the soul must be pure and simple, neither bounded by, nor attached to, any particular kind of intelligence, nor modified by any limitation of form, species and image. As God comes not within any image or form, neither is contained within any particular kind of intelligence, so the soul, in order to reach God, must likewise come within no distinct form or kind of intelligence.[288]

God is not an experience and cannot be contained in one. By way of pure theological virtue, the soul actually touches God and enters into union with him. Visions and other similar experiences do not offer the same security that faith affords the soul.

One's reaction to these phenomena ought to be to close one's eyes to them,[289] without entertaining any desire to examine the source of experience.[290] Elsewhere he counsels not admitting them or giving them any credit or attention,[291] since to admit them is tantamount to opening the door to the Evil One and his deceits and other similar things.[292]

Regarding imaginary visions, we are counseled to react in similar terms: suspicion, rejection, letting them die of neglect;

---

[288] A 2, chpt 16, 7.
[289] A 2, chpt. 17, 9.
[290] A 2, chpt. 11, 2.
[291] A 2, chpt. 27, 6.
[292] Loc. Cit. 7.

since these will always be limited, yet the wisdom of God – to which the intellect must be united – is not subject to the same limitations as human cognition which deals with particulars,[293] and, as a result, is an insufficient and disproportionate means for such matters.[294]

With regard to spiritual communications, one should neither desire nor seek them.[295] A pure and simple person knows to remain circumspect and humble in these matters and ought to energetically resist them, And if it is true that, for the reasons already described, it behooves the soul to close his eyes to the aforementioned revelations which come to it, and which concern the propositions of the faith, how much more necessary will it be neither to receive nor to give credit to other revelations relating to different things, wherein the devil habitually meddles so freely that I believe it impossible for a man not to be deceived in many of them unless he strive to reject them, such an appearance of truth and security does the devil give them.[296] Such spiritual communications are not necessary to love God wholly and the desire for them can actually be a hindrance to pure love of God.[297]

At this point it ought not shock us that St. John of the Cross counsels similar behavior with regard to spiritual visions that represent creatures.[298] Such knowledge as this, whether it be of God or no, can be of very little assistance to the progress of the soul on its journey to God if the soul desire it and be attached to

---

[293] Loc. Cit. 7
[294] Loc. Cit. 10.
[295] A 2, chpt. 21, 4.
[296] A 2, chpt. 27, 6.
[297] Ibid.
[298] A 2, chpt. 24, 8.

it; on the contrary, if it were not scrupulous in rejecting it, not only would it be hindered on its road, but it would even be greatly harmed and led far astray.[299]

If the soul remains strong in its resolve, humbly rejecting such communications and the devil, upon noticing that he cannot deceive this person, will attempt to sully that person's naked faith and poverty of spirit.[300]

Regarding revelations, one should "take great care to reject them,"[301] rather, with eyes closed, support himself in the Church's doctrine and the darkness of faith.[302] Locutions ought to receive the same treatment since they can harm the faith.[303] And let it be carefully noted that a soul should never act according to its own opinion or accept anything of what these locutions express, without much reflection and without taking advice of another. For strange and subtle deceptions may arise in this matter; so much so that I myself believe that the soul that does not set itself against accepting such things cannot fail to be deceived by many of them.[304]

Finally, regarding interior sentiments, one ought to not seek them out nor desire them. Otherwise, such a predisposition can prepare oneself for disaster. The devil is a master at taking advantage of these situations and presenting his counterfeits when the dispositions are there – especially using the sentiments or anything that might lull the soul into abandoning itself to his notions.[305]

---

299 A 2, chpt. 26, 18.
300 Loc. Cit. 9
301 A 2, chpt. 26, 18.
302 A 2, chpt. 27, 4.
303 A 2, chpt. 29, 12.
304 A 2, chpt. 30, 6.

Being well accompanied: By this our author means that we ought not trust ourselves too much, but rather recognize our indigence and benefit from the counsel of others. This requires humility, stripping oneself of whatever self-sufficiency and arrogance or presumption one might have. Of such humble ones, St. John says:

> Yet these humble souls, far from desiring to be anyone's teacher, are ready to take a road different from the one they are following, if told to do so. For they do not believe they could ever be right themselves. They rejoice when others receive praise, and their only sorrow is that they do not serve God as these others do. Yet these humble souls, far from desiring to be anyone's teacher, are ready to take a road different from the one they are following, if told to do so. For they do not believe they could ever be right themselves. They rejoice when others receive praise, and their only sorrow is that they do not serve God as these others do.[306]

A soul that must overcome the devil's strength will be unable to do so without prayer, nor will it be able to understand his deceits without mortification and humility.[307]

Not only is humility a requirement for a relationship with God, it protects the soul from the devil's onslaughts. Lacking this foundational virtue, the would-be contemplative opens himself up to the devil's thousand lies.[308] And this humility, to be authentic, must have body and soul, words and deeds – a

---

[305] A 2, chpt. 32, 6.
[306] D 1, chpt. 2, 7.
[307] C 3, 9.
[308] A 2, chpt. 26, 17.

true humility of heart without which one cannot repel demons.[309]

An aspect of this humility is the necessary dependence on others for spiritual perfection: angels and other people. The angels can communicate what they contemplate already in heaven, while men of virtue (confessors and spiritual directors) can transmit their counsel and common desire for the divine Spouse.[310] The angels instruct us interiorly, while people provide us with exterior aid.[311]

How saints die

At this point, it should be easy to understand that the death of the saints who have arrived at these heights must be of the most sweet and ineffable. Rather than an inherent punishment owed to fallen human nature because of sin, the saints see in death a prize and liberation. "They are no more afraid of death than they would be of a gentle rapture."[312] St. John of the Cross provides us with a beautiful page describing the death of these spiritual giants:

It should be known that the natural death of persons who have reached this state is far different in cause and mode from the death of others, even though it is similar in its natural circumstances. If the deaths of other people is caused by sickness or old age, the death of these persons is not so induced, in spite of their being sick or old; their soul as not wrested from them unless by some impetus of love far more sublime than those previously experienced; greater power, more valiant, since it tears through this veil and carries off the treasure, which is the soul.

---

[309] *Precautions*, 13.
[310] C 7, 6.
[311] Loc. Cit. 8.
[312] *Seventh Mansions*, 3, n.5.

The death of such persons is very gentle and very sweet, indeed sweeter and gentler than was their whole spiritual life on earth. For they died with the most sublime impulses and delightful encounters of love, resembling the swan whose song is much sweeter at the moment of death. Accordingly, David affirmed that the death of the saints is precious in the sight of the Lord (*cfr.* Ps. 116:15)."[313]

In the death of love, dreamed about so often by St. Therese of the Child Jesus, and which she in fact fully obtained, the same thing occurs in the deaths of all those transformed souls. Their death is nothing else than an immediate and direct transit of the soul to glory as saint John of the Cross says: "Since these souls – few that there be - are already extremely purged through love, they do not enter purgatory. St. Matthews says: *Blessed are the pure of heart for they shall see God* (Mt 5:8)."[314]

All of us can arrive to these heights

This sublime ideal of Christian perfection and holiness is open to all souls in grace, and the Lord indeed offers it to us. His command, *So be perfect, just as your heavenly Father is perfect* (Mt 5:48), is a universal injunction. The text of St. John of the Cross we have just considered confirms this. Since, if only the saints have arrived at this highest degree of love in the heights of transforming union and are the ones who do not pass through purgatory, it logically follows that this sublime state ought to be the normal terminus of the entire Christian life.

To hold otherwise, that God wants some souls to go to purgatory would be an error. The Christian life, developing

---

[313] Living Flame of Love, 1, n.30.
[314] Dark Night of the Soul, II, 2, n. 20.

itself gradually and without obstacles ought to lead to transforming union with God, which is a prelude to the beatific vision.

This teaching of theology has been fully confirmed by the experience of mystics throughout Church history. The lives of the saints prove it, and the teaching of the Church has always maintained it. St. Teresa says,

Remember, the Lord invites us all; and, since he is Truth itself, we cannot doubt him. If his invitation were not a general one, he would not have said: *I will give you to drink.* He might have said: "Come, all of you, for after all you will lose nothing by coming; and I will give drink to those I think fit for it." But, as he said we were all to come, without making this condition, I feel sure that none will fail to receive this living water unless they cannot keep to the path.[315]

Consider, and it is true, that God gives himself to those who give up everything for him. God is not an accepter of persons. He loves all; that there is no excuse for anyone, however wicked he may be, seeing that he has thus dealt with me, raising me to the state I am in.[316]

Not without some poignancy, St. Teresa leaves us with these thoughts.

For it is quite certain that, when we empty ourselves of all that is creature and rid ourselves of it for the love of God, that same Lord will fill our souls with himself.

Thus, one day, when Jesus Christ is praying for his apostles,

---

[315] Way of Perfection, 19.
[316] Life, 27.

he asked that they might become one with the Father and with him, even as Jesus Christ our Lord is in the Father and the Father is in him. I do not know what greater love there can be than this. And we shall none of us fail to be included here, for his Majesty went on to say: *Not for them alone do I pray, but also for all who believe in me* (Jn 17:20); and again: *I am in them* (Jn 17:23).

Ah, God help me! How true are these words and how well the soul understands them, for in this state it can actually see truth for itself. And how well we should all understand them were it not for our own fault!

The words of Jesus Christ our King and Lord cannot fail; but, because we ourselves failed by not preparing ourselves and departing from all that can shut out this light, we do not see ourselves in this mirror into which we are gazing and in which our image is engraved.[317]

Sic Transit Gloria Mundi – Stat Crux Dum Volvitur Orbis

---

[317] Seventh Mansions, 2, nn. 7-8.